Marital and Sexual Ethics in Islamic Law

Marital and Sexual Ethics in Islamic Law

Rethinking Temporary Marriage

Roshan Iqbal

LEXINGTON BOOKS
Lanham • Boulder • New York • London

Published by Lexington Books
An imprint of The Rowman & Littlefield Publishing Group, Inc.
4501 Forbes Boulevard, Suite 200, Lanham, Maryland 20706
www.rowman.com

86-90 Paul Street, London EC2A 4NE

British Library Cataloguing in Publication Information Available

Library of Congress Cataloging-in-Publication Data

Names: Iqbal, Roshan, author.
Title: Marital and sexual ethics in Islamic law : rethinking temporary marriage / Roshan Iqbal.
Description: Lanham : Lexington Books, 2023. | Includes bibliographical references and index.
Identifiers: LCCN 2022055299 (print) | LCCN 2022055300 (ebook) | ISBN 9781793606273 (cloth) | ISBN 9781793606280 (ebook)
Subjects: LCSH: Muta. | Marriage (Islamic law) | Sexual ethics--Religious aspects--Islam. | Sex--Religious aspects--Islam. | Husband and wife (Islamic law)
Classification: LCC KBP546.955 .I63 2023 (print) | LCC KBP546.955 (ebook) | DDC 346.01/6091762--dc23/eng/20230111
LC record available at https://lccn.loc.gov/2022055299
LC ebook record available at https://lccn.loc.gov/2022055300

∞™ The paper used in this publication meets the minimum requirements of American National Standard for Information Sciences—Permanence of Paper for Printed Library Materials, ANSI/NISO Z39.48-1992.

My life and this book have truly only been possible by the grace of others, so it is fitting then that it be dedicated to all those others, and by doing so I do not discharge my debt, nor is it a burden from which I wish to be relieved.

Contents

Acknowledgments

It is impossible to acknowledge all those who have made contributions to my book. This book, my graduate studies, much like my life, are the labor of many lives, without whose help this project would never have come to fruition. I am unable to name all the people who were instrumental in bringing this book to a close because the list would go on for pages. Nevertheless, the following people, among many others, deserve special thanks. My gratitude for those absent in name here is present in spirit.

I start with thanking God for this opportunity of which I was not worthy. This manuscript grew out of my PhD dissertation completed at Georgetown University. It is only fitting then that I start with thanking my adviser, Felicitas Opwis, who mentored me to maturation. In the same vein, I would like to thank Barbara Stowasser, who is no longer with us but who was instrumental in helping me develop my critical eye. John Voll was not my official adviser but was ever present with advice on work and life, and this continues even today. I would also like to thank John Esposito for both encouragement and funding opportunities. I would like to thank the last member of my dissertation committee, Maria Dakake, for her mentorship throughout this project. Special thanks goes to Meriem Tikue from my department at Georgetown University for her steadfast friendship, which continues to this day. I would also like to thank Emily Pollokof, Summar Sohaib, and Rebekah Zwanzig, whose editing and comments were indispensable in finishing this book and led to a significantly clearer manuscript. I would especially like to thank Summar for her personal friendship and warmth throughout the process. Many thanks to Omar Matadar of Qasid Institute. Without his knowledge of Arabic and his guidance, I would be completely lost in translation, and he saved me from errors of fact and interpretation. I have learned from and been inspired by a whole generation of Muslim feminist scholars, all of whom have had an important influence on my scholarship and to whom I am endlessly indebted. This book would not have been possible without several summer grants from Agnes Scott College for which I am also so very grateful. Of course, the usual disclaimer of all mistakes being solely mine applies.

Of the people not formally connected to this project and to whom I am indebted are Dr. Ault and Janet. Their generosity to me, their sincere and steadfast support, is outside of what language can capture. I would like to thank Zehra Baji and her father, Habib Uncle, without the generous help of whom my quest for knowledge would not have been possible. I would also like to thank, not in any particular order, Naila Bhabi, Hussain Bhai, Naveed Bhai, and Sabra Apa for discussions on larger existential dramas of life and for loving me like their blood-kin, and Thomosso, who not only put up with me but also put me up and whose generosity and company I reveled in. I would like to thank my new colleagues at Agnes Scott, Jan and Tina, for our weekly writing soirees filled with joy and laughter and for their life-sustaining companionship, and Scarlett, Mona, and Reem for their shimmering friendship, good cheer, and constant encouragement at every stage of this process. I owe a particular debt of gratitude to my siblings: Ronak, Roohi, Rukhsana, and Rani for succor and reality checks only sisters can give, and for their perpetual prayers and believing in my possibilities. To my academic siblings, Bindu and Nermeen, who stayed on skype and zoom writing for hours with me, I am at a loss for words to express my appreciation and sheer delight. This book is a small tribute to both my parents: to my mother whose personal piety and passion for faith first drew me to the study of Islam; to my late father, an avid reader, and to his encouragement since childhood to love the life of the mind. I trust I make them proud. It only remains for me to express my gratitude for my partner, Sohail, who, befitting a book on marital ethics, did not let me share in any household responsibilities, allowing me to focus on completing this book while being my at-home barista.

A shorter, edited version of Chapters 1 and 5 is forthcoming in *Harvard Journal of Islamic Law*, titled "Mutʿa, Temporary Marriage: Obsolete or Cutting Edge? Five Interrelated—Textual, Methodological, Lived, Moral, and Scientific—Pathways for Re-Interpretation."

Note on Transliteration

I have followed the transliteration guide of the *International Journal of Middle East Studies*. Words listed in *Merriam-Webster's Collegiate Dictionary* are spelled as they appear there; however, some words preserve the *ʿayn* and *hamza*, such as Qurʾan and Shiʿi.

Introduction

In my senior year of college, I visited my cousin in Toronto, Ontario, Canada, during spring break. One evening, they had friends over and the topic of *mutʿa*, temporary marriage, came up. My cousin's friend mentioned that her husband often traveled for work and had to live in Canada for long stretches without her. She exclaimed, "I told my husband he can enter a *mutʿa* marriage since he had to go without me for a long time." *Mutʿa* is most often associated with Shiʿi Islam, but despite my Shiʿi upbringing in Karachi, Pakistan and my family's regular attendance at *majālis* (sing. *majlis*), religious lectures, I had never heard about this type of marriage. When my ignorance became evident, the woman explained that the duration of a *mutʿa* is decided prior to the marriage, along with the amount of money gifted to the bride, and the marriage simply dissolves when this period of time comes to an end. Married and single men alike may partake in *mutʿa*, but the women must be single. This information came as a shock. At the time, having internalized colonial discourses around religion, particularly the Islamic oppression of women, I was unable to nuance my thinking and was troubled by the parallel with prostitution and what seemed like a loophole that allowed men to have sex outside of permanent marriage. I was further unaware that a Shiʿi man could partake in as many simultaneous *mutʿa* as he pleased, even in addition to the four permanent marriages Islamic law permits. My distaste did not begin to abate until I discovered that Muslim feminists stand on both sides of the debate about this type of marriage; they both approve and disapprove of *mutʿa*—each for sound reasons.

My simultaneous fascination and aversion to the practice led me to pursue a doctoral degree in Islamic studies. With sectarian and secular disagreement alike over the validity of the practice, what evidence do we have for the permissibility of *mutʿa*? A lengthy history of exegesis shows that one *āya* (pl. *āyāt*), verse, of the Qurʾan—Q 4:24—is used as a proof text for *mutʿa*. Thus, there are two questions central to my research on the topic: Can Q 4:24 be used as a proof text for the permissibility of *mutʿa*, as the Shiʿa have done?

Furthermore, what are the marital and sexual ethical implications of such a practice for men, women, children, the institution of marriage, and society?

To answer the first question, this book examines *tafsīr*[1] (pl. *tafāsīr*), exegesis, of Q 4:24 by a wide variety of exegetes who come from different schools and time periods—covering 1,400 years of intellectual history over three chapters (2, 3, and 4). My primary question, which relates to interpretive methodology or hermeneutics, explores whether the rules and regulations of Qur'anic hermeneutics validate the use of Q 4:24 to justify the permissibility of *mut'a*. The answers allow us to understand how historical contexts and sectarian influences have affected exegesis.

Why examine *mut'a* in *tafāsīr* when conventional wisdom suggests exploring the legal books of *fiqh*, jurisprudence, instead? First, to date, the *tafsīr* genre has been excluded from the study of *mut'a*. Second, *tafsīr* production preceded the legal writing of *fiqh*.[2] Third, *tafsīr* arguably has the longest history of seeking to understand the Islamic textual ethos because the Qur'an is at the center of Islamic legal thinking.[3] Even modernity, which disrupted all other Islamic sciences to a great degree, did not disrupt contemplation of the Qur'an and the Qur'anic sciences.[4] Finally, *tafsīr* contains a variety of exegetical opinions and methods and is therefore an interdisciplinary genre. Thus, a study of Qur'anic discussions about *mut'a* in works of *tafsīr* can help us locate *mut'a* within a larger religious discourse that encompasses the various disciplines that evolved from Muslims' responses to the Qur'an and that exists alongside other authoritative texts.

To answer the second question, this books' final chapter, chapter 5, explores sexual ethics and the consequences *mut'a* has for Muslim women, men, children, and the family structure as we know it. Allon Uhlmann notes that "sexuality in the Middle East and North Africa is one of the most charged themes that social sciences can hope to address."[5] The stakes in the political struggle over sexuality are high; the very nature of Islam and its social role are being questioned. The analysis presented in the chapter allows us to theorize new conceptualizations of sexual ethics, as it questions the fundamental conceptual and legal distinctions embedded in Shi'i assumptions concerning the "natural" differences between men and women, which makes the former "naturally need" more sex (and thus multiple partners) and therefore allows men to partake in *mut'a*. This final chapter presents methodological interventions in an attempt to rethink how marital and sexual ethics can be understood within jurisprudential discussions.

METHODOLOGY

Before proceeding, two disclaimers about my methodology are necessary. First, I have taken into account diverse voices from within the shared Islamic intellectual tradition, ones that have been neglected by mainstream Western academia—Shiʿi, Sufi, Ashʿari, Zaydī, and Ismaʿili; however, this study makes no claim to comprehensiveness. Similarly, while important works exist in Turkish, Malaysian, and other Islamicate languages, it was necessary to restrict my analysis to exegetical traditions in three languages that I am trained in and familiarity with: Arabic, Persian, and Urdu. Additionally, despite the growing number of commentaries available in print, far too many works remain inaccessible in manuscript form, and a multitude of sources exist, from the earliest centuries of Islam, from which several significant exegetical threads can be delineated and unearthed.

This book analyzes the works of nineteen commentators,[6] looking specifically at their exegesis of Q 4:24, and provides a broad chronology, ranging from the formative centuries and the first extant *tafsīr* by al-Balkhī (d. 150/767) to the present time. These selections reflect the diversity of voices within the shared intellectual heritage of Islam. Although contemporary discussions on *mutʿa* were revived after the Iranian Revolution, no one has examined and commented on contemporary *tafāsīr*, especially those by Persian Shiʿi scholars. Scrutinizing *tafāsīr* from this era is indispensable to understanding modern clerical arguments that are not defensive about the permissibility of *mutʿa*.

Most of the works used here are full commentaries, with three exceptions. There is no complete Ismaʿili *tafsīr* in the classical sense of the word. Hence, key commentators have been selected to represent this sect. Furthermore, because only men were involved in the actual recording and writing of *tafāsīr*, women's contributions have been lost, a complication that has been ignored until recently. As a corrective, this book treats ʿAʾisha as an exegete. Even though she does not have a proper *tafsīr* to her name, her recollection of the Prophet Muhammad's sayings, as well as her own comments, fit the practical definition of the earliest works of *tafsīr*. The final inclusion is Farḥat Ḥāshmī (b. 1957), who likewise does not have a written *tafsīr*, but her commentary on the Qurʾan is available in audio lectures.

Chapters 2, 3, and 4 more or less follow the same structure and proceed chronologically. First, I discuss the exegete's life and intellectual development. Next, I provide a detailed study of the selected *tafsīr* text. When examining each *tafsīr*, I ask questions about methodology. I am less concerned with the exegetes' conclusions than with their exegetical processes. To this end, I ask questions about organization, presentation, and hermeneutical principles:

How is meaning extracted from the words of the *āya*? What strategies do the exegetes employ in order to extract this meaning? Are methodological innovations introduced that align the interpretation of the *āya* with the ideology of the interpreter's legal school? Is there tension between sectarian affiliations and philology? What kinds of sources do the exegetes employ? What sources are acceptable, and why? Are there omissions, and if so, why?

Throughout this analysis, I explore the hermeneutical tools that exegetes use to construct different interpretations of Q 4:24. Comparing the works from the different schools alongside the intellectual history of the *āya*'s interpretation provides a history of various attitudes toward *mutʿa*. This allows us to learn whether the prohibition of *mutʿa* is universal among the Sunni and if permissibility is universal among the Shiʿa. This detailed investigation also enables us to determine which scholars speak in a tone of reconciliation, which scholars indulge in polemics, and why.

In each chapter, I not only pay attention to the examination of *tafāsīr* but also to intertextual references to *mutʿa* in each *tafsīr*; for example, these *tafāsīr* discuss other Qurʾanic *āyāt* (23:5, 4:12, 2:230, 2:234, and 65:1) as proof that the practice of *mutʿa* was abrogated, as well as responses to arguments in favor of or against abrogation. I also discuss *aḥādīth* (sing. hadith), variant readings, and aspects of *fiqh* that have a direct bearing on our understanding of *mutʿa*.

By providing a comparative analysis of different Islamic schools of thought and presenting the development of the genre of *tafsīr* over time and across each major school, this book aims to be the most comprehensive work on *tafāsīr* of Q 4:24. To date, no study has attempted such an undertaking, and it is my hope that this book serves as an important contribution to the study of the intellectual history of this *āya*.

BRIEF OVERVIEW OF CHAPTERS

Chapter 1—*Mutʿa*: Obsolete or Cutting Edge?

This chapter sets the stage for the following three chapters. It describes the institution, history, and practice of *mutʿa* and also provides a historical overview and critical discussion of contemporary popular works, thus addressing the growing interest in *mutʿa*.

Chapter 2—*Tafsīr*: Development of the Genre

This book situates *tafāsīr* of Q 4:24 within the historical framework of the development of Qurʾanic exegesis. A wide gap between the time of composition and the date some works were first transcribed complicates our analysis of the early phase of this genre's development. This section consists of a comprehensive collection of pronouncements thought to be made by the first generation of Muslims. These early works are concerned not just with the interpretation of the Qur'an but also with traditions of recording that were transmitted in the customary forms of *aḥādīth* and *akhbār* (sing. *khabar*), reports. These works are important sources, not only for studying the exegetical tradition but also for understanding historical traditions. This chapter proceeds from this early period, where most knowledge was transmitted orally, to a time when authors recorded their own works. This is also a period when the fortunes of Islam were rising steadily; by the end of this period, there is an active formation of sectarian self-identity. The relevant exegetes are:

ʿA'isha bt. Abī Bakr (d. 58/678), wife of the Prophet Muhammad;

Ibn ʿAbbās (d.68/687–8), cousin of the Prophet Muhammad;

Muqātil b. Sulaymān al-Balkhī (d. 150/767), author of the earliest extant commentary and a Murji'ī traditionalist;

Abū Jaʿfar al-Tabarī (d. 310/923), Sunni;

Abū Hātim al-Rāzī (d. 322/934–5), an Ismaʿili commentator;

Abū al-Nadr al-ʿAyyāshī (fl. late third/ninth century), a Shiʿi convert.

Chapter 3—*Tafsīr*: The Genre Evolves and Reaches Its Height

This chapter covers the middle period, when all the groundwork was laid for *tafsīr* as a robust genre and Muslims experienced social and political stability. Elaborate interpretations developed in the fourth/tenth century, since by then, *tafsīr* had combined its five constitutive elements: narrative, legal, textual, rhetorical, and allegorical.[7] The works in this period represent polyvalent readings of the Qur'an. Additionally, the middle period is also when sectarian concerns were solidified and there was a noticeable interest in relaying theological messages. This led to the process of citing authorities to declare loyalties, thus defining the tradition within which one works. The relevant exegetes are:

Aḥmad b. Muḥammad al-Thaʿlabī (d. 427/1035), Sunni;

Jār Allāh al-Zamakshsharī (d. 538/1144), a Muʿtazili thinker;

al-Faḍl b. al-Ḥasan al-Tabrisī (d. 548/1154), author of the most popular Shiʿi *tafsīr*;

Fakhr al-Dīn al-Rāzī (d. 606–1209), Sunni/Ashʿari;

Rashīd al-Dīn Maybūdī (fl. sixth/twelfth century), author of the earliest mystical commentary in Persian;

al-Qurtubī (d. 671/1272), Sunni.

Chapter 4—*Tafsīr*: The Modern Period

After sectarian contestations were settled, the modern period was characterized by colonization and its effects—postcolonialism and modernity—which were vital issues during this time. Exegeses from this period thus reflect responses to these conditions. According to political scientist and anthropologist Partha Chatterjee, the third-world bourgeois could not autonomously respond to their world without reinstating Enlightenment rationality.[8] This is evident in the form of competing modernizing discourses found within the works discussed in this chapter. The relevant exegetes are:

Muḥammad ʿAbduh (d. 1323/1905) and Rashīd Riḍa (d. 1354/1935), both Sunni;

Ibn ʿĀshūr (d. 1394/1973), Sunni;

Sayyid Abū al-Aʿlā Mawdūdī (d. 1399/1979), Sunni;

Muḥammad Ḥusayn Faḍl Allāh (d. 1330/2010), Shiʿi;

Farḥat Naseem Ḥāshmī (b. 1471/1957), Sunni;

Āyatullāh Sayyid Muḥammad Ḥusayn Tabātabāʾī (d.1400/1981), Shiʿi;

Nuṣrat Begum Amīn (d. 1403/1983), Shiʿi.

Chapter 5—Rethinking Marital and Sexual Ethics in Islamic Law

In this chapter, I argue that the question of *mutʿa*'s permissibility cannot be answered through an examination of classical texts alone. This analysis must be supplemented with a study that considers four interrelated factors: (1) Muslim feminist methodological interventions; (2) an ethnographic component that incorporates the voices and concerns of Muslim women, children, and men who are affected by *mutʿa*; (3) a study of moral philosophy that explores whether there is a connection between one's sexual activity and spiritual being; and (4) incorporating new research on the science of sexuality that may impact the premises upon which *mutʿa* is often based and justified. I attempt to answer the call for a "just sexual ethics" that was proposed by the renowned scholar of gender and Islam Kecia Ali. Although it is not within the scope of this book to perform the studies, or answer the questions presented in this chapter, I do point toward new methodologies for future research, suggest areas for further study, and provide questions that will bring us closer to an examination of *mutʿa* centered around sexual and marital ethics.

In addition to proposing future possibilities, this book provides several methodological interventions in the field of Islamic studies. First, by examining the development of the genre of *tafsīr* over 1,400 years and using works by scholars from various schools of thought on the issue of *mutʿa*, I challenge the idea that a *tafsīr* is an elevated practice of procuring exegesis solely from the text of the Qurʾan. Instead, I show that each *tafsīr* the book examines was shaped by the political, cultural, and regional contexts of the exegetes, as well as by their hermeneutical processes. Second, I highlight *aḥādīth* that exegetes use to explicate Q 4:24 and their understanding of *mutʿa*. By focusing on hadith as a medium for political commentary and sectarian allegiance, I emphasize the rich tradition of hadith commentary. Third, I underscore the contributions of female exegetes and do so by calling for a reevaluation of what "counts" as exegesis. For example, I include ʿAʾisha bt. Abī Bakr as an exegete due to her extensive contribution to commentary and the hadith corpus. I also include the audio lectures of Farḥat Ḥāshmī as a *tafsīr*, calling attention to the oral tradition, which, as recent ethnographic works have proven, address issues typically neglected by male commentators.[9] My book traces the tradition of commentary proceeding from the era of manuscript to audio, video, and live lectures on *tafsīr*. Finally, although I initially focus on the textual study of *tafāsīr*, I move away from studies of classical texts toward a discussion of the modern relevance of *mutʿa* by presenting a methodology through which we can rethink Islamic sexual and marital ethics and reinterpret Islamic law accordingly. Therefore, what I hope to craft here is a study with implications for contemporary Muslim marital law and sexual ethics, creating a compelling call for gender justice firmly grounded in the Islamic tradition.

NOTES

1. The term *tafsīr* is the most used Arabic term for interpretation or exegesis, including but not limited to the interpretation of the Qur'an. Labeling a work a *tafsīr*, therefore, reveals what it intends to cover. For more details, see the work of one of the pioneers in the field of *tafsīr*, Andrew Rippin, "Tafsīr," in *Encyclopaedia of Islam, Second Edition*, eds. P. Bearman, Th. Bianquis, C. E. Bosworth, E. van Donzel, and W. P. Heinrichs (Brill Online, 2012).

2. Walid A. Saleh, "The Last of the Nishapuri School of Tafsīr: Al-Wāḥidī (d. 468/1076) and His Significance in the History of Qur'anic Exegesis," *Journal of the American Oriental Society* 126 (2006): 235–36; Walid A. Saleh, "Preliminary Remarks on the Historiography of Tafsir in Arabic: A History of the Book," *Journal of Qur'anic Studies* 12 (2010): 6–40.

3. Michael Sells, *Approaching the Qur'án: The Early Revelations* (Ashland, OR: White Cloud Press, 2007).

4. Johanna Pink, "Tradition, Authority and Innovation in Contemporary Sunni Tafsīr: Towards a Typology of Qur'an Commentaries from the Arab World, Indonesia and Turkey," *Journal of Qur'anic Studies* 12, nos. 1–2 (2010): 56–82.

5. J. Uhlmann Allon, "Introduction: Reflections on the Study of Sexuality in the Middle East and North Africa," *Social Analysis: The International Journal of Social and Cultural Practice* 49, no. 2 (Summer 2005): 3.

6. Despite consulting several other works in addition to the ones selected and written about in detail, they are not cited because they are either redundant or do not address Q 4:24. I have also looked at related genres, such as *asbāb al-nuzūl*, occasions of revelation, and *gharīb al-Qur'ān*, obscure terms in the Qur'an, and mention them as needed.

7. The science of Qur'anic exegesis evolved considerably in the period between al-Qummī and al-Tha'labī. See Rashid Ahmed, "Qur'anic Exegesis and Classical Tafsir," *The Islamic Quarterly* 12 (1968): 71–119.

8. Partha Chatterjee, *Nationalist Thought and the Colonial World: A Derivative Discourse* (London: Zed Books, 1986).

9. Saba Mahmood, *Politics of Piety: The Islamic Revival and the Feminist Subject* (Princeton, NJ: Princeton University Press, 2005), 83–90.

Chapter One

Mut'a, Temporary Marriage

Obsolete or Cutting Edge?

Historically, marriage established a relationship between families, tribes, or clans rather than between individuals. It is only around the last century that it transformed into a personal, romantic relationship that focuses on the nuclear family in the global north, with the same changes appearing in urban centers of the global south. However, marriage still retains some need for community recognition and approval.[1]

The structure of the family is undoubtedly changing. Scholars discovered that trends indicating long-term change became noticeable during the 1970s and continued through the 1980s, and there is little sign of this trend easing. These broad changes witnessed in the global north have also started appearing in the global south, and they include: Fewer people marrying and many marrying later; more people divorcing and more divorces initiated by women; more marriages involving at least one divorced partner but the marriage rate among divorced people is falling; remarriages more likely to end in divorce than first marriages; more people cohabiting and births outside marriage are increasing; and more women are starting families later, having fewer children, or remaining childless, and more are raising children on their own.[2]

Research on Muslim American marriage trends has been sparse, particularly when it comes to divorce. A study by sociologist Ilyas Ba-Yunus mentions a divorce rate of 31.14 percent within the Muslim American community,[3] but this number was obtained using flawed methodology. Ba-Yunus derived this statistic by taking the number of Muslim divorces and dividing it by the number of Muslim marriages, and as clinical psychologists Aliya Chapman and Lauren Cattaneo point out, this fails to take into account Muslim Americans who may have married outside the United States or those who chose to marry without registering with the government.[4] Noha Alshugairi's work on Muslim marital trends in the United States is more recent and comes up with a divorce rate of 21.3 percent.[5] Chapman and Cattaneo find this statistic more acceptable, since it is close to the statistic on Asian American marriages—20 percent of Asian American marriages end in divorce; this is significant because one-third of Muslim Americans are South Asian.[6]

Due to globalization, shifts in Muslim marriage trends are not confined to the global north. In Turkey, not only has the number of divorces increased by 8 percent yearly, the number of couples getting married has decreased by 2.3 percent.[7] Turkish women are also choosing to marry later in life.[8] Between 1996 and 2007, Egypt saw an 83 percent increase in the national divorce rate.[9] And Egyptian women who divorce may remarry less often as a result of new Egyptian divorce laws, which favor granting the father custody of the children if the mother remarries.[10]

In addition to the research mentioned above, there is also evidence that more Muslim youth are having premarital sex. In 2016, psychologist Sobia Ali-Faisal published an article about her findings after conducting a survey of over four hundred Muslim young adults from the United States and Canada. The participants were recruited online, and she asked them questions regarding their sexual experience, sexual guilt, and sexual anxiety.[11] Ali-Faisal's research was groundbreaking, and Outburst, a Toronto-based organization that works with Muslim women to combat violence, created an infographic of its key findings. This infographic was circulated widely—among Muslim news sources and on social media.[12] According to this study, half of those surveyed had engaged in sexual intercourse, and two-thirds did so prior to marriage.[13] Thus, most of the sexually experienced Muslims surveyed had sex prior to marriage. Additional research showed that over half the Muslim college students surveyed reported having premarital sex.[14] Ali-Faisal also surveyed these young Muslims about the manner and medium of sexual education they had received; they reported that their greatest source of sex education was from the media, while the least likely source was their parents. This lack of sexual education puts Muslims at a higher risk for unhealthy and unhappy relationships.[15] As Muslim sexual health educator Sameera Qureshi states, "nuanced conversations about sexual health, rooted in Islamic spirituality, are not happening as much, as broadly, and as often as they need to be."[16] In a society where marriage rates are decreasing and divorce rates and premarital sex are steadily increasing, scholars must reexamine the function of Muslim marriage, particularly whether *mutʿa*, temporary marriage, could potentially play a new role.

Islam frames marriage as a religious duty and an important social institution that fulfills and protects the interests of the participants as well as society.[17] The Arabic word for marriage, *zawāj*, is derived from the root meaning "pair."[18] Islamic law defines it as a marital contract that permits both contracting parties to partake in sex and start a conjugal life together.[19] Islamic texts use several synonyms for *zawāj*; the most common is *nikāḥ*.

Although the dictionary defines *nikāḥ* as "sexual intercourse," colloquially it indicates matrimony, because marriage is the institution that makes sexual intercourse lawful.[20]

As indicated by the rich religious and legal literature produced on the subject, Muslims have shown considerable interest in the juridical aspects of marriage. Numerous *aḥādīth* (pl. of hadith) and Qur'anic *āyāt* (pl. of *āya*), verses, deal with marriage. These *āyāt* include: "And one of His signs is that He created for you spouses from among yourselves so that you may find comfort in them. And He has placed between you compassion and mercy. Surely in these are signs for people who reflect" (Q 30:21)[21]; "The believers, both men and women, are guardians of one another. They encourage good and forbid evil, establish prayer and pay alms-tax, and obey God and His Messenger. It is they who will be shown God's mercy. Surely God is Almighty, All-Wise" (Q 9:71); and "your spouses are a garment for you as you are for them" (Q 2:187). A hadith recalls the Prophet Muhammad's support for marriage: "Whoever wishes to follow my footsteps should know that marriage is one aspect of my heritage. So whoever loves me should follow my example."[22] According to Muslim scholars, this supports his recommendation that all men and women marry, unless they are restricted by a physical disability or are economically unable to do so. They also believe the Prophet Muhammad framed marriage as a sacred practice when he declared, "When a man marries, he has made his religion half perfect. Then let him fear Allah for the remaining half."[23]

Such *aḥādīth* affirm marriage as the basic building block of Muslim society; as a result, celibacy is frowned upon. The only classical scholar to sway from this position was al-Ghazālī (d. 505/1111), who encouraged celibacy for individuals committed to intellectual pursuits and advised them to marry only if remaining unmarried would cause them to be consumed with distracting sexual desires.[24]

Marriage in Islam is *ʿaqd*, a contract, unlike in Christianity, where it is considered a sacrament. An Islamic marriage contract, entered into by a man and woman, makes sexual intercourse legal (i.e., permissible) in the eyes of God and society and establishes reciprocal rights and duties between spouses. These rights and duties are often debated as being disproportionally in favor of men.[25] This inequity is evident in individual relationships and also supported by major social institutions.[26] As a result, many modern Muslim scholars, particularly female scholars, have dedicated their careers to researching questions related to sexual morality and gender within the Muslim marriage contract.[27] First and foremost among their concerns are marital ethics and gender inequality, particularly when dealing with the issue of *mutʿa*.

This chapter begins with the legal definition of *mut'a* and provides a comparative analysis of *mut'a* and *nikāḥ*, permanent marriage. Next, it briefly covers a broad history of temporary marriage prior to the advent of Islam and the rise of sectarian differences. This is followed by a history of *mut'a* after Islam, detailing differences between Sunni and Shi'i views of its permissibility and particular *aḥādīth* used to either justify or condemn *mut'a*. Finally, I address the contemporary practice of *mut'a* in Muslim societies.

LEGAL DEFINITION OF *MUT'A*

Mut'a comes from the Arabic root *mīm*, *tā'*, and *'ayn*, meaning "enjoyment," and it is a marital contract where a man—married, divorced, widowed, or single—and a woman—divorced or widowed, and some scholars allow a virgin with the permission of her father—marry for a specified period of time,[28] and the man gifts the woman a specified amount of money.[29] Of note here is that married men are allowed to partake in *mut'a* but married women are not, leading to what scholars call a double standard, which can be seen over and over again throughout this chapter. Additionally, married men can be in several simultaneous *mut'a* marriages. A few scholars allow an unmarried or virgin woman to partake in *mut'a*, while single men are unconditionally permitted. The duration of this type of marriage can be as long or short as the contracting parties want—from a single hour to ninety-nine years, for example—and the dowry-gift can be as meager or substantial as the parties decide in the contract. The woman does not receive *nafaqa*, monthly material support, or inherit from her temporary husband if he dies during the *mut'a*. At the end of the marital period, there is no divorce ceremony; the marriage automatically dissolves.[30] The man and woman may specify any conditions they like in their contract, as long as they do not conflict with Islamic law.[31] For example, they can stipulate that the marriage will not be sexually consummated or that the contract is solely to allow for companionship or travel. However, at the end of the allotted time, no matter how long, the woman must go through a shortened *'idda*, waiting period.[32] Here again, men do not have to observe a waiting period, but women do. Historically, its purpose was to determine the paternity of any child conceived as a result of the *mut'a*. For those that oppose *mut'a*, the shortened *'idda* suggests the wife is little more than a slave or concubine.[33] The *mut'a* contract can be renewed as many times as a couple wants and there is no waiting period between these contracts, but there needs to be a new dowry payment.

Unlike in a permanent marriage, there is no obligation to provide for the wife's monthly maintenance. At the end of the determined period, the spouses' part without reading a divorce formula and without any witnesses.[34]

Shi'i law further specifies that any children born from the *mut'a* are considered legitimate and, in theory, have the same status as children born within permanent marriages. This legal status and the corresponding inheritance rights of these children are important; they help distinguish *mut'a* from prostitution.[35] However, although this appears to be a safeguard to provide for the mother and child, historically the law supported the father if he denied paternity.[36] Today, with the availability of genetic testing for paternity, the matter is mitigated in favor of women.

Not all Shi'i jurists agree that a virgin woman can enter a *mut'a* contract, but a virgin man can. Some say only divorced and widowed women are legally permitted to do so, and others allow it only if the father gives his consent. Al-Kulaynī (d. 329/949) and Ibn Bābūya (d. 381/1002) give the father the right to decide for a virgin daughter, and al-Sharīf al-Murtaḍā (d. 436/1056) was the first to present the view that an adult virgin woman may arrange her own marriage.[37]

Traditional Shi'i legal doctrine does not require witnesses for a valid *mut'a*, nor does the marriage need to be registered.[38] Ziba Mir-Hosseini, a legal anthropologist who studies Islamic family law, points out that one of the main attributes of marriage is the public celebration and acknowledgment. However, in most circumstances, women who enter a *mut'a* cannot talk about it with others. She therefore calls it a "socially defective marriage."[39]

Finally, neither the Qur'an nor *aḥādīth* make any reference to the terms and conditions of a *mut'a* contract. Even Ibn 'Abbās and others who considered *mut'a* valid did not specify terms, except that it was for a definite period of time and the parties did not inherit from each other. Nothing, for example, was mentioned about the procedure for if a woman became pregnant. Who would maintain her? Or, after having the baby, which has a legal status, through what process would she get her *nafaqa*, monthly material maintenance, for the child? Despite this lack of process, *mut'a* has essentially become standardized and must meet certain terms and conditions: (1) *'aqd*, contract, which is comprised of an offer and acceptance; (2) *ajar*, recompense; (3) *ajal*, fixed duration; (4) *iftirāq*, separation when the predetermined period expires; (5) *'idda*, waiting period of six weeks; and (6) *'adm al-mirāth*, absence of inheritance.

DIFFERENCES BETWEEN *MUT'A* AND PERMANENT MARRIAGE

According to Islamic law, a valid marriage must meet certain conditions. If one or more of these conditions are not met, then the marriage is considered invalid. The Sunni define *mut'a* and permanent marriage differently, but the Shi'a make *mut'a* continuous with their rules and regulations about permanent marriage.

There are three basic conditions for a valid marriage:[40] (1) the two partners must be free of any conditions that would prevent them from marrying; (2) *ījāb*, consent of the woman or her guardian; and, (3) the acceptance of the groom. The Sunni require the proposal and acceptance be witnessed by qualified witnesses and presided over by a qadi in a ceremony or accompanied by some sort of public announcement. In contrast, the Shi'a do not require witnesses or that a religious authority preside over permanent marriages. *Mut'a* can be undertaken by two individuals who correctly read the formula[41] to themselves; this makes it legal.[42]

Mahr, dowry, is another essential part of the permanent marriage contract and should be set at the time of the marriage. If it is not, then *mahr al-mithal*, a dowry customary for the class, age, and status of the woman, is the default dowry. In *mut'a*, if the *mahr* is not set at the beginning, the marriage becomes invalid.[43]

According to both Shi'i and Sunni *fiqh* and in accordance with the Qur'anic edict, the parties in a permanent marriage inherit from each other, but in temporary marriage they do not. The Sunni emphasize that marriage's importance lies in settling questions of paternity and establishing inheritance.

Both the Sunni and Shi'a allow men, but not women, to enter into permanent marriages with women of the Book (Jews and Christians). According to the Sunni scholars Ibn Bābūya and al-Mufīd, *mut'a* with an unbeliever is forbidden, even with People of the Book. According to most Shi'i scholars, *mut'a* with Christian or Jewish women is permitted but *makrūh*, disliked.[44]

Both the Sunni and Shi'a allow for the man to engage in polygyny, with a limit of four wives. According to classical Shi'i jurists, men are permitted as many simultaneous temporary marriage partners as they desire,[45] and this is in addition to the four permanent wives. However, single, divorced, or widowed women can temporarily marry only one man at a time.

For both the Sunni and Shi'a, the man has a unilateral right to dissolve a permanent marriage. Yet there are some interesting differences in the divorce rules. The Sunni allow the three divorce statements to be pronounced at the same time, but the Shi'a do not allow this; nor do they allow them to be said in private, whereas the Sunni do. For the Shi'a, the husband must pronounce the divorce formula in front of a religious authority for it to be valid. This authority asks the couple to take a period to reconsider and have patience. They are asked to do this for a total of three cycles before they are finally legally divorced. It is important to note that the Shi'a require witnesses and religious authority for divorce proceedings but not for the marriage ceremony, something they have been able to argue for through the grammar of a Qur'anic *āya*. There is no divorce with *mut'a*; the separation takes place automatically when the time period lapses. When a permanent marriage ends, the Qur'an prescribes a waiting period for the wife—three menstrual cycles—but the Qur'an does not mention a waiting period for *mut'a*.[46]

There is some difference of opinion among the four Sunni schools. The Shafi'i, Maliki, and Hanbali schools consider *mut'a* completely invalid and any contract null and void. The Hanafi school considers the *mut'a* time limit an unsuitable condition and invalid, but the marriage remains valid. Hanafi scholars state that *mut'a* is a permanent marriage; the temporary aspect is invalid, but the recitation of the marriage formula has the power to create a marriage.[47]

The decision to forbid *mut'a* was not absolute or certain. And it is well known that Sunni scholars did not think corporal punishment should be imposed on anyone who practiced *mut'a*. The scholars explain their position by claiming a lack of certainty regarding *mut'a*'s status as forbidden: The four Sunni schools agree that the punishment for a person who enters a *mut'a* is not the same as for *zinā'*, fornication,[48] and the penalty for *zinā'* is not applied to *mut'a* due to confusion about its status, since a hadith from Ibn 'Abbās appears to support it.

And, according to Shi'i law, although *mut'a* is permitted, it is considered an inferior kind of marriage. In view of this inferior status, Imam Ja'far is quoted as saying that it is *makrūh*, blameworthy, to contract a temporary marriage with a virgin because of the wrong it does to her family. And Imam Mūsā al-Kāẓim is quoted as saying that temporary marriage is only acceptable for an unmarried man who needs it to preserve his modesty, or for a married man while he is absent from his wife.[49]

Since this is a major point of difference between *imāmī* Shi'i jurisprudence and the legal practice of other Muslim sects, it is surprising that *mut'a* has not been studied more comprehensively. This lack of scholarly attention is particularly alarming, considering the real-life consequences *mut'a* has for questions related to gender, sexuality, and marital ethics in Islam. A lack of clarity about or in-depth study of permissible sexual acts or issues concerning adultery can potentially create an environment in which abuse thrives.

TEMPORARY MARRIAGE BEFORE ISLAM

Forms of temporary marriage are found among various civilizations in the ancient world. For example, it was practiced among some Native American tribes, Inuit people, some sub-Saharan African tribes, and in Tibet.[50] Plato's *Republic* mentions his guardians being involved in this type of marriage.[51]

Temporary marriage also existed in the Middle East prior to the advent of Islam. Historian and anthropologist Raphael Patai mentions that Talmudic and Roman sources contain the first reports of temporary marriage in the Middle East. This form of marriage was legal "among the Jews of Babylonia in the third century" and "even sages and rabbis, when visiting another town, were said to practice this custom."[52] A Zoroastrian form of temporary marriage appears to be a hybrid between *mutʿa* and another pre-Islamic form of marriage known as *nikāḥ al-istibzāʿ*, which literally means marriage of intercourse. A husband would seek another man's assistance to impregnate his wife. When assured of his wife's pregnancy, the permanent husband would reunite with his wife, and the temporary husband would have no further contact with her. The permanent husband was considered the father and would raise the child as his own. This type of marriage was regarded as an act of "solidarity with a member of one's community."[53]

There have been a variety of commentaries on pre-Islamic marriage. Gertrude H. Stern writes that prior to the advent of Islam, marriage in the Arabian Peninsula was largely transitory.[54] Kamāl al-Dīn b. al-Humām states, "When a man came to a village and he had no acquaintance there, he would marry a woman for as long as thought he would stay, so that she would look after him and his property."[55] This arrangement continued until the Qurʾan revealed: "those who guard their chastity except with their wives or those bondwomen in their possession, for then they are free from blame" (Q 23:5–6). William Robertson Smith, on the other hand, writes that in its pre-Islamic form, *mutʿa* was a temporary alliance between a woman and a man, often a stranger seeking protection among the woman's tribe. Since the woman lived with her tribe, the tribe would protect both her and her husband.[56] Children born during such a union traced their lineage through their mother and would remain with the tribe, regardless if the father stayed.[57] Smith characterizes pre-Islamic society as having a predominantly matrilineal character. Collectively, these findings show that prior to Islam, almost any man could find temporary sexual companionship wherever he went, and either this is an exaggeration, or the temporary nature of sexual relations was not thought to be remarkable.[58]

This brief overview of the history of marriage institutions prior to Islam suggest that, broadly speaking, marriage was not understood to be permanent in the way it is in the modern era, and biological parents were not considered directly responsible for their children. A father might leave before his child was born if he was a temporary visitor in the mother's village or, in the case of *nikāḥ al-istibzāʿ*, if he served as a father only to produce respectable offspring for another man. More research is necessary before we can uncover a realistic and comprehensive picture of the realities of women's lives in pre-Islamic societies. However, there is sufficient evidence indicating that various types of marriage and cohabitation were practiced in pre-Islamic Arabia.

A BRIEF OVERVIEW OF SECTARIAN DIVISIONS IN ISLAM

Fully understanding the Sunni and Shiʿi perspectives on *mutʿa* requires understanding how these doctrinal groups developed. The Prophet Muhammad died in 11/632 without nominating an official successor, leaving his followers to appoint a leader. The Ansar, Companions of the Prophet Muhammad, were about to appoint a leader from their group when ʿUmar urged them to accept Abū Bakr (d. 13/634), who was given the title *Khalīfat Rasūl Allāh*, Deputy of the Messenger of God. There were people who did not accept Abū Bakr as their leader and thought ʿAli was the rightful heir.[59] These people were the proto-Shiʿi community.

However, the main difference between the Shiʿa and Sunni is not the issue of *khilāfa* but *imāma*.[60] The Shiʿi theory of the imamate evolved gradually during the first Islamic century and took definite shape in the middle of the second/eighth century. For approximately the next 100 years, until the death of the eleventh imam,[61] al-Ḥasan al-ʿAskarī, in 260/874, no significant changes were introduced into the doctrine.[62]

The first major addition appears in the mid-fourth/tenth century: the belief that there are twelve imams, the last of whom remains in perpetual *ghayba*, concealment, until his ultimate return as the Mahdi.[63] The *ghayba* is divided into two periods: *al-ghayba al-sughrā*, a lesser concealment, (260–329/874–94) during which time the imam was represented on earth by four successive representatives, and *al-ghayba al-kubrā*, a greater concealment, whose duration is known only by God.[64]

The Shiʿa and Sunni differ in their sources of law. Shariʿa is based on two sources: the Qurʾan and the sunna. The Prophet Muhammad in his last sermon is said to have declared, "I have left among you two things, and as long as you hold fast to them, you will not go astray: the Book of Allah and the sunna of his Prophet."[65] The Qurʾan and sunna are complementary: one is read in conjunction with the other because many of the commands in the Qurʾan cannot be understood without explanation. The Prophet Muhammad often provided this exegesis and is considered a source of "extra-Qurʾanic" judgment; however, this "extra-Qurʾanic" element is contained within the general principles outlined by the Qurʾan and does not stand as a separate source.

For the Sunni, the sunna is restricted to referencing the person of the Prophet Muhammad; while for Twelver Shiʿa it also includes a body of statements and actions ascribed to the twelve imams. A group of legal specialists focusing on the sunna and *aḥādīth* arose from among the Successors of the Companions of the Prophet. The Successors' were preoccupied with studying religious discourse that would help them formulate legal doctrines. They amassed many traditions, and the large number of *aḥādīth* they collected alarmed many Muslims. Some of these specialists blatantly used the Prophet Muhammad's name to support all kinds of embellishments and authorizations; as Burton puts it, these were cases of "pious self-deception."[66] Feminist Muslim scholars, as will be discusses later in chapter 5, also take a fresh, critical approach to *aḥādīth*.

Scholars developed methods for the verification and counter verification of each *isnād*, chain of transmission, and *matn*, subject; for example, al-Bukhārī (d. 256/870) found that out of the 20,000 *aḥādīth* he collected, only 7,225 seemed sound. Sunni Muslims generally recognize six correct or authentic collections: al-Bukhārī; Muslim b. al-Ḥajjāj (d. 261/875); Ibn Mājah (d. 258/877); Abū Dāwud (d. 270/889); al-Tirmidhī (d. 279/892); and al-Nasāʾī (d. 303/915). Aḥmad b. Ḥanbal (d. 241/855), whose great encyclopedia of traditions, called the *Musnad*, contains nearly 29,000 traditions, has also "been a subject of pious reading."[67] The Shiʿa consider four collections canonical (usually referred to as *akhbār*): al-Kulaynī (d. 939/340); Ibn Bābūya (d. 381/991–92); al-Tūsī (d. 459/1066–67); and al-Mufīd (d. 413/1032). Al-Kulaynī's *al-Kāfī fī ʿilm al-dīn*,[68] the earliest of the four, is the largest, the most detailed, and the most revered by Twelver Shiʿa. It was compiled a few decades after the disappearance of the twelfth imam in 260/873.

In addition to the Qurʾan and *aḥādīth*, Sunni and Shiʿi law rely on *ijmāʿ*, scholarly consensus—of Sunni and Shiʿi scholars respectively. They also each rely on one additional source: Sunni law incorporates *qiyās*, analogy, while Shiʿi law prefers *ʿaql*, reason.[69] Twelvers and Ismaʿilis totally reject *qiyās*, but Zaydīs generally accept it.

A distinct Shiʿi legal doctrine was first formulated by Muḥammad al-Bāqir and then expanded upon by his son Jaʿfar al-Ṣādiq, the fifth and sixth imams respectively, to whom the bulk of the Shiʿi legal tradition is attributed.[70] Al-Bāqir (d. 735/117) was a contemporary of the Kufan legal scholar Ibrāhīm al-Nakhāʾī and the Medinan al-Zuhrī. The lifetime of Jaʿfar al-Ṣādiq (80–148/700–65) coincided almost exactly with that of Abū Ḥanīfa (80–150/699–767), the founder of the Hanafi school of Kufa, while Mālik b. Anas (97–179/765–95), the founder of the Maliki school of Medina, was somewhat younger.[71]

There are three main points of difference between Shiʿi and Sunni law: (1) only the Shiʿa allow *mutʿa*; (2) only the Sunni allow the prohibition of *ṭalāq al-bidaʿ*, three-fold repudiation;[72] and, (3) the Shiʿa favor treating paternal and maternal relatives equally and remove the privileged position of paternal relatives that exists in Sunni inheritance law.[73] While Shi'i law does not differ from Sunni law any more than the laws of the four Sunni schools differ among themselves, the differences between Sunni and Shi'i law appear greater because of the underlying social antagonism between the two sects.

The Shi'a were separated into two main branches: the Zaydīs,[74] known as the Fiver Shi'a, and the Isma'ili,[75] or the Sevener Shi'a. The mainstream Zaydīs did not permit *mut'a*.[76] Why did Zaydīs adopt a solution that was so contrary to the Twelver doctrine at that time? Islamic law scholar Joseph Schacht argues it was because the Shi'i doctrine of *mut'a* simply did not exist yet, and he dismisses the *Majmū' al-fiqh* as being a later fabrication.[77] The Zaydī tradition that is opposed to *mut'a* is noteworthy because it only mentions that the Prophet Muhammad forbade *mut'a* on the occasion of the campaign at Khaybar.[78] A Twelver report of the same tradition from Zayd also contains the prohibition of eating the flesh of domesticated donkeys,[79] which is an al-Zuhrī hadith.[80] Thus, it is likely that the Zaydīs adopted this al-Zuhrī hadith and gave it credibility through an 'Alid *isnād*, chain of transmission, at a later date.

The Isma'ilis do not permit *mut'a*, and they never developed a systematic doctrine of their own regarding *mut'a*. Their objection to Sunni principles of *uṣūl al-fiqh*, the sources of law, which paralleled the Twelver objections, are expressed in Qāḍī al-Nu'mān's (d. 363/974) *Ikhtilāf uṣūl al-madhāhib*. And they also hold the position that the Prophet Muhammad forbade *mut'a*.[81]

HISTORY OF *MUT'A* AFTER ISLAM

This section will draw a picture of *mut'a* after the advent of Islam. Here we have three types of evidences: Sunni *aḥādīth*, the sermon of 'Umar, and Shi'i *aḥādīth*. The Sunni and Shi'a alike agree that the Prophet Muhammad recommended *mut'a* to his Companions and soldiers. 'Abdullah, as reported by Qays, said, "We used to be on expedition with the Prophet and had no women with us, so we asked the Prophet whether we could get ourselves castrated, which the Prophet prohibited, and permitted us to marry women in return for a robe [dowry] for a definite period."[82]

All major Sunni hadith collections include *aḥādīth* on *mut'a* and end by concluding that Islam forbids it. The traditions quoted in each collection differ considerably in number, form, and the order in which they are presented. However, they do agree that *mut'a* is not permitted. The Sunni tradition differs mainly concerning the time and place that the Prophet Muhammad forbade *mut'a*, and the opinions include:[83] after the raid on Khaybar (7/628); at the raid of the minor hajj; in the year of Awṭās (8/629); in the year of the conquest of Mecca (8 or 9/629 or 630); at the battle of Hunayn (9/630); at the battle of Tabuk (9/630); or even during the last pilgrimage (11/632). Some *aḥādīth* are more general, claiming the Prophet Muhammad disallowed it but not saying when. Islamic scholars have dealt with apparently contradictory *aḥādīth* by claiming that *mutʿa* was allowed and disallowed several times. The numerous dates given for the impermissibility of *mutʿa* make it difficult to determine the truth. All that is certain is that there is confusion about when it was disallowed. Only a few Sunni sources mention *mutʿa* without immediately mentioning it is forbidden, including *al-Masnad* by Ibn Ḥanbal, which asserts that *mutʿa* was permitted by the Prophet Muhammad and does not mention that it was abrogated or forbidden, as well as Muslim b. Ḥajjāj's (d. 261/875) *Saḥīḥ* and al-Haythami's (d. 807/1404) *Majmaʿ*.

In most Sunni collections, it is related from ʿAli that he said, "Verily the Prophet of God banned the *mutʿa* of temporary marriage and the eating of the meat of domesticated donkeys."[84] In Shiʿi sources, the words "on the day of the battle of Khaybar" are added. In another hadith, Ibn Sabra related from his father the following: "I came upon the Prophet of God early in the morning [. . .] leaning against the Kaʿba. He said, 'O people! I commanded you to seek enjoyment from these women, but now God has forbidden that to you until the day of Resurrection. So if you have a temporary wife, let go of her way; and do not take back anything of what you have given her.'"[85] The Sunni consider this hadith important and center most of their arguments around it. The Shiʿa point out that although the hadith is related by many chains of authority, they all go back to one Companion, Ibn Sabra. They assert the principle that a Qurʾanic verse cannot be abrogated by even the most authentic hadith.

Another hadith, related from Salman b. al-Akwa through his father, reports that the Prophet Muhammad permitted *mutʿa* in the year of Awṭās (8/629) for three days, and then he prohibited it. This hadith is related in many sources, with numerous discrepancies in the text. The Sunni affirm that *mutʿa* was allowed due to special circumstances at the advent of Islam—Muslims were often at war during this period. The Shiʿa respond to this hadith in a familiar way: first citing that a hadith related from one Companion cannot abrogate the Qurʾan. Additionally, the Shiʿa question how this hadith could be authentic when Abū Bakr did not forbid *mutʿa* during his caliphate and ʿUmar only banned it toward the end of his caliphate during a sermon (discussed below). The conflicting Sunni views have benefited Shiʿi scholars, who use the confusion and conflicting dates to cast doubt on the veracity of the Sunni claim and solidify their own position on the permissibility of *mutʿa*.

A key area of contestation regarding the issue of *mutʿa* is the sermon of ʿUmar in which he outlawed *mutʿa*: "Two *mutʿas*[86] were practiced during the time of the Prophet, but I forbid both of them and will punish anyone who practices either."[87] The Sunni interpret the Companions' silence and lack of protest as indicating their knowledge that *mutʿa* had already been abrogated.

The Shiʿa, on the other hand, claim ʿUmar's sermon demonstrates that *mutʿa* was permitted during the lifetime of the Prophet Muhammad and, therefore, attribute the banning of *mutʿa* to ʿUmar and his opinion. If the Prophet Muhammad had indeed prohibited *mutʿa*, then ʿUmar would not have needed to ban it.[88] A detailed study of this will be provided in chapter 3, when al-Rāzī discusses the sermon in detail.

There is a general Shiʿi method for presenting this issue within *aḥādīth* compilations. An author begins with speaking about Q 4:24 as a proof text for the permissibility of *mutʿa*. For example, al-Kulaynī starts his chapter on *mutʿa* by narrating a hadith that mentions the *āya* and that *mutʿa* is permitted. This hadith has a Shiʿi chain of transmission and goes back to Abū Basīr, who reports: "I asked Abū Jaʿfar, peace be upon him, about *mutʿa*. He replied, "It has been revealed in the Qurʾan that 'so for whatever you enjoy [of marriage] from them, give them their due compensation as an obligation. And there is no blame upon you for what you mutually agree to beyond the obligation [Q 4:24].'"[89] Shiʿi scholars then proceed to mention a hadith from ʿAli that illustrates the strong disapproval of ʿUmar. This hadith serves as evidence for the second opinion held by the Shiʿa: ʿUmar banned *mutʿa* on his own authority rather than on the Prophet Muhammad's authority. ʿAli is quoted saying, "Were it not for the little son of al-Khattab, who preceded me, only a scoundrel would be guilty of fornication."[90] This hadith works as a foil for the Shiʿa in two ways: First, there is apparent tension in the belittling language of ʿAli, and it establishes a rivalry with ʿUmar, whose authority is not accepted by the Shiʿa; his teachings are contradicted and rejected whenever possible. Second, citing this hadith allows the Shiʿa to mention *taqiyya*, denial of religious belief and practice when facing persecution, a Shiʿi notion sometimes held almost as high as an article of faith.

The polemical nature of these discussions is emphasized by the large number of *aḥādīth* that extol the merits of *mutʿa*. According to one story, a Shiʿi man approached Muḥammad al-Bāqir and asked him about the merits of *mutʿa*, and he replied:

> "If he [any man] desires the face of God, [he should strive] to oppose those who reject it. Thus every time he extends his hand to her, God inscribes it as a good deed, when he approaches her, God forgives him a sin; and when he bathes, God forgives him in accordance [with the] amount of water that was poured on his hair." I said, "According to the numbers of hairs?" And he said, "Yes."[91]

No modern Shiʿi hadith collection lacks a chapter, or at least part of one, that contains a tradition on *mutʿa*. The prominence of the subject indicates its importance in Shiʿi hadith literature, which goes into extensive detail, unlike Sunni hadith literature; this can perhaps be explained by *mutʿa*'s role as a defining aspect of Shiʿi communal identity. Since the Qurʾan is treated as a fixed text, *aḥādīth* are the arena in which positions are more likely to be defended.

Examining *aḥādīth* on *mutʿa* provides insight into the history of early hadith in general. Classical jurists looked at a hadith and evaluated its *isnād* and issues related to its *matn*, as well as some components of *zarf al-riwāya*, the historical circumstances of its utterance. Modern Muslim scholars sort through discrepancies in *aḥādīth* in different ways. Mernissi's double investigation of hadith, a simultaneous "historical and methodological" approach to evaluating authors and the condition of a hadith's first use, is a good template for investigating *mutʿa*. Asking who uttered a hadith, to whom, and in what context helps reveal the underlying motivations for the opinions on *mutʿa* that are conveyed in *aḥādīth*.

CURRENT PRACTICE OF *MUTʿA*

Mutʿa slowly disappeared from the Sunni world after ʿUmar banned it. The Shiʿa, on the other hand, continued to insist *mutʿa* was lawful and trace the origin of its jurisprudence to Jaʿfar al-Ṣādiq, one of the Prophet Muhammad's descendants and the sixth Shiʿi imam.[92] And *mutʿa* briefly returned to the Shiʿi community in an official capacity when Caliph Maʿmun reapproved it in the ninth century, but because a consensus on the unlawfulness of *mutʿa* emerged in the Sunni community before this period, they did not accept Maʿmun's edict.[93]

Prior to the 1979 Iranian Revolution, a marginal population in Iranian and Iraqi shrine pilgrimage towns covertly practiced *mutʿa*. However, the Iranian public's knowledge of *mutʿa* was vague, and people considered the practitioners social deviants. But clerics approved of this practice as part of an effort to resist the modernizing policies of the Pahlavis, who did not legally recognize *mutʿa*.[94] Men entered into *mutʿa* with lower-class women, widows, or women who frequented shrines to offer sexual services to pilgrims and travelers.[95]

After the Iranian Revolution, it was reintroduced by the Islamic regime for various reasons, using two strategies to counter the negative public perception of *mutʿa*: The first strategy involved redefining the practice. *Mutʿa* was presented as a brilliant Islamic edict that responded to human sexual needs; however, these needs mostly signified male needs. This is not to say that Iranian scholars did not recognize female sexual needs, but they did so mostly in the service of men, and in a less comprehensive manner. Both classical and modern scholars have viewed sexuality as anchored in nature in a particular way. For example, in his book, *The Rights of Women in Islam*, Ayatollah

Muṭahharī (d. 1979) writes that woman is by nature monogamist; thus, polyandry is incompatible with her natural tendencies—good women do not seek sex or enjoy multiple sexual partners.[96] Man, however, is not a monogamist, and polygyny is in his nature; suppressing this nature could have negative psychological and social results. The connection between public health and male sexual satisfaction implies that if men are sexually satisfied, then public health will be maintained. Additionally, Muṭahharī suggests this will result in higher public morality since men will be less likely to seek out prostitutes. Haeri critiques him and says that the notion of public health here is "hypothetical and ideological."[97] Neither scholar links *mut'a* with the possibility of health hazards like sexually transmitted infections; nor is there any consideration of the effect *mut'a* might have on the psychological well-being of both temporary and permanent wives and their children.

The second strategy was to make *mut'a* familiar to the public. This was done by including information about *mut'a* in as many forums as possible, including high school textbooks, sermons in mosques and during religious gatherings, on radio and television shows, and in newspapers. Even then president Hashemi Rafsanjani took part in the campaign during a Friday sermon in 1990. He encouraged young men who did not have the economic means to maintain a permanent marriage to use *mut'a* to satisfy their sexual needs, stating that *mut'a* is a shari'a ruling compatible with "modern" times. Rafsanjani's speech garnered angry responses from the women's press and activists who saw it as another attack on women's rights, dignity, and security in marriage.[98]

The reasons for using these strategies to promote *mut'a* were tied to historical realities. Ayatollah Khomeini took power in 1980 after the devastating eight-year Iran–Iraq War, during which Iran suffered an unfathomable loss of life. This resulted in a decreased population, leaving the country with a substantial gender imbalance. Thus, the government adopted policies to increase the birth rate, including promoting early marriage, remarriage, *mut'a*, large families, and motherhood as the main role of women. It also displaced women from educational institutions and curtailed employment opportunities, policies that had many feminists up in arms.[99] Since then, however, state attitudes have changed and so have societal demographics. For example, present numbers show that more Iranian women graduate from university than men, and the government has implemented a family planning program to counter the population boom in the 1980s and 1990s.[100] Since the 1990s there has been another major demographic shift. A recent *BBC* article speaks of another demographic shift due to late marriages and fewer children. The government fears if action is not taken and people are not encouraged to marry and have more children, in three decades Iran could have one of the oldest populations on the planet.[101]

In the modern era, *mutʿa*, called *sīgha* in Iran, has three main categories. The first type of *sīgha* is called "trial marriage." It allows two people to live together to see if they are compatible. It is also used by young university students who want to live together in an apartment.

"Travel *sīgha*" is the second category,[102] and it allows people to bypass Islamic laws that segregate the sexes and travel together. It can be used for sexual or nonsexual purposes. Tourism companies use it to facilitate unmarried couples going on cruises, and a cleric provides officiating documents as couples enter the cruise ship. One family traveling with a male can use it to have women from another family travel with them, since *mutʿa*/*sīgha* makes them family. In these cases, it prevents accusations of *zinā*ʾ, fornication.

The third type is used for reproductive purposes. Robert Tappan describes how *mutʿa* is utilized to gain access to third-party surrogacy. It allows a couple to use donor gametes and embryos, which are inserted into the infertile wife (or even a surrogate). Here, *mutʿa* also prevents accusations of inappropriate sexual behavior and guarantees the child's lineage, even if scholars ultimately disagree about which of the women is the "mother."[103]

Using *mutʿa* to address infertility can be complicated. The process is simple if it is the wife who is infertile. However, if the husband is infertile, the process is a burden for the woman. Islamic law does not allow a woman to have more than one husband at a time—permanent or temporary. Women can still contract a *mutʿa*, but they must first divorce their husbands, observe a waiting period of three months, and then contract the *mutʿa* with the sperm donor. Once the predetermined period of the *mutʿa* comes to an end, the wife must observe another waiting period before she can remarry her original husband. However, the child belongs to the temporary husband according to Islamic law; thus, the woman and the donor must sign a separate agreement that grants custody of the child to the permanent husband.

Despite their desperate pleas, contemporary scholars refuse to give a verdict favoring women and thus allowing them bypass this long and circuitous process. In two of Makarem Shirazi's rulings addressing donor semen, he remains firms that a child should be produced only within the bounds of a religiously sanctioned marriage. He does not invoke applicable juristic principles like *durūra*, necessity, or *al-ʿadam al-haraj*, protection against distress and constriction, to offer an alternative solution.

Those in Iranian society who are in favor of *mutʿa* are primarily the religious elite, as well as those already practicing it, while the public often has a negative view of it because it can foster abuse. Speaking for the religious elite in an interview at his home in Qom, the conservative scholar Sayyid Reza Borghei Mudaris offered a list of those who might benefit from *mutʿa*: a financially strapped widow; a young widow, who can use it to fulfill her sexual needs; a man who cannot afford a permanent marriage; and a married man who is experiencing domestic strife and needs "a kind of medicine."[104] Some feminists support *mut'a,* such as Shala Sherkats, editor of the feminist monthly *Zanan.* She explains her position: "First, relations between young men and women will become a little bit freer. Second, they can satisfy their sexual needs. Third, sex will become depoliticized. Fourth, they will use up some of the energy they are putting into street demonstrations. Finally, our society's obsession with virginity will disappear."[105]

Other scholars have reservations, saying regardless of its benefits, *mut'a* destroys families and morality and is not justifiable within Islam. And some feminists point out that these marriages are the prerogative of wealthy (mostly married) men, while the majority of women they temporarily marry are divorced, widowed, or poor.[106] Haeri maintains that neither clerics nor leading thinkers have analyzed *mut'a*'s implications in a coherent way, claiming "if they are really serious, they should study the matter in the context of sexuality, birth control, sexually transmitted diseases, morality, religion and gender relations,"[107] to which I would also add male and female psychology, Islamic marital and sexual ethics, and a serious study of current research within the science of sexuality.

Few statistics exist on the practice of *mut'a* within Shi'i populations, because even when legally permitted after the Islamic Revolution, no registration was required.[108] Nevertheless, anecdotal evidence suggests the practice has gained ground around the world. *Mut'a* has been the focus of several news stories and documentaries by Western media intrigued by the idea of an institution that authorizes sex in societies where illicit sex is a crime resulting in serious punishment, including 100 lashes for unmarried individuals or death by stoning for married ones. Major news outlets like *Mother Jones,* the *Guardian*, *Huffington Post,* the *BBC*, and the *New York Times* have all published on *mut'a/sīgha.*[109] NPR and podcasts have also covered the practice of temporary marriage.[110] The film industry has demonstrated a similar interest, and a few documentaries with provocative titles have been made on the subject, such as *Married for a Minute* (aired on the BBC in May 2013),[111] *In the Bazaar of Sexes,*[112] *Iraq's Secret Sex Trade,*[113] and *Fereshteh: Daughter of Ahmad.*[114] These media sources compile interviews with clerics and practitioners, giving us a flavor of the lived experience of *mut'a,* the current state of its practice, and the backgrounds of the various parties involved. They discuss various aspects and interpretations of its practice, including the benefit of encouraging couples get to know one another freely before committing to permanent marriage, as well as the detriment caused when *mut'a* serves as legalized prostitution or exploits vulnerable women.

In Iraq, *mut'a* was banned during the reign of Saddam Hussein but became permitted and gained ground after the US invasion, especially because *mut'a* helped provide for families in severe economic hardship. Nagham Kadhim runs a women's rights organization in Najaf and states, "*mut'a* marriage happens when there is an economic factor, like when the woman is poor and [does] not have money and the religious institution would offer her those job opportunities, through working for a kindergarten," for example, where she would receive 100,000 dinars (about $100 USD) per month.[115] Kadhim further explains that the institution hosts seminars about *mut'a* to convince newly employed women of the practice's religious permissibility.[116] Other women in Najaf stated that religious offices only help poor women if they are pretty, because beauty makes them good candidates for *mut'a*.

In Tajikistan, *mut'a* was unheard of until recently. Now, the mosques in Dushanbe frequently warn attendees about the unlawfulness of *mut'a*. Tajikistan has a sizable Iranian community living in its major cities, and there have been a number of incidents where Tajik women found themselves in *mut'a*s and then abandoned.[117]

In Lebanon, anthropologist Lara Deeb originally thought she would include a discussion on new ideas and practices regarding *mut'a* among youth in her project about leisure in the southern suburbs of Beirut.[118] As the project proceeded, she abandoned the idea because she discovered that interviewing people practicing it would be difficult given its social stigma. She also did not want to add to the already sensationalized representation of Islam, and Shi'i Islam in particular. Nonetheless, she concludes that the practice has increased among youth looking to simultaneous live moral lives and date in the Western sense; thus, they are reshaping moral norms around these issues.

In India,[119] cases have been reported of men from the Arabian Gulf visiting and using *mut'a* to marry women, often young girls and orphans, for short periods of time until they go back home. Sometimes, this is done with the approval of the parents, and in other cases, such marriages are facilitated by orphanages under the guise of helping young orphaned girls get settled or be provided for financially. One social worker and activist in the state of Kerala reported that over two thousand young children in the region have been born from such marriage arrangements.[120] Men can even choose between unions lasting a week or two or ones in which the bride accompanies the man to his home country, where she might be forced into both sexual and domestic servitude.[121]

On the other side of the world, we see more examples of young people utilizing *mut'a* to date and cohabitate. *Mut'a* helps them reconcile their religious beliefs with their modern context, and it is clear that the practice of *mut'a* is on the rise in the West. One young man in New York, on his thirty-fifth *mut'a*, says he is looking to get married but needs to find someone who is compatible.[122] In London, another young man, on his thirteenth, is also ostensibly looking for the "right one."[123]

Dearborn, Michigan has the largest population of Arab Muslims in the United States; the majority are Lebanese Shi'a from the Beqaa region and believe that *mut'a* is permissible. *Mut'a* was not a major issue in this community before the Iranian Revolution. Several immigrants only become aware of it after coming to the United States. In Dearborn, it is certainly not viewed as a Lebanese tradition, although the idea is not foreign to Lebanon;[124] however, it was likely only practiced by shaykhs and women on the periphery of society, much like Haeri discovered in Iran.

There are also other variations. *'Urfi*, marriage without documentation, and *misyār*, traveler's marriage, are conducted among the Sunni.[125] In a secular Western context, the Mexican government now allows a type of temporary marriage that gives the couple a two-year trial period, after which they may dissolve the marriage without excessive paperwork or hassle, saving the courts time and money and the individuals' emotional pain.

CONCLUSION

The Shi'a have recently labeled *mut'a* as one of the most progressive institutions in Islam, but *mut'a* cannot be specifically labeled a Shi'i juridical innovation; it existed in pre-Islamic Arabia. According to Sunni *aḥādīth, mut'a* existed at the beginning of Islam but was subsequently prohibited, as shown in various *aḥādīth*. However, according to Shi'i *aḥādīth*, *mut'a* was not abolished, and the Shi'a use Q 4:24 as a proof text for its permissibility. But there is still disagreement within Shi'ism, since both Zaydīs and Isma'ilis do not permit it.

The dispute concerning *mut'a* continues today and contains political dimensions that exist at a regional level; for example, following the 1979 Islamic Revolution in Iran and Khomeini's rise to power, the regime in Iran began to pursue a policy aimed at raising the national popularity of *mut'a*. This popularity eventually extended to Shi'i communities all over the world. The practice thus transformed from being simply accepted to becoming commendable, a position that challenges previous historical understandings of the concept.

It has become an amorphous tool that can be used as a loophole to transgress strict religious edicts, surpass gender segregation, allow women to travel without a guardian, and rebalance population disruption in the aftermath of war. Socially, *mut'a* may have little to do with religious or doctrinal matters, and it can be viewed as an appropriate social solution to difficult problems; for example, a solution to the pressures of a highly sexualized modern environment. In addition, this chapter has indicated possible future developments where *mut'a* might be used for fertility treatment. Feminist scholars have both reservations (for its potential to abuse vulnerable women) and praise (it can depoliticize sex), and their diverse opinions add a layer of complexity when evaluating *mutʿa*.

Whether *mutʿa* is morally wrong and obsolete or cutting edge and just right for the times depends on the relationship between sex and permanent marriage in Islam. The following three chapters analyze the existing theological material in *tafsīr* to examine whether the permissibility of *mutʿa* is justified within Qurʾanic hermeneutics. The final chapter proposes a more holistic methodology for the reinterpretation of *mutʿa* and presents a compelling call for gender justice grounded in the Islamic legal tradition. I hope this attention to the formative and classical texts, in combination with a discussion about a method for reinterpreting *mutʿa*, will serve as a model for how gender studies and Islamic law may be incorporated and studied by researchers in the future.

NOTES

1. G. Robina Quale, *A History of Marriage Systems* (Westport: Greenwood, 1988). See also Edward Westermarck, *A Short History of Marriage* (New York: Macmillan, 1926); Nancy F. Cott, *Public Vows: A History of Marriage and the Nation* (Cambridge, MA: Harvard University Press, 2000).

2. Most contemporary studies of marriage attest to this. Everyday observations also point to changes in the historical institution of marriage, especially in the West, where gay marriage is making headway, but also in the East, where there is more divorce and single parenthood than before. See also, John M. Eekelaar and Mavis Maclean, eds., *A Reader on Family Law* (Oxford: Oxford University Press, 1994), 31–41.

3. Ilyas Ba-Yunus, "Divorce Among Muslims," *Islamic Horizons* (July/August 2000), quoted in Samana Siddiqui, "Divorce Among American Muslims: Statistics, Challenges & Solutions," Sound Vision, https://www.soundvision.com/article/divorce-among-american-muslims-statistics-challenges-solutions (accessed August 9, 2020).

4. Ilyas Ba-Yunus, "How Do Muslims in North America Divorce?" in *Muslim Family in a Dilemma: Quest for a Western Identity*, ed. M. Akhtar (Washington, DC: University Press of America, 2007), 9–18, quoted in Aliya R. Chapman and Lauren Bennett Cattaneo, "American Muslim Marital Quality: A Preliminary Investigation," *Journal of Muslim Mental Health* 7, no. 2 (2013): http://dx.doi.org/10.3998/jmmh.10381607.0007.201.

5. Noha Alshugairi, "Marital Trends in the American Muslim Community: A Pilot Study," *Journal of Muslim Mental Health* 5, no. 3 (2010): https://doi.org/10.1080/15564908.2010.551275.

6. Chapman and Cattaneo, "American Muslim Marital Quality."

7. "Marriages Down, Divorces Increase in Turkey," *Daily Sabah,* February 26, 2020, https://www.dailysabah.com/turkey/marriages-down-divorces-increase-in-turkey/news.

8. Fariba Nawa, "Divorce Turkish Style," *The New York Review of Books*, February 20, 2019, https://www.nybooks.com/daily/2019/02/20/divorce-turkish-style/.

9. Lolwa Reda, "On Marriage and Divorce in Egypt," *Egypt Today*, February 28, 2019, https://www.egypttoday.com/Article/6/66379/On-Marriage-and-Divorce-in-Egypt.

10. Lorena Rios, "'Biased' Changes to Egypt's Divorce Laws Over Custody Prompt Outcry," *Huffington Post*, January 26, 2017, https://www.huffpost.com/entry/egypt-divorce-laws-custody_n_588a0396e4b0737fd5cbaf46.

11. Sobia Ali-Faisal, "What's Sex Got to Do With It? The Role of Sexual Experience in the Sexual Attitudes, and Sexual Guilt and Anxiety of Young Muslim Adults in Canada and the United States," *Journal of Muslim Mental Health* 10, no. 2 (2016): 27–41.

12. Sobia Ali-Faisal, "North American Muslims & Sex Ed: Looking at Sexual Guilt with Researcher Sobia Faisal-Ali," interview by Chelby Daigle, June 2, 2015, https://muslimlink.ca/stories/muslim-sex-ed-sexual-guilt.

13. Ali-Faisal, "What's Sex Got to Do With It?," 28.

14. Sameera Ahmed, "Religiosity and Presence of Character Strengths in American Muslim Youth," *Journal of Muslim Mental Health* 4, no. 2 (2009), quoted in Sobia Ali-Faisal, "What's Sex Got to Do With It?," 30.

15. Ali-Faisal, "North American Muslims."

16. Sameera Qureshi, "I'm a Muslim Sexual Health Educator. 'Ramy' Shouldn't Surprise You," *Medium*, July 10, 2020, https://medium.com/@sameeraq/im-a-muslim-sexual-health-educator-ramy-shouldn-t-surprise-you-a144de565863.

17. Any Islamic *fiqh*, jurisprudence, book with a chapter on *nikāḥ*, sexual intercourse or marriage, will confirm this point. More specifically, see Abū Ḥāmid al-Ghazālī, *Iḥyā' 'ulūm al-dīn* (Beirut: Dār al-Marifat, 1981).

18. Muḥammad b. Mukarram Ibn Manẓūr, *Lisān al-'Arab* (Beirut: Dār al-Sadir, 1990), 2:292–93.

19. As a contract, it conveys legal rights and obligations to each spouse. As a legal institution, it is defined in terms of *arkān*, pillars, and *aḥkām*, statutes. See Muḥammad Abū Zahra, *al-Aḥwāl al-shakhṣīyya* (Cairo: n.p., 1957), 18.

20. Ibn Manẓūr, *Lisān al-'Arab*, 2:626.

21. All translations, except for the translation of Q 4:24, are from Mustafa Khattab, trans., *The Clear Quran: A Thematic English Translation of the Message of the Final Revelation* (Lombard, IL: Book of Signs Foundation, 2016).

22. Al-Ghazālī, *Iḥyā' 'ulūm al-dīn*, 2:22.

23. Ibid.

24. Madelain Farah, *Marriage and Sexuality in Islam: A Translation of al-Ghazali's Book on the Etiquette of Marriage from the Ihya* (Salt Lake City: University of Utah Press, 1984).

25. See, for example, Kecia Ali, "The Feminist Sexual Ethics Project," Brandeis University, September 26, 2003, https://www.brandeis.edu/projects/fse/muslim/articles.html.

26. Catharine MacKinnon's dominance theory argues that men are privileged and women are subordinate to them, and this male privilege receives support from most

social institutions, as well as from a complex set of cultural beliefs. It differs from equal treatment theory and cultural feminism, criticizing sameness and difference approaches for allowing men to be the metric for the norm: "Under the sameness standard, women are measured according to our correspondence with man, our equality judged by our proximity to his measure," while "[u]nder the difference standard, we are measured according to our lack of correspondence with him." The goal of equal treatment theory and cultural feminism is equity between men and women; the goal of dominance theory is liberation from men. In particular, dominance theory provided a different perspective on the social and political practices that subordinate and exploit women. Subordination occurs through complex patterns of force, social pressures, and traditions, rituals, and customs. See Nancy Levit and Robert M. Verchick, eds., *Feminist Legal Theory: A Primer* (New York: New York University Press, 2006), 23.

27. See, among others, the work of Kecia Ali, *Sexual Ethics and Islam: Feminist Reflections on Qur'an, Hadith, and Jurisprudence*, 1st ed. (Oxford: Oneworld Publications, 2006); Aysha A. Hidayatullah, *Feminist Edges of the Qur'an*, 1st ed. (Oxford: Oxford University Press, 2014); Amina Wadud, *Qur'an and Woman: Rereading the Sacred Text from a Woman's Perspective*, reprint ed. (New York: Oxford University Press, 1999); Amina Wadud, *Inside the Gender Jihad: Women's Reform in Islam* (Oxford: Oneworld, 2006); Hadia Mubarak, *Rebellious Wives, Neglectful Husbands: Controversies in Modern Qur'anic Commentaries* (Oxford: Oxford University Press, forthcoming January 2022); Celene Ibrahim, *Women and Gender in the Qur'an* (Oxford: Oxford University Press, 2020); Zahra Ayubi, *Gendered Morality: Classical Islamic Ethics of the Self, Family, and Society* (New York: Columbia University Press, 2019); and Asma Barlas, *Believing Women in Islam: Unreading Patriarchal Interpretations of the Qur'an* (Austin: University of Texas Press, 2002).

28. Muḥammad b. Yaʿqūb al-Kulaynī, *al-Furūʿ min al-kāfī*, ed. ʿAlī Akbar al-Ghaffārī (Tehran: Dār al-Kutub al-Islāmiyya, 1968), 5:455; Muḥammad b. al-Ḥasan al-Ḥurr al-ʿĀmilī, *Wasāʾil al-Shiʿa*, ed. Ḥasan al-Amīn (Beirut: Dār al-Taʿāruf, 1986), 14:465; Muḥammad Bāqir b. Muḥammad Taqī al-Majlisī, *Biḥār al-anwār* (Beirut: Muʾassasat al-Wafāʾ, 1983), 100:308; Ruhollah Khomeini, *A Clarification of Questions: An Unabridged Translation of* Resaleh Towzih al-Masael, trans. J. Borujerdi, 1st ed. (Boulder, CO: Westview Press, 1984), all give similar instructions for *mutʿa* marriage.

29. Al-Ṭūsī says, "The conditions for *mutʿa* are that the time period and the compensation must be mentioned. This is what distinguishes it from permanent marriage." Ibn Jaʿfar Muḥammad b. al-Ḥasan al-Ṭūsī, *Taḥdhīb al-aḥkām* (Najaf: n.p., 1380/1960–61), 7:262.

30. See Umar b. Muhammad Daudpota and Asaf Ali Asghar Fyzee, "Notes on *Mutʿa* or Temporary Marriage in Islam," *Journal of the Bombay Branch of the Royal Asiatic Society* 8, (1932): 79; see also Ignaz Goldziher, *Introduction to Islamic Theology and Law* (Princeton, NJ: Princeton University Press, 1981), 9:207–8; Khomeini, *A Clarification of Questions*; ʿAllama Sayyid Muḥammad Muḥammad Ḥusayn Ṭabāṭabāī, *Shi'ite Islam*, trans. Seyyed Hossein Nasr (Albany, NY: SUNY Press, 1977); W. Heffening, "Mutʿa," in *Encyclopaedia of Islam, Second Edition*, eds. P. Bearman, Th. Bianquis, C. E. Bosworth, E. van Donzel, and W. P. Heinrichs

(Brill Online, 2012); Harald Motzki, "Marriage and Divorce," in *Encyclopedia of the Qur'ān*, ed. Jane Dammen McAuliffe (Brill Online); and Shahla Haeri, "Temporary Marriage," in *Encyclopedia of the Qur'ān*.

31. Khomeini, *A Clarification of Questions*.

32. It consists of two menstruation periods, rather than the three for permanent marriage; if she does not menstruate, it is forty-five days. The waiting period of a slave is half that of a free woman.

33. See I. K. A. Howard, "*Mut'a* Marriage Reconsidered in the Context of the Formal Procedures for Islamic Marriage," *Journal of Semitic Studies* 2, no. 1 (1975): 82–92, https://doi.org/10.1093/jss/XX.1.82.

34. Jurists are in consensus that there is no divorce in *mut'a*. Murata writes that a saying of Imam Ja'far is explicit about this. He was asked if a husband and wife who are married by *mut'a* can become separated without a formal divorce and replied, "Yes." See Sachiko Murata, *Mut'a: Temporary Marriage in Islamic Law* (Qum: Ansariyan Publishers, 1986), 44.

35. Shahla Haeri, *Law of Desire*: *Temporary Marriage in Shi'i Iran* (Syracuse, NY: Syracuse University Press, 1989), 60.

36. Since a *mut'a* is not registered, the only way to receive maintenance if a child is conceived is if the man accepts his responsibility; his only pressure to do so is his conscience. In a permanent marriage, he would be put through the procedure of taking, *li'an*, the oath of damnation. He is not put through the same kind of legal and moral testing after a *mut'a*.

37. Al-Sharīf al-Murtaḍā, *al-Intiṣār* (Najaf: Manshūrat al-Matba'a al-Ḥaḍāriyya, 1971), 119–21. He gives this as the Shi'i doctrine without hinting that there might be an alternative teaching and claims *ijmā' al-ṭā'ifa* as support. See Howard, "*Mut'a* Marriage Reconsidered," 84, fn 11.

38. According to Shi'i doctrine, *mut'a* is a type of marriage that "nobody needs to know about." Haeri writes that al-Ṭūsī, the great Shi'i theologian, specifies that "at no time are taking witness or making *mut'a* public conditions of *mut'a*, unless the man fears accusation of fornication, in which case taking two witnesses is recommended." Haeri, *Law of Desire*, 233.

39. Ziba Mir-Hosseini, *Marriage on Trial: A Study of Islamic Family Law*, rev. ed. (New York: I. B. Tauris, 2001), 166.

40. See Ibn Dāwud, *Arkān al-nikāḥ wa-shurūṭuhu* (Cairo: Maktabat al-tarbiya al-islamiya, 1963), 63–69. More generally, see Maḥmūd 'Alī al-Sarṭāwī, *Sharḥ qānūn al-aḥwāl al-shakhṣiyya* (Amman: Dār al-Fikr, 1997), 60–62; Abū al-'Aynayn Badrān, *Aḥkam al-zawāj wa-l-ṭalāq fī al-Islām* (Cairo: Dār al- ma'ārif, 1964) 76–77; and Maḥmūd al-Qasabī Zalat, *Fiqh al-usra* (Beirut: Dar al-Qalam, 1999), 45–48.

41. The formula is simple and is phrased something like this: "I, [First Name, Last Name], marry you, [First Name, Last Name], for X period and Y amount of money."

42. Muhammad Alī al-Tabātabā'ī, *Riyād al-masā'il* (Tabriz, 1990–91), 2:94.

43. 'Abd al-Rahmān al-Jazīrī, *al-Fiqh 'alā al-madhāhib al-arba'a* (Cairo: n.p., 1969), 4:24.

44. Seyyed Hossein Nasr, "Ṭabāṭabā'ī, Muḥammad Ḥusayn," in *The Oxford Encyclopaedia of the Modern Islamic World*, ed. John L. Esposito (Oxford: Oxford University Press, 2001), 227–30.

45. Al-Majlisī quotes a number of traditions that permit a man to simultaneously contract *mut'a*s with an unlimited number of women. For example, Ja'far al-Ṣādiq is quoted as saying, "Marry a thousand of them," which is clearly an exaggeration; al-Majlisī, *Biḥār al-anwār*, 100:309. Haeri quotes al-Ṣādiq, the founder of Shi'i law. When asked, "Is [a] *mut'a* wife one of [the] four (legally permitted in Islam) wives?" The imam responded, "Marry from among them one thousand, for they are wage earners, *ajir*." Haeri, *Law of Desire*, 2.

46. A woman, on the other hand, cannot divorce a man independently, but she can ask for a *khul'*, which is a separation from the husband issued by the qadi and requires the wife to return the bridal money originally given to her. See Murata, *Temporary Marriage in Islamic Law*, 18–23.

47. Murata, *Temporary Marriage in Islamic Law*, 70; see also Heffening, "Mut'a."

48. See R. Peters, "Zinā or Zināʾ," in *Encyclopaedia of Islam, Second Edition*. If someone is found guilty of fornication, their punishment is the *ḥadd* punishment, which is one hundred lashes for each party if they are unmarried and stoning to death if they are married. The four schools agree that the punishment for *mut'a* is *ta'zīr*, less than the full punishment for *zināʾ*, depending on the circumstances and the opinion of the judge. See Murata, *Temporary Marriage in Islamic Law*, 71.

49. Al-Kulaynī, a Shi'i legal authority and author of *al-Kāfī*, one of the sect's most important early books, quotes many *aḥādīth* on *mut'a*. He dedicates a relatively extensive chapter to them in *al-Kāfī*, where he discusses the various conditions and aspects of *mut'a*, as well as its legal ramifications. See al-Kulaynī, *al-Kāfī*, 5:448–60.

50. Edward Westermarck, *The History of Human Marriage* (New York: The Allerton Book Company, 1922), 267–68.

51. Daudpota and Fyzee, "Notes on Mut'a," 79.

52. Raphael Patai, *Golden River to Golden Road: Society, Culture, and Change in the Middle East* (Philadelphia: University of Pennsylvania Press, 1967), 127.

53. Haeri, *Law of Desire*, 18–19.

54. Gertrude H. Stern, *Marriage in Early Islam* (London: The Royal Asiatic Society, 1939).

55. Kamāl al-Dīn Ibn al-Humām, *Fatḥ al-qadīr* (Cairo: al-Maktaba al-Tijāriyya al-Kubrā, 1974), 3:51; and see also, Abū 'Īsā Muḥammad al-Tirmidhī, *Ṣaḥīḥ* (Cairo: n.p., 1350–53/1931–34); "Bāb Nikāḥ," as quoted in Mohammad Muslehuddin, *Mut'a: Temporary Marriage* (Lahore: n.p., 1974), 3; Haeri, *Law of Desire*, 241–46.

56. William Robertson Smith, *Kinship and Marriage in Early Arabia* (Boston: Beacon Press, 1903), 35.

57. Khalid Sindawi, *Temporary Marriage in Sunni and Shi'ite Islam: A Comparative Study* (Wiesbaden: Harrassowitz Verlag, 2013), 23.

58. For more on *mut'a* in pre-Islamic Arabia, see Jawād 'Alī, *al-Mufaṣṣal fī tārīkh al-'Arab qabla al-Islām* (Beirut: Dār al-'Ilm li-l-Malāyīn, 1976), 536–37.

59. For more on this period, see Andrew J. Newman, *The Formative Period of Twelver Shi'ism: Ḥadīth as Discourse Between Qum and Baghdad* (Richmond,

Surrey: Curzon Press, 2000); and Wilferd Madelung, "Imāma," in *Encyclopaedia of Islam, Second Edition.*

60. Etan Kohlberg, "Imam and Community in the Pre-Ghayba Period," in *Authority and Political Culture in Shi'ism*, ed. Arjomand Said Ami (Albany, NY: SUNY Press, 1988), 34.

61. The term "imam" refers to the concept of "supreme leadership" after the death of the Prophet Muhammad. Most often, it refers to the Shi'i concept of the right of leadership belonging to those related to the Prophet Muhammad by blood. Thus, the Shi'a, or those who felt that 'Ali had a divine right as the immediate caliph after the Prophet Muhammad, denied the legitimacy of the caliphates of Abū Bakr, 'Umar, and 'Uthmān and founded the imamate, a continuation of divine leadership based on the character and perception of the imam as sinless and divinely guided, as well as on the imam's blood relationship to the Prophet Muhammad. For more, see Madelung, "Imāma."

62. Kohlberg, "Imam and Community," 34.

63. The term refers to the Islamic belief that a "rightly guided one," the Mahdi, will return before the end of time to rule and restore faith and justice. For a deeper understanding of the history of the meaning, see Wilferd Madelung, "al-Mahdī," in *Encyclopaedia of Islam, Second Edition.*

64. For more details, see, for example, Abdulaziz Sachedina, *Islamic Messianism: The Idea of Mahdī in Twelver Shī'ism* (Albany, NY: SUNY Press, 1981), 85ff.

65. Al-Tirmidhī, *Ṣaḥīḥ*. The sermon is mentioned in hadith nos. 1628, 2046, 2085.

66. John Burton, *An Introduction to the Hadīth* (Edinburgh: Edinburgh University Press, 1994), xvi.

67. J. Robson, "Ḥadīth," in *Encyclopaedia of Islam, Second Edition.*

68. It is comprised of three parts: *Uṣūl al-kāfī*, *Furū' al-kāfī*, and *al-Rawda min al-kāfī*, which together represent the crystallization of Twelver Shi'i religious thought as it had developed during the first two centuries after the death of 'Alī b. Abī Ṭālib (d. 40/661). Al-Kulaynī usually cites several versions of each tradition, with different chains of transmission, and the one he judges to be the most authentic comes after the "weaker" ones. Al-Kulaynī lived during the "smaller occultation" of the twelfth imam and was in touch with his last agent.

69. Wilferd Madelung, "Shī'a," in *Encyclopaedia of Islam, Second Edition.*

70. The Shi'a call Abū Ja'far Muḥammad al-Ṭūsī (d. 460/1068) the "Elder of the Denomination," since he is the founder of Shi'i demonstrative jurisprudence, the first person to give Shi'i law a systematic basis.

71. Joseph Schacht, "Abū Ḥanīfa al-Nu'mān," in *Encyclopaedia of Islam, Second Edition.*

72. The Shi'i denial of the validity of *ṭalāq al-bidā'* reflects its founders readiness to break not only with the political institutions of the Muslim community but also with some of its social practices that take a different attitude toward women.

73. In contrast with previous cases, Shi'i law in this instance does not seem to have had much of a precedent in early Islamic practice, or in the moral sentiment of law scholars. Again, it is apparent that the founders of Shi'i law were more willing than Sunni scholars to repudiate the actual legal practice of the early Muslim community.

74. For a detailed discription, see Wilferd Madelung, "Zaydiyya," in *Encyclopaedia of Islam, Second Edition.*

75. For a detailed descrption, see Wilferd Madelung, "Ismāʿīliyya," in *Encyclopaedia of Islam, Second Edition.*

76. The Jārūdiyya sect of the Zaydīs did permit *mutʿa*. The Jārūdiyya were former supporters of Muḥammad al-Bāqir, which could simply indicate that al-Bāqir upheld this doctrine, leading to continuity between some Zaydī and the Twelver (*imāmī*) Shiʿa. See Wilferd Madelung, *Der Imam al-Qasim Ibn Ibrahim und die Glaubenslehre der Zaiditen* (Berlin: Walter de Gruyter, 1965), 47.

77. Joseph Schacht, *Origins of Muhammadan Jurisprudence* (Oxford: Clarendon Press, 1950), 260, 262, 267.

78. Zayd b. ʿAlī, *Corpus Juris*, ed. Eugenio Griffini (Milan: Ulrico Hoepli, 1919), 718; referred to in Arthur Gribetz, *Strange Bedfellows: Mutʿat al-Nisāʾ and Mutʿat al-Ḥajj: A Study Based on Sunnī and Shīʿī Sources of Tafsīr, Ḥadīth, and Fiqh* (Berlin: Klaus Schwartz, 1994), 6.

79. Abū Jaʿfar Muḥammad b. al-Ḥasan al-Ṭūsī, *al-Mabsūt fi fiqh al-imāmiyya* (Tehran: n.p., 1967), 2:251.

80. Ibn Isḥāq has three reports of the Prophet Muhammad's prohibition of eating the flesh of domestic donkeys at Khaybar, but none of the prohibitions of *mutʿa* are present there. He does not, however, use al-Zuhrī as a source for this incident; see ʿAbd al-Malik Ibn Hishām, *The Life of Muhammad: A Translation of Isḥāq's* Sīrat Rasūl Allāh, trans. Alfred Guillaume (Karachi: Oxford University Press, 1978), 758. Al-Wāqidī does join the prohibition of eating the flesh of donkeys and *mutʿa* and attributes the prohibition to Khaybar; see Muḥammad b. ʿUmar al-Wāqidī, *Kitāb al-Maghāzī* (London: Oxford University Press, 1966), 2:660–61. The effectiveness of al-Zuhrī's ʿAlid *isnād* is seen in Ibn Khallikan's report of Yaḥyā b. Aktham persuading al-Maʾmūn to rescind his proclamation allowing *mutʿa* on the strength of al-Zuhrī's tradition. Al-Maʾmūn was also under the impression that ʿUmar abolished *mutʿa*.

81. Al-Qadi Numan b. Muhammad, *Ikhtilāf uṣūl al-madhāhib*, ed. Sham'un T. Lokhandwalla (Shimla: Indian Institute of Advanced Studies, 1972), 2:267.

82. Muslim b. al-Ḥajjāj, *Tafsīr al-ṣahīh* (Cairo: n.p., 1374/1916), 38.

83. Murata, *Temporary Marriage*, 62–63.

84. Ibid., 62.

85. Ibid.

86. The two are *mutʿa al-ḥajj* and *mutʿa al-nisāʾ*. To understand *mutʿa al-ḥajj* we need to start with *ḥajj*, the pilgrimage to Mecca, which is one of the five pillars of Islam. It is the obligation for Muslim adults once in their lifetime, if they can financially afford it after taking care of all their responsibilities (Q 3:97). It takes place at an appointed time, in the month of Dhū al-Ḥajj, and in appointed places, namely Mecca and its surroundings. *ʿUmra*, on the other hand, is a voluntary pilgrimage and can be performed at any point in the year. It is lawful to perform *ʿumra* and *ḥajj* in the same journey, first *ʿumra* and then *ḥajj*. After the pilgrims perform *ʿumra*, they are free to resume worldly affairs, including sexual intercourse with their spouses. *ʿUmra* is thus an enjoyment of an additional benefit in *ḥajj*; therefore, it is called

mut'a al-ḥajj. History books tell us that 'Umar thought this to be too indulgent or distracting and banned *mut'a al-ḥajj*. His words were, "I know that the Prophet and his companions allowed it, but I dislike it and they [the pilgrims] should go into their wives under the thorny trees and then proceed to perform hajj while the drops of water are falling from their head." Gribetz, *Strange Bedfellows*, 27.

87. Gribetz, *Strange Bedfellows*, 56.

88. Haeri, *Law of Desire*, 10, 11.

89. Al-Kulaynī, *al-Furū' min al-kāfī*.

90. Murata, *Temporary Marriage*, 68.

91. See al-'Āmilī, *Wasā'il al-Shi'a*, 14:442.

92. Imam Ja'far produced the definitive source of Shi'i jurisprudence. In Shi'i thought, the imams are considered infallible and divine authority is thought to be vested in their sayings.

93. Haeri, *Law of Desire*, 1.

94. Ibid., 2, 7.

95. The practice of sacred prostitution was a common act of worship in many ancient nations. In Babylon, a woman was expected to sit in the courtyard of the temple of Ishtar at least once during her lifetime and have sexual intercourse with a stranger. In Canaan, there were women who served in the temple and had sexual relations with priests and pilgrims. And in India, girls served as priestesses in the temple. They danced and sang and then the doors of rooms around the temple would open, and the priestesses would have sexual intercourse with the pilgrims in order to placate the gods.

96. Murtaẓa Moṭahharī, *The Rights of Women in Islam* (Tehran: World Organization for Islamic Services, 1981), 15.

97. Haeri, *Law of Desire*, 2, 193.

98. For an analysis of the Friday sermon (November 1990) where President Rafsanjani advocated for *mut'a,* see Haeri, *Law of Desire,* 113, see also, 10, 12.

99. Annalee Newitz, "How Iran Became One of the World's Most Futuristic Countries," IO9, last modified May 2, 2014, http://io9.com/how-iran-became-one-of-the-worlds-most-futuristic-count-1570438769.

100. Haeri, *Law of Desire,* 80.

101. "Iran Unveils State-Approved Dating App to Promote Marriage," *BBC News*, July 13, 2021, https://www.bbc.com/news/world-middle-east-57818758.

102. Haeri, *Law of Desire,* 54.

103. Robert Tappan, "Beyond Clerics and Clinics: Bioethics and Assisted Reproductive Technology in Iran" (PhD diss., University of Virginia, 2011).

104. Nadya Labi, "Married for a Minute," *Mother Jones*, March/April 2010, http://www.motherjones.com/politics/2010/03/temporary-marriage-iran-islam.

105. Elaine Sciolino, "Love Finds a Way in Iran: 'Temporary Marriage,'" *New York Times*, October 4, 2000, http://www.nytimes.com/2000/10/04/world/love-finds-a-way-in-iran-temporary-marriage.html.

106. *Iran Rooyan*, "Trafficking Fact Sheet," http://iranrooyan.org/wp-content/uploads/2011/12/TRAFFICKING-FACT-SHEET-final.pdf; and *Al-Bawaba*, "Iran Permits Brothels Through Temporary Marriages," last modified June 7, 2010,

http://www.albawaba.com/behind-news/iran-permits-brothels-through-temporary-marriages.

107. Haeri, *Law of Desire*, 24.

108. This is one reason why women's rights groups have vehemently objected to it.

109. Labi, "Married for a Minute"; Homa Khaleeli, "I Was a Temporary Bride," *The Guardian*, July 11, 2015, https://www.theguardian.com/lifeandstyle/2015/jul/11/i-was-a-temporary-bride-in-iran; Mehrnaz Samimi, "Online 'Sigheh'in Iran: Revolutionary or Restricting?" *HuffPost*, November 18, 2014, https://m.huffpost.com/us/entry/6182110/amp; Sciolino, "Love Finds a Way in Iran"; Shabnam Mahmood and Catrin Nye, "I Do, for Now Anyway," *BBC News*, May 13, 2013, https://www.bbc.com/news/uk-22354201.

110. Kelly McEvers, "Abuse Of Temporary Marriages Flourishes In Iraq," NPR, last modified October 19, 2010, http://www.npr.org/templates/story/story.php?storyId=130350678; Shoshana Shmuluvitz, "Temporary Marriage in Islam: Exploitative or Liberating?" *Tel Aviv Notes* 6, no. 5 (March 11, 2012): http://dayan.org/content/tel-aviv-notes-temporary-marriage-islam-exploitative-or-liberating.

111. BBC Asian Network Reports, *Married for a Minute*, May 13, 2013, https://www.bbc.co.uk/programmes/b01sdpfp.

112. Sudabeh Mortezai, dir., *In The Bazaar of Sexes*, FreibeuterFilm, 2019. Trailer available at: https://www.filmplatform.net/product/in-the-bazaar-of-sexes/.

113. *Frontline*, season 2019, episode 6, "Iraq's Secret Sex Trade," November 12, 2019, https://www.pbs.org/wgbh/frontline/film/iraqs-secret-sex-trade/.

114. Hassan Akhondpour, dir., *Fereshteh: Daughter of Ahmad*, 2016.

115. McEvers, "Abuse of Temporary Marriages."

116. Planet Iran, "Temporary Marriage Has Turned into a Career and Source of Income in Iran," *Iran Press News*, last modified August 9, 2010, http://planet-iran.com/index.php/news/21112.

117. Farangis Najibullah and Kayumars Ato, "Tajik Mullahs Warn of New Threat in Temporary Marriages," Radio Free Europe Radio Liberty, last modified June 17, 2012, http://www.rferl.org/content/tajik-mullahs-warn-against-temporary-marriages/24616875.html.

118. Lara Deeb, "On Representational Paralysis, Or, Why I Don't Want to Write About Temporary Marriage," *Jadaliyya*, last modified December 1, 2010, http://www.jadaliyya.com/pages/index/364/on-representational-paralysis-or-why-i-dont-want-t; and Lara Deeb and Mona Harb, "Sanctioned Pleasures: Youth, Piety and Leisure in Beirut," *Middle East Report* 37, no. 245 (2007): http://www.merip.org/mer/mer245/sanctioned-pleasures.

119. Ajaz Ashraf, "What is Mut'a Marriage—and Why It May Be Difficult for India's Supreme Court to Invalidate It," Scroll.in, https://scroll.in/article/874702/what-is-muta-marriage-and-why-it-may-be-difficult-for-the-supreme-court-to-invalidate-it (last accessed September 4, 2021).

120. Surabhi Tandon, "'Temporary' Marriages Still Going on in Kerala State," television newscast, FRANCE 24 English, November, 18, 2013, https://www.youtube.com/watch?v=lyLvD2Hneco.

121. Rol Srivastava, "Indian Child Brides Sold in 'Package Deals' to Men from Gulf States," Thomson Reuters Foundation, October 10, 2017, https://www.reuters.com/article/us-india-trafficking-marriage/indian-child-brides-sold-in-package-deals-to-men-from-gulf-states-idUSKBN1CF1F7.

122. Betwa Sharma, "Islam's Sex Licenses," *Daily Beast*, last modified April 29, 2009, http://www.thedailybeast.com/articles/2009/04/29/islams-sex-licenses.html.

123. Mahmood and Nye, "I Do"; and Soeren Kern, "Britain: Islamic Temporary Marriages on the Rise," Gatestone Institute, last modified June 4, 2013, http://www.gatestoneinstitute.org/3748/uk-islamic-temporary-marriages.

124. Linda S. Walbridge, *Without Forgetting the Imam: Lebanese Shi'ism in an American Community* (Detroit, MI: Wayne State University Press, 1996).

125. *'Urfī* marriage has been on the rise in Egypt for a while. As given in the journal *al-Buḥūth al-fiqhiyya al-mu'āṣira*, the correct definition is: "A written or unwritten contract of matrimony, without an official document." See Sindawi, *Temporary Marriage in Sunni and Shi'ite Islam*, 36. These types of marriages are usually contracted without the woman's guardian's knowledge or permission, without the presence of witnesses, without bride money, and without making the act known. In Egypt, this kind of marriage is common among students. *Zawāj al-misyār*, travel marriage, has no basis in canonical law and is therefore not mentioned by early jurists. It arose out of the practical necessities of life. The most prominent feature of this marriage is that the wife freely and readily agrees to waive some of her rights to support and to have her husband stay the night. Scholars like Yūsuf al-Qaraḍāwī write that *misyār* marriage is different from *mut'a* because it cannot be annulled without a divorce; see Yūsuf al-Qaraḍāwī, *Zawāj al-misyār* (Cairo: Maktabat wahba, 1999), 23. In addition, the *misyār* wife counts as one of the four wives allowed. This is a legally valid marriage, even if socially unacceptable.

Chapter Two

Tafsīr

Development of the Genre

The Qur᾿an is the foundational text of Islam, and from the advent of Islam onward, it has been one of the main sources of Islamic legislation, despite contradictory interpretations. Qur᾿anic interpretation or exegesis has been a central preoccupation of Muslim scholars. The Arabic word for exegesis is *tafsīr* and comes from the verbal root *fa*, *sīn*, and *ra*, which means "to explain."[1] *Tafsīr* works reflect on each *āya*, verse, of the Qur᾿an. This intellectual engagement has existed since the beginning of Islam and continues today. The Qur᾿an states: "He is the One who has revealed to you O Prophet the Book, of which some verses are precise—they are the foundation of the Book—while others are elusive. Those with deviant hearts follow the elusive verses seeking to spread doubt through their false interpretations—but none grasps their full meaning except God" (Q 3:7).

The *tafsīr* genre attempts to explain *āyāt* (pl. of *āya*) by putting them into conversation with each other, as well as *asbāb al-nuzūl*, occasions of revelation, and *nāsikh wa mansūkhuhu*, abrogation. Works of *tafsīr* often systematically cite scholars' varying opinions on particular *āyāt* and, therefore, serve as a sort of encyclopedia of scholarly opinions and interpretations. Exegetes use scholarly tools such as history, grammar, semantics, and poetry, and also drawn on law and theology to various degrees, depending on their objectives. A *tafsīr* might, for example, attempt to illustrate certain legal frameworks or debate specific theological viewpoints.[2]

Early on, a *tafsīr* was not written down. It was not yet part of a cohesive and easily identifiable genre; it was more hadith-oriented. If there was a question about the meaning of an *āya*, the Companions tried to remember whether or not Prophet Muhammad had said something in reference to it. *Tafāsīr* (pl. of *tafsīr*) gave others the opportunity to understand the meaning of the Qur᾿an and made the Word of God applicable to daily life. In this chapter, I provide a broad historical treatment of the genre, starting with the early oral transmission of information about the Qur'an through *aḥādīth* (pl. of hadith) and *khabar*, reports, and progressing to the period when authors first began recording their exegetical works. I address the most prominent *āya* cited in discussions of *mut'a*, Q 4:24, and look at its Qur'anic context. I then look at a variety of exegetical works and discuss six prominent exegetes, starting with 'A'isha bt. Abī Bakr, the wife of the Prophet Muhammad. She is not normally treated as an exegete, but I treat her as one here as a corrective—my justification is that in this period, *aḥādīth* were used to explicate the Qur'an, and she is one of the main transmitters of *aḥādīth*. This discussion of exegetes and exegetical works from varying sectarian allegiances helps me to broadly illustrate how prominent issues in the classical era were illustrated in contemporary Qur'anic commentaries.

Understanding the Islamic position on *mut'a* requires understanding whether or not the Qur'an has anything to say on the matter. Over time, various tools were developed to extract meaning from the text, and they eventually became categorized as grammar, lexicography, theology, legal principles, and narrative, among others.[3] The *tafsīr* texts available to us are a representation of the attitudes and approaches of the male intellectual elite. It is only in the twenty-first century that we have two complete and one partial *tafsīr* by women.[4] Other than these three women, we do not have a single *tafsīr*—or even references in the margins of *tafāsīr* to ones—by a female exegete among the works available to us. Chapter 4 provides a complex and full discussion of the works by these three women. Today, many scholars, both male and female, approach the Qur'an through the analytical lens of gender.[5]

A variety of twentieth-century writers have addressed the significance of gender issues in the context of *tafsīr* and other areas of study. The Qur'an addresses itself to men and women. This is done by using the singular and plural grammatical forms of the masculine in Arabic, which can be interpreted as referring to both men and women.[6] General command statements often begin with "You who believe" or "O People," referring to men and women. Other *āyāt* use the neutral term *nafs*, soul, to encompass both genders.[7] Exploring the detailed discussions of interpretations or translations of particular Qur'anic terms that are relevant to the issue of gender in Q 4:34, for example, *qawwāmūn*, in charge of, or *nushūz*, rebellion, are beyond the scope of this brief introduction, but they have been addressed by many key female Islamic and Qur'anic studies scholars.[8] As a general trend, classical exegetes cited every existing interpretation or philological connotation; conversely, modern commentators excavate the past to recover historical authorities' comments and discussions that allow for readings of the Qur'an that to modern sensibilities, are more progressive or egalitarian.

Gendered readings of the Qur'an often involve discussions of marriage. In legal parlance, *mut'a* is understood as temporary marriage. Except for one possible reference in Q 4:24, the Qur'an does not contain any reference to this type of marriage, its procedure, or the rights and duties involved.[9] The Shi'a understand this *āya* as granting Muslims the right to practice *mut'a*.[10] According to Shi'i scholars, the context of the *āya* indicates that the verb *istamta'a* refers to *mut'a* in addition to its dictionary meaning, "to enjoy." According to Sunni exegetes' final consensus, in this *āya* the meaning of *istamta'a* is related to pleasure; it refers to deriving (sexual) pleasure or benefit from marriage. On the other hand, Shi'i exegetes hold that in a legal context, the verb has a technical meaning and refers to a marriage contract for which a time limit is set and that was practiced at that time. Thus, Q 4:24 is subject to different and contradictory interpretations, especially the phrase "So, such of them with whom you have *mut'a*"—Shi'i translation—or "those with whom you seek enjoyment"—Sunni translation.

This *āya* is one of the most debated passages in *tafsīr* literature due to the meaning of certain words, the grammatical questions it raises, and issues related to the transmission of the Qur'an. The meaning of the terms *muḥṣin* and *mut'a* are endlessly contested, and the grammatical issues this *āya* raises include whether the particle *mā* refers to animate objects and what the role of the particle *fa* is in this context. Additionally, whole phrases have contested meanings: Q 4:24 states "Give those you have consummated marriage with their due dowries," but the text attributed to Ubayy b. Ka'b, Ibn 'Abbās, and Ibn Mas'ūd reads, "And those of whom you seek [sexual] enjoyment *for a definite period* give them their wages as settled"[11] From the Shi'i point of view, the phrase "for a definite period" is an integral part of understanding the *āya*, although Shi'i scholars have different views on whether these words are also an integral part of the received text. Some Sunni sources also mention the alternative reading, but they do not use it as a proof for the legitimacy of *mut'a*.[12]

Though the purpose of Qur'anic commentaries has been to elucidate the text and clarify incomprehensible passages, in the case of the *mut'a āya*, commentaries based on conflicting explications of the text have often obscured rather than clarified the meaning.[13] The following sections will look at exegetical discussions of the *āyāt* surrounding Q 4:24 and then at classical commentaries specifically on Q 4:24.

NEIGHBORING *ĀYĀT*

Qur'anic discussions of issues related to marriage start at Q 4:19. The Qur'an forbids acts of injustice toward women: "Oh believers! It is not permissible for you to inherit women against their will or mistreat them to make them return some of the dowry as a ransom for divorce—unless they are found guilty of adultery. Treat them fairly. If you happen to dislike them, you may hate something which God turns into a great blessing" (Q 4:19). The most accepted interpretation of this *āya* is that it forbids the pre-Islamic Arab custom of inheriting stepmothers. According to this custom, when a man who has remarried dies, one of his sons can inherit his stepmother and make her his wife. The process involves the stepson placing a cloth over his dead father's face and thereby becoming the owner of his stepmother. This allows him to treat her in any manner he wants, whether that means marrying her off to someone else and keeping her dowry for himself or forbidding her from marrying again while he is alive.

The next *āya* reads as follows: "If you desire to replace a former wife with another and you have given the former even a stack of gold as a dowry, do not take any of it back. Would you still take it unjustly and very sinfully?" (Q 4:20). In other words, if a man divorces his wife to marry a different woman, he must not take back any of the dowry that he gave the first wife, even if it is exceptionally large and he desires only a small part. The next *āya* continues discussing this point,[14] and then Q 4:22 again refers to marrying one's father's wife: "Do not marry former wives of your fathers." Both this and Q 4:19 were revealed after Abū Qays b. al-Aslat died and his wife was inherited and married by his son Muḥṣin, who refused to pay the daily expenses of his stepmother-cum-wife, give her the due share of the inheritance, or allow her to visit her relatives. She therefore went to the Prophet Muhammad and told him what had happened. He then told her to return to her husband and wait; perhaps God would send down a statute that would clarify her situation. These *āyāt* were then revealed.

The following *āya*, Q 4:23, describes the women men are forbidden to marry, such as their own mothers and daughters. There are fourteen types: seven prohibited because of blood relations and seven for various other causes, such as relations through breastfeeding or milk mothers.[15] The next *āya* begins by stating that married women are forbidden to men. It goes on to say, "All other women are permitted to you, provided you seek them by means of your wealth, desiring chastity, not committing fornication" (Q 4:24). This defines acceptable sexual relationships with women: either through marriage or by purchasing slaves. The next portion of Q 4:24 states, "So for the enjoyment you have enjoyed from them give them their wages as settled." Murata writes that the word "so," *fa*, shows that this part of the *āya* is the conclusion reached by the previous part.[16] Since the previous section deals with the different kinds of legitimate sexual relationships, one can conclude that this section represents the exposition of a new kind of marriage; one not mentioned previously and which requires the man to pay his wife wages. The

Shiʿa also claim that the use of the word *ajr*, compensation or wages, instead of *mahr*, dowry, is additional proof that this *āya* is referring to *mutʿa*.[17]

Next, Q 4:25 states that if a man is too poor to marry a free Muslim woman, he should marry a Muslim slave girl. It also presents statutes related to these types of marriages.[18]

The final *āya* we will consider here is: "It is God's Will to make things clear to you, guide you to the noble ways of those before you, and turn to you in mercy. For God is All-Knowing, All-Wise" (Q 4:26). This is a general reference to the social and collective directives that appear in this *sūra* and the ones preceding it.

Now that we have looked at the text of Q 4:24 and its surrounding *āyāt*, we can turn to individual exegetes and their discussions of it.

ʿAʾISHA BT. ABĪ BAKR (D. 58/678)

ʿAʾisha bt. Abī Bakr is possibly the most important, as well as the most controversial, female figure in early Islamic history,[19] and her biography intersects with crucial early religiopolitical developments.[20] I am specifically interested in her role as someone knowledgeable about religion[21] and treat her as an exegete for two reasons: 1) because her oral transmission of *aḥādīth* qualifies her as such in a period when the sunna of Prophet Muhammad was considered exegesis; 2) to recover the voices of women within the corpus of knowledge about the historical past. Rehman puts it best when she writes,

> Reinstating the voice of ʿĀ'isha to the very core of the *ḥadīth* literature would be a step in the direction of normalizing a female voice at the epicenter of the Islamic tradition. This move goes beyond the typical feminist hermeneutical approaches in interpreting the Quran. Beyond interpreting the tradition from the position of women, it is imperative that the voices of women like ʿĀ'isha be permitted to form the very tradition itself.[22]

Women's direct and indirect contributions to intellectual traditions have often been overlooked. This calls for a reevaluation of what scholars can and should consider intellectual contributions. ʿAʾisha not only transmitted numerous *aḥādīth*, she also commented on them. Despite the lack of an extant, comprehensive exegesis, her commentary on the types of marriage present in pre-Islamic Arabia, as well as her discussions about which were permissible within Islam, can be considered her exegesis on Q 4:24. ʿAʾisha's voice is preserved in chains of oral transmission; thus, the ʿAʾisha we know is forever mediated. Yet ʿAʾisha played a central role in the development and transmission of a world religion, and so her contributions, however indirect, are integral to our understanding of Islam.

About one-third of al-Bukhārī's collection of *aḥādīth* is attributed to her, and she issued many *fatāwā* (pl. of fatwa), legal opinions, on a variety of topics. In addition to the Prophet Muhammad, ʿAʾisha transmitted from Abū Bakr, ʿUmar, Fāṭima, Saʿd b. Abī Waqqāṣ, Usayd b. Ḥuḍayr, and others; and those who transmitted from her include ʿUmar b. al-Khaṭṭāb, ʿAbdallāh b. ʿUmar, Abū Hurayra (d. 57/678, 58/679, or 59/680), Abū Mūsā al-Ashʿarī (d. c. 42/662), and Ibn ʿAbbās (d. 68/687–88).[23] She was also a respected Qurʾan commentator and transmitted her exegesis to her student ʿUrwa b. al-Zubayr (d. 93/711–12 or 94/712–13).[24] ʿAṭāʾ b. Abī Rabāḥ (d. 114–15/732–33) glowingly described her as "the most perspicacious and learned among people and the best among them in her opinions."[25] Additionally, we also have a little studied or commented upon book of 220 *aḥādīth* attributed to her, where she contradicts, corrects, or explicates *aḥādīth* that were then in circulation from male Companions of the Prophet.[26] These were not included within the *ṣaḥiḥ*, sound, collections, particularly those of al-Bukhārī and Muslim,[27] despite meeting the highest standards of authentication, and they have on many occasions been overlooked in favor of the statements of other Companions. In addition to *fiqh*, jurisprudence, it is also said that she excelled in the recitation of poetry and in *ṭibb*, medicine.[28] The Prophet Muhammad reportedly counseled his Companions "to take half your religion from al-Ḥumayrāʾ (i.e., ʿĀʾisha)."[29] Thus, it is crucial to acknowledge that the failure to rightfully recognize ʿAʾisha as a key exegete is a historical shortcoming.

Despite a wealth of data, the (largely sectarian) conflict over ʿAʾisha's life makes it difficult to construct a historically accurate picture of her. However, she was born in Mecca around 614 and was the daughter of Abū Bakr, a trusted ally and close Companion of the Prophet Muhammad who later became the first caliph.[30] When the Prophet Muhammad died, she was eighteen and childless. She lived for forty-six more years and died in Medina in 58/678 at the age of sixty-four. She was his third wife and remained his favorite, even though he married several other women after her. Her beauty, intelligence, charm, and wit are thought to be the reasons she was favored by the Prophet Muhammad—and also why later she was dear to the community. The Prophet Muhammad nicknamed her al-Ḥumayrāʾ, the little ruddy one, and *ḥabībat ḥabīb Allāh*, the beloved of the beloved of God, which speaks volumes about her special position in the Prophet Muhammad's household.

ʿAʾisha was also embroiled in the succession story after the Prophet Muhammad's death, when conflict flared between the supporters of ʿAʾisha's father, Abū Bakr, and the Prophet Muhammad's son-in-law, ʿAlī b. Abī Ṭālib.[31] Two events lent her inordinate notoriety and made her the focus of medieval communal debate; the first happened during the Prophet Muhammad's lifetime and the other occurred after his death.

The first is referred to as *ḥadīth al-ifk*, the incident of the lie. It occurred after the expedition of Banū al-Muṣṭaliq in 6/628. ʿAʾisha accompanied the Prophet Muhammad, and at some point, she left the area where the caravans were located and walked a distance to relieve herself. While there, she realized she had lost her necklace along the way and started looking for it, losing track of time. Meanwhile, the caravan proceeded without anyone realizing she was missing. She got back to the campsite, discovered she had been left behind, and waited for help to come. Ṣafwān b. al-Muʿṭṭal al-Sulaymānī, supposedly a handsome young man, found her and escorted her back to Medina. Meanwhile, ʿAʾisha's absence led to all kinds of rumors about her character and loyalty to the Prophet Muhammad. These rumors were spread by ʿAbd Allāh b. Ubayy, the leader of the *munāfiqun*, hypocrites, who was disturbed by the Prophet Muhammad's rising prestige and power in the community. Without any witnesses to validate her story, ʿAʾisha had no way to prove her innocence, even though there was no solid evidence against her. Her situation became perilous, but the Prophet Muhammad received a revelation regarding her innocence and reputation. She was saved by divine intervention (Q 24:7–11).[32] This incident conferred special prestige on her: God spoke in her defense. And these *āyāt* became the foundation for classical rulings that required the accuser to provide four eyewitnesses to establish proof of illicit sexual conduct. They also established the precedent of viewing slander of chaste women as harmful and worthy of the *ḥadd* punishment of eighty lashes.[33]

The second event that elicited controversy was ʿAʾisha's opposition to the fourth caliph, the Prophet Muhammad's son-in-law ʿAli, whom some sources say advised him against trusting her version of what happened at Banū al-Muṣṭaliq—something which she, supposedly, never forgave or forgot.[34] Her opposition led her to instigate a civil war, which was called the Battle of the Camel because the most ferocious part of the battle took place in the vicinity of a camel she was riding.

The third caliph, ʿUthmān b. ʿAffān (r. 23–35/644–56), whose character was tainted by serious accusations of nepotism during his reign, was killed by Egyptian rebels in his home. ʿAʾisha was returning from performing hajj in Mecca, and upon her return, she publicly demanded that ʿAli, now appointed the fourth caliph, take revenge for ʿUthmān's wrongful death. ʿAli refused. She, along with her two staunch allies, Ṭalḥa b. ʿUbayd Allāh (d. 36/656) and al-Zubayr b. al-ʿAwwām (d. 36/656), gathered forces in Basra in southern Iraq and instigated the first civil war in Islam. It was a bloody war, and both sides suffered heavy losses. Both Ṭalḥa and al-Zubayr were killed, and although ʿAʾisha lost, ʿAli escorted her back to Medina with the respect due to the Prophet Muhammad's widow.

ʿAʾisha's role in the civil war is heavily debated. Shiʿi sources tend to vilify her, while Sunni sources focus on her roles as a hadith transmitter and the most beloved wife of the Prophet Muhammad and suggest that her less than amicable sentiments toward ʿAli were exploited by others.[35] Additionally, Sunni sources portray her as remorseful for her actions at the end of her life, "an interpretation that grants her exculpation."[36] Whatever the case, this battle effectively ended ʿAʾisha's role in politics; however, it did not end her public role or her roles as a hadith transmitter, teacher, and counselor.[37] She continued to be widely revered by her contemporaries for her knowledge and was consulted by the senior *akābir*, Companions, for her detailed understanding of *farāʾiḍ*, inheritance shares.[38]

Accounts about the Prophet Muhammad (including his actions and events during his lifetime) are a key part of the Islamic literary corpus, are revered as the authentic annals of early Islam, and serve as a model for Muslim conduct and a source for Islamic law. Although, in general, early records were written down by men, a significant portion of these accounts was recounted on the authority of women like ʿAʾisha. These records can be traced back to a woman from the Prophet Muhammad's generation; usually a female Companion. Therefore, women, and ʿAʾisha in particular, have played an important role in authoring Islam's official history and the literature that established Islamic society's normative practices. This indicates that the first generation of Muslims (the generation closest to the Jahiliya period and its attitudes toward women), as well as their immediate heirs, had no difficulty accepting women as authorities.

There are a couple *aḥādīth* on the issue of marriage that fit our purposes here, and the most important of them involves ʿAʾisha describing the different types of marriage present during Prophet Muhammad's time. The full tradition recorded by al-Bukhārī is as follows:

A. One was the marriage of people as it is today, where a man betroths his ward or his daughter to another man, and then later assigns a dower (bride wealth) to her and then marries her.
B. Another type was where a man said to his wife when she was purified from her menses: Sent her to someone and then asks her to have intercourse with him; her husband then stays away from her and does not touch her at all until it is clear that she is pregnant from that (other) man with whom she sought intercourse with if he wants. He acts simply from the desire for a noble child. This type of marriage was (known as) *nikāḥ al-istibzāʾ*, the marriage seeking intercourse.

C. Another type was where a group (*raht*) of less than ten used to visit the same woman and all of them would have intercourse with her. If she became pregnant and bore a child, when some night had passed after the birth, she sent for them, and not a man from them might refuse. When they had come together in her presence, she would say to them, "You know the result of your acts; I have borne a child, he is your child," naming whomever she will by his name. Her child is attached to him and he may not refuse.

D. The fourth type of marriage is where many men frequent a woman, and she does not keep herself from any who comes to her. These women are like the *baghāya*, prostitutes. They used to set up at their doors banners as a sign. Whoever wanted them went to them. If one of them conceived and bore a child, they gathered and summoned the physiologists. Then they attached her child to him, and the child was called his son, no objection to this course being possible.[39]

Only the first marriage that ʿAʾisha describes is long-term; the other three are temporary. ʿAʾisha concludes the hadith by saying that except for the first form of marriage, all were prohibited, which clearly eliminates *mutʿa* as a permissible form of marriage.

Another hadith from ʿAʾisha regarding marriage states: "The Prophet said: There can be no marriage without a *walī* [a guardian], and the sultan is the *walī* of the one who has no other."[40] *Mutʿa*, as defined by the Shiʿa, does not require a *walī* unless the woman is a virgin.

Another relevant hadith from ʿAʾisha asserts: "The Prophet said: If a woman has not been given in marriage by one of her *walī*s, her marriage is void."[41] She reports that the Prophet Muhammad repeated the word "void" three times. If the couple had intercourse, the woman receives a marriage portion in accordance with what her husband regarded as lawfully his. If they cannot agree, the sultan is the *walī* of the one who has no one else.[42]

In al-Zaskashī's collection of 220 *aḥādīth*,[43] where ʿAʾisha contradicts the Companions on various issues, we also find a hadith where she comments on the impermissibility of *mutʿa*. It says that she was asked about the *mutʿa* of women and responds, saying between me and you is the Qurʾan, and then recites "Who abstain from sex, except with those joined to them in the marriage bond, or (the captives) whom their right hands possess—for (in their case) they are free from blame" (Q 23:6). She continues by saying that those who desire more than their wife and the captive their right hand possesses have gone beyond the bounds that God has prescribed. The editor notes that this hadith meets the conditions that al-Bukhārī and Muslim used for determining *ṣaḥiḥ*, sound, *aḥādīth*. This hadith is not included in their collections, but it is a *ṣaḥiḥ*.

If we take ʿAʾisha's narrations in these *aḥādīth* as exegetical evidence, we find she argues against the permissibility of *mutʿa*. However, the legacy of ʿAʾisha bt. Abī Bakr is heavily contested because of the political and gender implications it presents to historians.[44] The Shiʿa do not include *aḥādīth* by ʿAʾisha in their collections, whereas the Sunni hold her up as a primary source for their tradition (though they do censure her for her role in the civil war against ʿAli). ʿAʾisha's biography reveals the process by which Islamic gender ideals as well as Sunni and Shiʿi community identities were constructed through the evolution of two conflicting interpretations of a shared past.

IBN ʿABBĀS (D. C. 65–68/684–88)

Abū al-ʿAbbās ʿAbd Allāh b. ʿAbbās b. ʿAbd al-Muṭṭalib b. Hāshim b. ʿAbd al-Manāf al-Qurashī al-Hāshimī is referred to as Ibn ʿAbbās in most sources. He had five sons and two daughters. The eldest son, Abū Muḥammad ʿAlī al-Hāshmī al-Sajjād, was the father of the ʿAbbasid caliphs, and because of this, it is thought that Ibn ʿAbbās's biography is ʿAbbasid propaganda.[45] Ibn ʿAbbās is thought to have either died as early as sixty-eight years old (65/684–85) or as late as seventy-one or seventy-two (68/687–88). He lived for fifty years or more after the Prophet Muhammad's death and was his paternal cousin and Companion. He is called the *baḥr*, ocean, of the Muslim community and the interpreter of the Qurʾan. Not surprisingly, he is said to have excelled in all fields of knowledge, including what we consider secular fields of knowledge today, such as pre-Islamic poetry, the genealogy of Arabs, and the history of *maghāzī*, military expeditions. His religious knowledge included the words and deeds of the Prophet Muhammad, legal matters, exegesis, pilgrimage rites, and the portions for each share of an inheritance.

He is considered the creator of the science of *tafsīr* and holds a special place in Islamic literature[46]—and the hagiographic references to his intelligence border on legendary. It is said that before Ibn ʿAbbās was born, Prophet Muhammad identified him as a wise man. In other stories, we learn that after Ibn ʿAbbās was born, he rubbed his saliva in Ibn ʿAbbās's mouth and predicted he would become a great, wise man and would leave a phenomenal legacy for Islam. The Prophet Muhammad is said to have prayed specifically that he be granted the ability to interpret the Qurʾan, which is what he is historically best known for.[47] Given these extraordinary anecdotes and the authority that his name elicits, modern scholarship is hesitant to accept every report ascribed to him.

Separating history from myth in Ibn ʿAbbās's biography is difficult.[48] For example, it is uncertain how old he was when the Prophet Muhammad died.

A conservative estimate is that he spent only two and half years in Prophet Muhammad's presence, but according to later historical records, he could have been ten, twelve, thirteen, or even fifteen years old when he died. It is thought that later historians falsified his age at the time of Prophet Muhammad's death in order to substantiate his authority on the issues to which his name was ascribed.[49] If he was only five when the Prophet Muhammad died, how could he have all the knowledge later ascribed to him?

There is also confusion about his role during the first three caliphates.[50] A conservative rendering is that he was not involved and kept to himself during their rule. According to hagiographic accounts by later historians, all the caliphs sought his counsel and held it in high regard; however, the only evidence of him playing a political role is during the rule of ʿAli, the fourth caliph. We know that ʿAli appointed Ibn ʿAbbās governor of Basra in 36/655. According to some sources, he stayed there until ʿAli's murder in 40/659; after this, he went to Mecca and then established himself in al-Taif. Other sources say he resigned from his governorship in Basra. Neither the circumstances nor the date of his departure from Basra are certain. Many sources indicate he misappropriated funds from the treasury in Basra and then was sacked by ʿAli. Other sources claim it was his brother who misappropriated the funds. The reason for this is obvious: It is important to maintain a pristine and pious legacy for Ibn ʿAbbās, a celebrated Muslim authority.

Despite the fragmentary evidence, we can deduce that he was the first to memorize the latter part of the Qurʾan and wrote parts of it down during Prophet Muhammad's lifetime. Ibn ʿAbbās is credited with a codex that is arranged in a different chronological order than the ʿUthmānic codex.[51] More importantly, some of his readings differed from the ʿUthmānic codex, and this is why he is included here.

Before we speak about the variant reading that is pertinent to our topic here, let us look at his other contributions to Qurʾanic studies.[52] Ibn ʿAbbās was the first to teach Qurʾanic commentary—specifically on *Sūrat al-Baqara*, Chapter of the Cow—in Basra. During the pilgrimage, he is said to have commented on and taught *Sūrat al-Nūr,* Chapter of the Light. "[Ibn] ʿAbbās is considered the founder (for us, both real and mythical—real because he has played a certain role in the foundation of exegesis and mythical because Islamic sources have transformed him into a kind of *persona sacra* in this field of Qurʾānic exegesis)."[53] However, because there are contradictory interpretations transmitted under his name, it difficult to ascertain which interpretations are actually Ibn ʿAbbās's and which are other early transmitters ascribing their thoughts to him.

The same problem can be observed with the transmission of *aḥādīth* in his name.[54] If we look at al-Ṭabarī, we find 5,835 exegetical *aḥādīth* on the authority of Ibn ʿAbbās.[55] According to al-Ḥākim (d. 214/829) and al-Shāfiʿī

(d. 240/820), he transmitted no more than one hundred *aḥādīth*. According to Ja'far (d. 194/809) he could have only heard nine *aḥādīth* from the Prophet Muhammad, but according to al-Qaṭṭān (d. 558/1163) it could be ten, while according to al-Ghazālī (d. 505–1111) he could have only heard four. Regardless of the number, it is known that he was turned to for his opinion on Prophetic traditions.[56]

This led to the construction of him as a master at delivering legal positions. These positions are interesting; some seamlessly coincide with what later became Shi'i interpretations, while others coincide with Sunni legal rulings. The five most prominent rulings that differ between Shi'i and Sunni law involve:[57] (1) *wuḍū'*, ablution: Ibn 'Abbās prescribes washing the face and hands and wiping the head and feet, which the Shi'a do, while the Sunni wipe their heads and wash their feet;[58] (2) *ṭalāq*, divorce: Ibn 'Abbās does not allow divorce by triple repudiation uttered on the same occasion, like the Shi'a, but the Sunni allow it; (3) *umm al-walad*, mother of the child: Ibn 'Abbās prescribed that if a slave woman gives birth to the master's child, she is free after his death, a practice followed by Shi'i law but not by Sunni law; (4) *al-mash 'alā l-khuffayn*, wiping of shoes: Ibn 'Abbās prescribed wiping shoes instead of washing the feet, which is prohibited by Shi'i law but permitted by Sunni law; and (5) *zawāj al-mut'a*, *mut'a* marriage: Ibn 'Abbās permitted it, and the Shi'a allow it but not the Sunni.

Various manuscripts and *tafsīr* titles are attributed to Ibn 'Abbās.[59] However, attempting to establish the origins of these texts and trace them to him presents a series of problems. First, when evaluating these texts, we must determine whether they are compilations extracted from later works, which were then unified, or later reformulations whose authorship editors attributed to Ibn 'Abbās. Scholarly consensus reveals that the work of Ibn 'Abbās has gone through multiple compilations and therefore cannot be completely his. Regardless of whether the *tafsīr* ascribed to Ibn 'Abbās is entirely or partially his, it does provide information on the discussions taking place at a relatively early point in Islamic history.

Bearing this in mind, we can turn to his variant reading of Q 4:24 in *Tanwīr al-miqbās*,[60] which has been attributed to Ibn 'Abbās numerous times. It has also incorrectly been attributed to Muḥammad b. Ya'qūb al-Fīrūzābādī (d. 817/1414).

"Also forbidden are married women—except female captives in your possession." Ibn 'Abbās explains that all married women are forbidden, unless they are captives of war; if they are captives of war, they are not forbidden, even if they had living husbands prior to their capture. However, it is only permissible to have sexual contact with these women after it has been determined that they are not pregnant. This is done by waiting for one menstruation period.

"Lawful to you are all beyond these—as long as you seek them with your wealth." He writes that this means seeking to marry up to four women, buying captives with one's wealth, and marrying for an agreed period of time for an agreed amount of money (i.e., *mutʿa*). It is unclear if the editor put this in or if it is Ibn ʿAbbās further clarifying that the lawfulness of *mutʿa* was later abrogated.

"In a legal marriage, not in fornication." He comments that this means being with them as legitimate husbands, not indulging in adultery, and having a proper marriage.

"Give those you have consummated marriage with their due dowries." He writes that you are obligated to give a full dowry to those you derive benefit from.

"It is permissible to be mutually gracious regarding the set dowry." This means you may increase or decrease the dowry amount as long as it is by mutual agreement and after the original obligation has been fulfilled.

"God is All-Knowing, All-Wise." In this last section of the *āya*, he claims that God wisely made *mutʿa* impermissible. Again, it is unclear if the editor has inserted this or if it is in the original text. It is worth mentioning that no other *tafsīr* I have encountered interprets the last section of the *āya*, a salutation, as speaking about the prohibition of *mutʿa*.

It appears that Ibn ʿAbbās's view of *mutʿa* as permissible attracted quite a lot of criticism—due to the fact that he was very young when the Prophet Muhammad died—and it was argued that he was not present when the Prophet Muhammad declared it forbidden. According to a hadith found in several collections, Sālim b. ʿAbd Allāh is reported to have stated:

> ʿAbd Allāh b. ʿUmar came and was told that Ibn ʿAbbās stated that *mutʿa* was permitted. Whereupon ʿUmar said, "Praise be to God, I do not believe that Ibn ʿAbbās would say so." They said, "He did indeed. He allows it." ʿUmar said, "Was not Ibn ʿAbbās but a young lad in the lifetime of the messenger of God, may God grant him peace?" He then added, "The Messenger of God forbade it, and we are not fornicators."[61]

And a number of sources quote a tradition in the name of Saʿīd b. Jubayr, who scolded Ibn ʿAbbās concerning *mutʿa*, chiding,

> "Do you know what you did? Your legal opinion has become known so far and wide even the poets have mentioned it." Ibn ʿAbbās said, "What did they say?" Saʿīd b. Jubayr said, "He said to the shaykh when he remained sitting for a long time, O Ibn ʿAbbās do you have a legal ruling? Do you permit young women to be your abode until the people's origin?" Whereupon Ibn ʿAbbās said, "We

> belong to God and we return to him. By God, this is not what I ruled, nor is it what I wanted, I did not permit what God did not permit, a dead flesh, blood, and flesh of pig."[62]

This tradition indicates Ibn ʿAbbās gave the ruling that *mutʿa* was only permissible out of necessity. There are several unresolved problems surrounding these *aḥādīth*, including their historical and historiographical significance,[63] and the theological motivations for transmitting such *aḥādīth* remain in question as well.

Other sources indicate that Ibn ʿAbbās came to the conclusion that *mutʿa* was valid even after Caliph ʿUmar had forbidden it.[64] Al-Qurṭubī (d. 671/1272) notes that Ibn ʿAbbās subsequently changed his mind; so the consensus among Sunni scholars was that it was forbidden.[65] However, this debate is ostensibly still ongoing, so Ibn ʿAbbās's view deserves to be considered in more detail. Specific details of his perspective are reported in the hadith literature: (1) there is evidence that he stated without reservation that *mutʿa* was permissible;[66] (2) there is evidence that he subsequently recanted and adopted the position that it was forbidden;[67] and (3) there is evidence that even later he once again thought it was permissible, but only in cases of necessity.[68]

MUQĀTIL B. SULAYMĀN AL-BALKHĪ (D. 150/767)

Abū al-Ḥasan Muqātil b. Sulaymān b. Bashīr al-Azdī al-Khurasānī al-Balkhī[69] was born in Balkh (modern day Afghanistan) and lived in Marw and Iraq. He traveled widely for his scholarly pursuits—from Beirut to Mecca. Muqātil holds a significant position in the field of *tafsīr*: most evidence points toward him being the first person to write a complete exegesis. Scholars have been skeptical about the authenticity of earlier texts, but are less so when it comes to Muqātil's *tafsīr*,[70] *Tafsīr al-kabīr*, which has several extant manuscripts; this is because the style of writing is consistently uniform and the author's approach to the Qurʾan is also consistent with what we know about Muqātil's theology from later sources that mention him.

Muqātil's exegesis is noteworthy for his three theological convictions. First, he made abundant use of *isrāʾīliyyāt*, biblical narratives, in his comments on Judeo-Christian events.[71] Additionally, he interprets the anthropomorphic verses in the Qurʾan literally; for example, concluding that God has a body, which sits on a throne. Finally, he believed all Muslims would eventually go to heaven, even if they were sinners, because their punishment would end one day due to their belief in *tawḥīd*, the oneness of God, and this would redeem them.

He also wrote two other books on the Qurʾan: *Kitāb Tafsīr al-khams miʾat āya min al-Qurʾān al-karīm* organizes verses by legal topic and provides interpretation; *al-Ashbāh wa-l-naẓāʾir fī al-Qurʾān al-karīm* examines Qurʾanic sentence structure, discusses the various possible meanings of certain words, and then lists those words' meanings and where in the Qurʾan the words have been used according to those meanings. His other works on the Qurʾan are not extant. Some studies have suggested unsuccessfully that he had Zaydī leanings, and it has even been suggested that he was politically a Zaydī, but there is no historical evidence to support either claim. There is, on the other hand, sufficient evidence that he was Murjiʾī, at least in terms of theology.[72]

Interestingly, although his *tafsīr* was reproduced by later exegetical writers, such as al-Ṭabarī (d. 450/1058), they do not acknowledge him as the source.[73] Scholars suggest several reasons for this: he disregarded *isnād*, chain of transmission, in his work; he relied on *isrāʾīliyyāt* material; and he interpreted the anthropomorphic verses in the Qurʾan literally.

Muqātil's *tafsīr* begins by analyzing the words in each *āya* and discussing their meanings.[74] At the end of the *āya*, he gives a one-sentence conclusion, which sometimes is related to the entire *āya* and sometimes to the most important or confusing aspect of it. For Q 4:24, his final analysis concerns *mutʿa*.

He interprets *muḥṣināt* as women one can marry; they are not prohibited through lineage or marital relations. He goes on to indicate there is an exception, "except female captives in your possession," and he explains this section of the *āya* by saying, "from the free, two, three, or four." This is interesting because the phrase "except female captives in your possession" is generally thought to mean "slave women." He explains "This is God's commandment to you" by saying that God has permitted four wives. In the next section of the *āya*, "lawful to you are all beyond these," he explains that "all beyond these" means "four." Then, the *āya* states, "as long as you seek them with your wealth in a legal marriage," and Muqātil interprets this to mean "the vulva." This is followed by, "not in fornication," which Muqātil explains as "adultery in the open." Then he writes that the *āya* speaks about *mutʿa*, a marriage that is for a limited time. For the section of the *āya* that is translated as "give them their *ajr*," he writes "give them their *mahr*." The last section of the *āya* states "it is permissible to be mutually gracious regarding the set dowry." Muqātil explains that after the original contract has been fulfilled, there is no harm if the amount or the time is extended.

His final comment on this *āya* is that the permissibility of this type of marriage has been abrogated by the *āyāt* on divorce and inheritance. He assumes the reader will understand which marriage he is referring to when he says, "this marriage" (i.e., *mutʿa*). Interestingly, his exegesis on the next *āya* starts by emphasizing that *mut'a* was prohibited by the revelation of Q 59:7.[75] However, the next *āya* has nothing to do with *mut'a*; rather, it speaks about the permissibility of marrying a slave woman if one cannot afford to marry a free woman. It is possible that the editor made a mistake when deciding where the exegesis for Q 4:24 ended and that for Q 4:25 began.

Muqātil does not deny that the *āya* refers to *mut'a*, but he also clearly states that *mut'a*'s permissibility has been abrogated. Muqātil is using the Qur'an to explain the Qur'an, not just by referencing *āyāt* on divorce and inheritance but also by mentioning the moral prerogative to follow what the Prophet Muhammad has allowed and to prohibit what he has disallowed.

ABŪ JA'FAR AL-ṬABARĪ (D. 310/923)

Abū Ja'far Muḥammad b. Jarīr b. Yazīd al-Ṭabarī was born in Amul, Tabaristan in 224–25/839 and died in Baghdad, Iraq in 310/923.[76] It is unclear whether his family was indigenous to the region or whether they were of Arab descent. He was a polymath and famous for his universal history and Qur'an commentary.[77] Al-Ṭabarī's work is the second major commentary to have survived—Muqātil's is the first.

Al-Ṭabarī's father Jarīr was a moderately prosperous landowner. He provided his son with a consistent income during his life, and when he died, al-Ṭabarī's inheritance was substantial enough that he was able to dedicate himself entirely to the pursuit of knowledge. This financial support enabled him to travel extensively as a student and later gave him financial independence, which meant he was able to avoid outside pressures and influences on his work.

He memorized the Qur'an at seven years old, qualified to lead the Muslim prayer at eight, and studied the Prophetic traditions at nine. It is well authenticated that he left home at twelve to seek knowledge and stayed in northern Persia, in Rayy, for five years; his intellectual formation during his time there gave him a solid grounding for his future career. Still under seventeen years old, he left Rayy and traveled to the intellectual center of the Islamic world, Baghdad, and then proceeded to Egypt. Al-Ṭabarī then returned to Baghdad around 256/870, and this marked the end of his student years. He settled down for the remaining fifty years of his life, devoting himself to teaching and writing.

In Baghdad, he was able to specialize in multiple branches of knowledge. He embraced history, *tafsīr*, hadith, and *fiqh*, possibly wrote in the field of ethics, and had an intellectual interest in Arabic literature and poetry. His scholarly approach is notable for its emphasis on *ijtihād*, the independent exercise of judgment. After quoting his sources—he depended on existing written works and reports—he presents what he considers to be the most acceptable view. His own beliefs appear to have fit within the framework of then-orthodox Islam (i.e., within the environment of his predecessor Ibn Ḥanbal and al-Ashʿarī who came after).

On the question of the imamate—the fiercely disputed question of his time, because Shiʿism was gaining authority in the heartland of the caliphate—he defended the preeminence of all four caliphs, venerating Abū Bakr and ʿUmar and defending the rights of ʿAli equally. However, since accusing someone of Shiʿi sympathies was a standard weapon at the time, al-Ṭabarī was accused of such sympathies by his Hanbali opponents, who stirred up a Baghdad mob against him on more than one occasion.[78]

Al-Ṭabarī began his work in *fiqh* as a Shafiʿi, but as his views developed into a distinct and self-sustaining corpus of law, he and his followers formed a separate *madhhab*, legal school, the Jarīriyya.[79] In al-Ṭabarī's later years, his students were considered adherents of this school, and its ranks included several leading scholars of the age. However, its principles were apparently not distinct enough from Shafiʿi ones to have ensured its future growth and development after al-Ṭabarī's death, particularly since the three well-established Sunni *madhāhib*, the Maliki, Hanafi, and Shafiʿi, were by now firmly entrenched and competing for supremacy in various regions of the Islamic world.

His *History, Tārīkh al-rusul wa al-mulūk*, more commonly known as *Tārīkh al-Ṭabarī*, and his *Commentary*, *Jāmiʿ al-bayān ʿan taʾwīl al-Qurʾān*, are the most extensive extant early works of Islamic scholarship, and they preserve the greatest array of citations from lost sources. Thus, they furnish modern scholarship with the richest and most detailed sources for the political history of the early caliphate, as well as for the early stages of the development and subsequent variety and vitality of Islam as a religious institution and corpus of legal knowledge and practice. Hence, al-Ṭabarī's works are compilations of two-centuries worth of written material (50–250/670–864); in general, he did not incorporate any works by his contemporaries.

The *Commentary* is known as the *tafsīr* par excellence. Al-Ṭabarī worked on it for many years, and it was not ready for dissemination until sometime between 283/896 and 290/903. It was immediately highly regarded and is probably considered al-Ṭabarī's most outstanding achievement, even more so than his works on law and tradition; indeed, it is still an important work for present-day scholars. Al-Ṭabarī provides a grammatical and lexicographical analysis of Qurʾanic *āyāt* and also makes theological and legal deductions. This was "the first major work in the development of traditional Quranic sciences," and it became a standard text that later commentators drew upon.[80] Being the earliest complete Qurʾanic commentary, it contains "the compilation and material arrangement of the first two centuries and a half of Muslim exegesis."[81] Al-Ṭabarī cites material from the standard authorities, noting even the insignificant variations in transmission. Below, I quote his classic interpretation of the opening *āyāt* of *Sūrat al-Nisā'*, since it sums up the various earlier interpretations that had become widely accepted by the first part of the tenth century.

The sources al-Ṭabarī uses in his discussion of *mut'a* reveal his nuanced perceptions of early Islam.[82] He begins his commentary on Q 4:24 as follows: "The exegetes have disputed the meaning of the passage: 'So, those with whom you seek enjoyment give them their dowries as settled.'" After this, he provides four traditions as evidence that the *āya* refers to permanent marriage and not to *mut'a*. This is followed by the comment that "others, however, say that the words 'you enjoy' refer to women who one enjoys in return for compensation, not the absolute kind of marriage that is contracted with a guardian, witness, and bridal money." He then quotes eleven traditions that support *mut'a*. Next, al-Ṭabarī writes, "As for what has been related in the name of Ubayy b. Ka'b and Ibn 'Abbās who read the Qur'anic verse as, 'So for whatever you enjoy from them for a determined time,' that is a version that contradicts the codices of the Muslims. It is forbidden for anyone to add to God's book anything that has not been confirmed in a way that cannot be denied."[83] And he ends his discussion of this issue with the following brief commentary: "We have shown elsewhere in our book that *mut'a* is not valid like a true marriage and have therefore dispensed with repeating it here."[84]

Al-Ṭabarī and the earlier exegetes he records display a remarkable degree of disagreement and apparent confusion about what the Qur'an means when it uses the word *mut'a*—this continued even almost three centuries after the Qur'an was revealed. The presence of contradictory reports and evidence suggests sophisticated editorial work. Al-Ṭabarī made his exegesis as vague as the term he is trying to explain (i.e., *mut'a*). Using multiple reports, he seems to present a strong case for neutrality, without directly casting doubt on the legitimacy of *mut'a*, thus leaving the reader in some doubt.

ABŪ ḤĀTIM AL-RĀZĪ (D. 322/934–35)

Abū Ḥātim al-Rāzī[85] was an Isma'ili missionary in charge of *da'wa*, missionary work, in Rayy, Iran.[86] He succeeded in converting the ruler of the city, Aḥmad b. 'Alī (d. 311/924) and received his patronage. After the Sunni Samanids took Rayy, Abū Ḥātim fled to the court of the Daylamī prince Mardavij in Tabaristan, where he conducted his famous debate with the physician-philosopher Abū Bakr Zakariyya al-Rāzī (Rhazes, d. after 311/924).

After Mardavij turned against the Isma'ilis, Abū Ḥātim fled to Azerbaijan, where he died in 322/934–35.

It is important to understand Isma'ili history, as it provides context for the scholarship that emerged from this group.[87] Within the Shi'i community, the Isma'ilis are the second largest group. However, our knowledge of their history and doctrines has remained fragmentary and distorted because our knowledge has largely depended on the accounts of their opponents, as the authentic Isma'ili writings preserved by the community were inaccessible to outsiders for a long time. This has changed radically in the past few decades due to the discovery of large private collections. Numerous Isma'ili works have now been edited and many more have become accessible in public libraries. The most noteworthy Isma'ili manuscript collections are in Bombay and London;[88] the former was donated by Asaf Ali Asghar Fyzee to the library of Bombay University in 1957, while the latter is held by the Institute of Ismaili Studies, founded in 1977.

Abū Ḥātim was an early exponent of Isma'ili Neo-Platonism and wrote works, such as *Kitāb al-Iṣlāḥ*,[89] on the cosmology and cosmogonic schemes of Isma'ili philosophy. He also produced a defense of prophecy called *A'lam al-nubuwwa*.[90] Like many Persians of his time, he did not revere the Fatimid caliph-imam but remained a Qarāmaṭī dedicated to the awaited Mahdi, the Hidden Imam, Muḥammad b. Ismā'īl b. Ja'far al-Ṣādiq.[91]

Al-Rāzī's *Kitāb al-Zīna* is a two-volume lexicon of theological terms.[92] The first volume considers the significance and origins of language as well as the believer's need to understand the Arabic language and technical Islamic terms; it contains a dictionary of technical religious terms and liberally quotes passages from the Qur'an, *aḥādīth*, and classical Arabic verse and prose. The second volume focuses on periphrasis and the lexigraphy of these terms, beginning with the key Qur'anic phrase "Most Beautiful Names of God"; al-Rāzī's central thesis is that to understand Islam, you must know the meaning of the names of God.

Volume one is divided into three chapters. The first chapter discusses: why the Arabic language is superior and the intricacies of its pronunciation; the difference between Arabic and other languages that use the same characters; and the history of Arabic grammar. In the second chapter the excellence of Arabic rhetoric is discussed, including the laws of Arabic poetry. He differentiates between the characteristics of good poetry and bad poetry, the difference between poetry and song, and finally, the significance of orality in relation to Islam and Arabic poetry. In the third chapter, terms that are either entirely new or took on a new meaning within the context of Islam are listed, defined, and discussed; for example, the words *ṣalāa*, *ḥajj*, and *ṣiyām* existed before Islam but have a specific meaning within Islam. This illustrates how previous practices were incorporated into Islam and given a clear Islamic identity. He also discusses non-Arabic words, and this is the section that interests us. There is no mention of *mutʿa*, which indicates that this was not a new term—as mentioned earlier, *mutʿa* existed in pre-Islamic Arabia—but he does include a small section on polygamy, where he discusses one, two, three, and four wives and the linguistic issues in the numbering.

This exegesis does not appear to be exclusively Ismaʿili, and although Abū Ḥātim often quotes the authority of the sixth Shiʿi imam, Jaʿfar al-Ṣādiq, he also cites Ibn ʿAbbās, Abū ʿUbayda, and others. Maybe this work was written for a general Muslim audience. The volumes fit into the early Muslim genre of grammatical and lexicographical works; by analyzing and investigating the Arabic language, they sought to understand and explain the religious language in the Qurʾan and in the narrations of the Prophet Muhammad.

ABŪ AL-NAḌR AL-ʿAYYĀSHĪ (FL. LATE THIRD/NINTH CENTURY)

Abū al-Naḍr Muḥammad b. Masʿūd al-Samarqandī al-ʿAyyāshī, a contemporary of al-Kulaynī, was a prominent third–fourth/ninth–tenth-century scholar who lived in the Islamic east and Transoxiana.[93] Al-ʿAyyāshī holds a special place in Shiʿism because he was a Sunni convert. He studied in the Shiʿi centers of Baghdad, Kufa, and Qum, and his main teachers were al-Ḥasan b. ʿAlī b. Faḍḍāl (d. 244/838–39) and ʿAbd Allāh b. Muḥammad b. Khālid al-Ṭayālisī al-Tamīmī, both Kufan traditionalists who transmitted reports from the eighth imam, ʿAlī al-Riḍā (d. 203/808).[94]

He was a prolific author and was considered "trustworthy." His student, Abū ʿAmr al-Kishshī (d. 340/951), compiled the first Shiʿi biographical dictionary. Al-ʿAyyāshī is reported to have written one, but it is not extant, and his influence upon his student is a matter of speculation. His extant Qurʾanic commentary is incomplete and only extends to the end of the eighteenth chapter, *Sūrat al-Kahf*. Although al-ʿAyyāshī's comments on later verses are cited in other Shiʿi *tafsīr* works, like the *Majmaʿ al-bayān* of Abū Faḍl al-Ṭabarsī (d. 548/1154) and the work of Ibn Tāwūs (664/1266), who also attested to having a copy in his library, at some point in the Timurid period parts of it seem to have been lost and only portions of it are available to us.

Despite the confusion that occurred within the Shiʿi community due to the *ghayba*, occultation, of the imam, this led to a period of intense intellectual discussion among scholars who were trying to make sense of what the occultation meant. Thus, Twelver works in this period were often preoccupied with combating extremist views on the status of the imam, as the more moderate mainstream scholars attempted to forge a middle path that would defend the Shiʿi faith against other Shiʿi groups, including the *ghulāt*, extremists, and

Sunni detractors. The narrations in al-ʿAyyāshī's work are significant because they stress the imam's knowledge, a central issue for Twelver Shiʿism during that period, and refute the positions of the Twelvers' opponents.

Most of the legal compositions mentioned in biographical works do not suggest overtly Shiʿi content. Nevertheless, the title of two legal works indicate that they dealt with issues that were disputed by the Sunni and the Shiʿa; these are *Kitāb al-Mutʿa* and *Kitāb al-Mash ʿalā al-qadamayn* (The book of wiping feet [for purification to pray]).

As a traditionalist, his commentary is confined to reports from the imams explaining the meaning and import of the *āyāt*. He does not offer his own opinions on the meaning but rather relies on the narrations being self-explanatory. He has eight narrations on Q 4:24: four on the definition of *muḥṣanāt* and four on *mutʿa*;[95] out of the four on *muḥṣanāt*, three describe them as married women and one describes them as chaste women.

The first hadith about *mutʿa* is from Jābir b. ʿAbd Allāh, who narrates from the Prophet Muhammad that they were on a *ghazwa*, expedition, (he does not mention which one) when they asked him about *mutʿa*, and he did not forbid it. The hadith proceeds to say that ʿAli said had it not been for ʿUmar, there would be no one so wretched as to commit *zināʾ*, fornication.

The next hadith is from Ibn ʿAbbās, who is reported to have said that *fa-mā istamtaʿtūm*, "So, those with whom you seek enjoyment," is followed by *illā ajal musammā*, "for a prescribed time," and that the Prophet Muhammad permitted *mutʿa* and never prohibited it.

The next hadith is from Abū Jaʿfar, who is narrated as saying that this section of the verse should be read with the addition of "for a prescribed time," and it is directed at the type of marriage that is for a limited time. Next, he is asked if these women are among the four one is allowed to marry, and he answers no, they are not from the four; they are wage earners. He then mentions that if both parties agree, the time can be extended without the woman going through a waiting period.

Since he only gives us pro-*mutʿa* hadith narrations, we can conclude that al-ʿAyyāshī is in full agreement with the Shiʿi viewpoint that *mutʿa* is allowed. We can also gather that at this point, about three hundred years after the death of the Prophet Muhammad, there seems to be a Shiʿi consensus that *mutʿa* is part of the legal system that distinguishes them from the Sunni.

CONCLUSION

Early exegetes exhibited a substantial array of opinions on the meaning of the divine command in Q 4:24. At this point in the *tafsīr* literature, the most important problem concerns the word *istamtaʿa*. As mentioned at the beginning of the chapter, this word means "pleasure," but in legal language, it denotes "temporary marriage," a pre-Islamic Arabian practice.

ʿAʾisha is clear that *mutʿa* is not allowed. Neither the Sunni nor the Shiʿa refer to *aḥādīth* she recorded or include her sayings anywhere in their discussions of this *āya* or in other works concerning *mutʿa*. This is noteworthy because it contradicts what is otherwise said about respect for her authority, and it is connected to the later practice of recycling a handful of authorities to develop discussions about *mutʿa*.

Ibn ʿAbbās, the father of *tafsīr*, is first recorded as permitting *mutʿa* and then as not permitting it. His view of *mutʿa*'s permissibility attracted quite a bit of criticism because he was still quite young when the Prophet Muhammad died and likely was not present when he declared it forbidden. Given Ibn ʿAbbās's authority within the Sunni tradition, it was important for the Shiʿa to cast doubt on the clarity of what he said.

Muqātil b. Sulaymān, the author of the earliest extant Qurʾanic commentary, writes that *mutʿa* was abrogated by the *āya* of inheritance and divorce and we can note that the Qurʾan is being used to explicate itself. At this stage, the *āya* is unequivocally considered in terms of the permissibility or impermissibility of the practice of *mutʿa*.

Al-Ṭabarī offers two possible interpretations—allowed and forbidden—each supported by a set of Prophetic reports from early authorities. At first, al-Ṭabarī does not seem to express a preference for either meaning, possibly because he is unclear about the permissibility or prohibition of *mutʿa*. However, the way he organizes the material is not unbiased: six reports are cited; two against the permissibility of *mutʿa* and four in favor. Furthermore, the less supported reading is prefaced as the opinion of the majority of the pious ancestors. Finally, he mentions that he has discussed this previously and finds the prohibition of *mutʿa* correct. It is noteworthy that almost three centuries after the Qurʾan was revealed, there is still no consensus on *mutʿa*.

Al-Rāzī did not prepare a typical *tafsīr*—it is the first Ismaʿili one we examine. He discusses new vocabulary that Islam introduced and words that existed in pre-Islamic Arabia but acquired a different meaning after the advent of Islam. He does not mention *mutʿa* in his discussion of new vocabulary, which indicates that *mutʿa* was not considered a new institution. However, the advent of Islam did change *mutʿa* from a matrilineal institution into a patrilineal one. Al-Rāzī not mentioning this change leaves us in doubt about its currency in his time.

The Ismaʿili commentator Abū Ḥātim does not discuss this *āya*. This could be because he was a persecuted minority and had other, more important issues (like theology) to defend and discuss. It could also mean that *mutʿa* was not a significant issue at the time he was writing.

Al-ʿAyyāshī cites the standard authorities. He gives his own judgment on the validity of *mutʿa* and says the only correct reading is that *mutʿa* is allowed; no other reading is acceptable. We must remember that he was a convert to Shiʿism, and he might have had more incentive to prove himself to be an authentic Shiʿi.

With the exception of al-ʿAyyāshī, none of these scholars unequivocally claim *mutʿa* is permissible. In Sunni scholars' writings, both interpretations of *mutʿa*—permissible and prohibited—in general had equal authority. The fact that Sunni scholars held such contradictory views proves that the issue of *mutʿa* was not yet decided. The ultimate outcome of the legal debate among the Sunni on this matter cannot be treated in isolation from sectarian developments, especially the emergence of the Twelver school, which treated the subject of *mutʿa* in a manner quite inconsistent with the Sunni position. The minor sects that we considered from this period, however, refrain from commenting on the institution of *mutʿa*. In this chapter, we saw the developments in the *tafsīr* genre that occurred in the classical period; however, this science and the sectarian concerns illustrated through it are solidified in the middle period.

NOTES

1. B. Carra de Vaux, "Tafsīr," in *Encyclopaedia of Islam, First Edition (1913–1936)*, eds. M. Th. Houtsma, T. W. Arnold, R. Basset, and R. Hartmann (Brill Online).

2. Andrew Rippin, "Tafsīr," in *Encyclopaedia of Islam, Second Edition*, eds. P. Bearman, Th. Bianquis, C. E. Bosworth, E. van Donzel, and W. P. Heinrichs (Brill Online, 2012).

3. The science of Qurʾanic exegesis evolved considerably over time. For a short discussion, see Rashid Ahmed, "Qur'anic Exegesis and Classical Tafsir," *The Islamic Quarterly* 12 (1968): 71–119; and Norman Calder, "Tafsīr from Ṭabarī to Ibn Kathīr: Problems in the Description of the Genre, Illustrated with Reference to the Story of Abraham," in *Approaches to the Qur'an*, eds. Gerald R. Hawting and Abdul-Kader A. Shareef (London: Routledge, 1993), 101–40.

4. In earlier eras, there was no formal training for women, and most female religious scholars were the relatives of male clerics. In the modern era, however, women are largely excluded from the formal clerical hierarchy in most Muslim countries. For example, although most Shiʿi clerics agree that women can reach the rank of a *mujtahid*, a religious authority able to decide on religious matters, they cannot act as, *marjaʿ al-taqlīd*, a source of emulation, for other believers. Women preachers do not preach in front of men, yet they exercise great influence over their female followers. They lead rituals held by women at home, or in a shrine, mosque, or another religious building—this includes giving sermons, Qurʾan reading, invocations, and recitations. Learned preachers also give religious lessons on a daily or weekly basis at homes or

at religious seminaries and schools. The basis of their knowledge and prestige differs. Some have obtained their education informally from a religiously learned relative or as a disciple of another male or female religious authority. In the last decades, an increasing number of women have studied at religious seminaries or in university theological faculties. Consequently, women have begun to challenge the male monopoly over the interpretation of religious source. For more, see Hilary Kalmbach, "Social and Religious Change in Damascus: One Case of Female Islamic Religious Authority," *British Journal of Middle Eastern Studies* 35, no. 1 (2008): 37–57.

5. See Amina Wadud, *Qur'an and Woman: Rereading the Sacred Text from a Woman's Perspective*, repr. ed. (New York: Oxford University Press, 1999); Anitta Kynsilehto, *Islamic Feminism: Current Perspectives* (Tampere: Tampere Peace Research Institute, 2008); Aysha A. Hidayatullah, *Feminist Edges of the Qur'an*, 1st ed. (Oxford: Oxford University Press, 2014); Nicholas Awde, *Women in Islam*, 2nd rev. ed. (London: Bennett and Bloom, 2005); Karen Bauer, *Gender Hierarchy in the Qur'ān: Medieval Interpretations, Modern Responses* (Cambridge: Cambridge University Press, 2015).

6. Brannon Wheeler, "Representations: Qurʾān: Overview," in *Encyclopedia of Women & Islamic Cultures*, ed. Suad Joseph (Brill Online, 2014).

7. In the *āyāt* that use *nafs*, soul, the gender category gets blurred. For example, Q 4:1 states that God created humanity from a single soul, dividing the soul to create partners. Some exegetes say that God created Adam as an androgynous being and then split humanity into male and female.

8. In general, among others, see Wadud, *Qur'an and Woman*; Amina Wadud, *Inside the Gender Jihad: Women's Reform in Islam* (Oxford: Oneworld, 2006); Kecia Ali, *Sexual Ethics and Islam: Feminist Reflections on Qur'an, Hadith, and Jurisprudence*, 1st ed. (Oxford: Oneworld Publications, 2006); Kecia Ali, *Marriage and Slavery in Early Islam* (Cambridge, MA: Harvard University Press, 2010); Hidayatullah, *Feminist Edges of the Qur'an*; Asma Barlas, *Believing Women in Islam: Unreading Patriarchal Interpretations of the Qur'an* (Austin: University of Texas Press, 2002); Hadia Mubarak, *Rebellious Wives, Neglectful Husbands: Controversies in Modern Qur'anic Commentaries* (Oxford: Oxford University Press, forthcoming in January 2022); Amira A. Sonbol, *Women, the Family, and Divorce Laws in Islamic History*, 1st ed. (Syracuse, NY: Syracuse University Press, 2007); Ziba Mir-Hosseini et al., eds., *Men in Charge?: Rethinking Authority in Muslim Legal Tradition* (London: Oneworld, 2015); Ziba Mir-Hosseini et al., eds., *Gender and Equality in Muslim Family Law: Justice and Ethics in the Islamic Legal Tradition* (New York: I. B. Tauris, 2017); Juliane Hammer, Dina El Omari, and Mouhanad Khorchide, eds., *Muslim Women and Gender Justice: Concepts, Sources, and Histories*, co-edited with Dina El Omari and Mouhanad Khorchide (London: Routledge, 2019); Juliane Hammer, *American Muslim Women, Religious Authority, and Activism: More Than Prayers* (Austin: University of Texas Press, 2012); Asma Lamrabet, *Women in the Qur'an: An Emancipatory Reading*, trans. Myriam Francois-Cerrah (New York: Kube Publishing, 2016); Ayesha S. Chaudhry, *Domestic Violence and the Islamic Tradition: Ethics, Law, and the Muslim Discourse on Gender* (Oxford: Oxford University Press, 2015); Sa'diyya Shaikh, *Sufi Narratives of Intimacy: Ibn ʿArabī, Gender, and Sexuality* (Chapel Hill:

University of North Carolina Press, 2012); Saba Mahmood, *Politics of Piety: The Islamic Revival and the Feminist Subject* (Princeton: Princeton University Press, 2005); Zahra Ayubi, *Gendered Morality: Classical Islamic Ethics of the Self, Family, and Society* (New York: Columbia University Press, 2019); Hina Azam, *Sexual Violation in Islamic Law* (Cambridge, UK: Cambridge University Press, 2015); and Celene Ibrahim, *Women and Gender in the Qur'an* (Oxford: Oxford University Press, 2020).

9. See Appendix A.

10. As mentioned earlier, Shiʿi commentators accept this *āya* as a valid source permitting the practice of *mutʿa*; Sunni commentators do not.

11. See, for example, Abū Jaʿfar Muḥammad b. al-Ḥasan al-Ṭūsī, *al-Tibyān fī tafsīr al-Qurʾān*, ed. Āghā Buzurg al-Ṭihrānī (Najaf: al-Maṭbaʿa al-ʿIlmiyya, 1957–63), 3:166; al-Faḍl b. al-Ḥasan al-Ṭabrisī (Ṭabarsī), *Majmaʿ al-bayān fī tafsīr al-Qurʾān*, eds. Hāshim al-Rasūlī and Faḍl Allāh al-Ṭabāṭabāʾī al-Yazdī, (Mashhad: al-Maʿārif al-Islāmiyya, 1976), 3:32. For the text of the Qurʾan attributed to these three companions, see Arthur Jeffery, *Materials for the History of the Text of the Qur'an: The Old Codices* (Leiden: E. J. Brill, 1937), 36, 126, 197. For a history of the evolution of the Qurʾanic text see Frederik Leehmuis, "Codices of the Qur'an," in *Encyclopaedia of the Qurʾān*, ed. Jane Dammen McAuliffe (Brill Online).

12. For more on this issue, see Arthur Gribetz, *Strange Bedfellows:* Mutʿat al-Nisāʾ *and* Mutʿat al-Ḥajj*: A Study Based on Sunnī and Shīʿī Sources of* Tafsīr*,* Ḥadīth*, and* Fiqh (Berlin: Klaus Schwartz, 1994), 161.

13. On Qurʾanic exegesis's function and its terminological and linguistic meaning, see Muhammad b. ʾAbdullāh al-Zarkashī, *al-Burhān fī ʿulūm al-Qurʾān* (Beirut: Dār al-Fikr, 1988), 2:162–69; Jalāl al-Dīn al-Suyūṭī, *al-Taḥbīr fī ʿilm al-tafsīr* (Beirut: Dār al-fikr, 1983), 36–41; see also Rippin, "Ṭafsīr." For more on the historical evolution of exegesis and its multiple schools, see Musa O. A. Abdul, "The Historical Development of Tafsir," *Islamic Culture* 50 (1976): 141–53.

14. Q 4:21, "And how could you take it back after having enjoyed each other intimately and she has taken from you a firm commitment?"

15. Q 4:23, "(Also) forbidden to you for marriage are your mothers, your daughters, your sisters, your paternal and maternal aunts, your brother's daughters, your sister's daughters, your foster-mothers, your foster-sisters, your mother-in-law, your stepdaughters under your guardianship if you have consummated marriage with their mothers—but if you have not, then you can marry them—nor the wives of your own sons, nor two sisters together at the same time—except what was done previously. Surely God is All-Forgiving, Most Merciful."

16. Sachiko Murata, *Mutʿa: Temporary Marriage in Islamic Law* (Qum: Ansariyan Publishers, 1986), 53.

17. See Abū Jaʿfar Muḥammad b. al-Ḥasan al-Ṭūsī, *Tahdhīb al-aḥkām* (Najaf: n.p., 1380/1960–61), 7:249–50.

18. Q 4:25, "But if any of you cannot afford to marry a free believing woman, then (let him marry) a believing bondwoman possessed by one of you. God knows best (the state of) your faith (and theirs). You are from one another. So marry them with the permission of their owners, giving them their dowry in fairness, if they are chaste, neither promiscuous nor having secret affairs. If they commit indecency

after marriage, they receive half the punishment of free women. This is for those of you who fear falling into sin. But if you are patient, it is better for you. And God is All-Forgiving, Most Merciful."

19. Hoda Elsadda, "Discourses on Women's Biographies and Cultural Identity: Twentieth-Century Representation of the Life of Aisha Bint Abu Bakr," *Feminist Studies* 27, no. 1 (2001): 37–64.

20. Leila Ahmed, "Women and the Advent of Islam," *Signs* 11, no. 4 (1986): 665–91.

21. Ashley Manjarrez Walker and Michael A. Sells, "The Wiles of Women and Performative Intertextuality: 'A'isha, the Hadith of the Slander, and the Sura of Yusuf," *Journal of Arabic Literature* 30, no. 1 (1999): 55–77; Aisha Geissinger, "The Exegetical Traditions of ʿĀʾisha: Notes on Their Impact and Significance," *Journal of Qur'anic Studies* 6, no. 1 (2004): 1–20.

22. Sofia Abdur Rehman, "ʿĀ'isha's Corrective of the Companions: A Translation and Critical Ḥadīth Study of al- Zarkashī's *al-Ijāba li-īrādi mā istadrakathu ʿĀ'isha ʿala al ṣahāba*" (PhD diss., University of Leeds, 2019), 3–4.

23. Shihāb al-Dīn Aḥmad Ibn Ḥajar al-ʿAsqalānī, *al-Iṣāba fī tamyīz al-ṣahāba*, ed. Khayrī Saʿīd (Cairo: al-Maktabah al-Tawfiqiyya, n.d.), 8:141.

24. Geissinger, "The Exegetical Traditions of ʿĀʾisha."

25. Al-ʿAsqalānī, *al-Iṣāba*, 8:140.

26. Al-Zarkashī's *al-Ijāba* is a very important work for hadith history and gender. Unfortunately, it has not been studied, neither in English nor in Arabic. The first somewhat detailed study of it in English is the PhD dissertation by Sofia Abdur Rehman.

27. Rehman, "ʿĀ'isha's Corrective of the Companions," 3.

28. Al-ʿAsqalānī, *al-Iṣāba*, 8:140; Yusūf b. ʿAbd Allāh Ibn ʿAbd al-Barr, *Jām bayān al-ʿilm* (Cairo: n.p., 1346), 4:437.

29. Asma Afsaruddin, "ʿĀʾisha bt. Abī Bakr," *Encyclopaedia of Islam, THREE*, eds. Kate Fleet, Gudrun Krämer, Denis Matringe, John Nawas, and Everett Rowson (Brill Online).

30. W. Montgomery Watt, "ʿĀʾisha Bint Abī Bakr," *Encyclopaedia of Islam, Second Edition*.

31. Maya Yazigi, "Defense and Validation in Shiʿi and Sunni Tradition: The Case of Muḥammad b. Abī Bakr," *Studia Islamica* 98/99 (2004): 49–70.

32. Q 24:7–11, "[A]nd a fifth oath that God may condemn him if he is lying. For her to be spared the punishment, she must swear four times by God that he is telling a lie, and a fifth oath that God may be displeased with her if he is telling the truth. (You would have suffered,) had it not been for God's grace and mercy upon you, and had God not been Accepting of Repentance, All-Wise. Indeed those who came up with that (outrageous) slander are a group of you. Do not think this is bad for you. Rather, it is good for you. They will be punished, each according to their share of the sin. As for their mastermind, he will suffer a tremendous punishment."

33. Hina Azam, "Rape as a Variant of Fornication (Zina) in Islamic Law: An Examination of the Early Legal Reports," *Journal of Law and Religion* 28, no. 2 (2012): 441–66.

34. D. A. Spellberg, *Politics, Gender, and the Islamic Past: The Legacy of A'isha Bint Abi Bakr* (New York: Columbia University Press, 1994), 60.

35. For a more detailed discussion of these debates, see Spellberg, *Politics, Gender, and the Islamic Past.* Spellberg focuses on the medieval communal debate about ʿA'isha, because as a woman with a high profile, her behavior had to be considered by later male definitions of feminine ideals and appropriate female roles.

36. Afsaruddin, "ʿĀ'isha bt. Abī Bakr."

37. Mohammad Fadel, "Two Women, One Man: Knowledge, Power, and Gender in Medieval Sunni Legal Thought," *International Journal of Middle East Studies* 29, no. 2 (1997): 185–204.

38. Abū ʿAbd Allāh Muhammad Ibn Saʿd, *Kitāb al-Ṭabaqāt al-kabīr*, ed. Eduard Sachau (Leiden: E. J. Brill, 1904–40), 8:66; al-ʿAsqalānī, *al-Iṣāba*, 8:140.

39. Al-Bukhārī, *Kitāb al-Jāmiʿ al-ṣaḥīḥ* (Leiden: n.p., 1862–1908), 3:427. W. Montgomery Watt translates this hadith in *Muhammad at Medina* (Oxford: Oxford University Press, 1962), 378–79.

40. ʿAbd Allāh b. Muḥammad Ibn Abī Shayba, *al-Musannaf* (Beirut: n.p., 2004), 3:272, no. 15. For this use of "sultan," see J. H. Kramers, C. E. Bosworth, O. Schumann and Ousmane Kane, "Sulṭān," in *Encyclopaedia of Islam, Second Edition.* In legal texts from the formative period, this word is used abstractly to mean political authority. In the context of this tradition and in reference to marriage and divorce in general, it means qadi.

41. Much attention is given to the *walī*'s authority in Islam. In most Sunni schools of thought there is a problem if a marriage is concluded without a *walī*. For example, Ibn Ḥanbal says such a contract is not valid and that a new one must be contracted. He mentions the legal maxim, "There can be no marriage without a *walī*." For the historical discussion of this maxim, see Joseph Schacht, *Origins of Muhammadan Jurisprudence* (Oxford: Clarendon Press, 1950), 182–83. Al-Shāfiʿī agrees with Ibn Ḥanbal. Mālik agrees but with some qualifications. Abu Ḥanīfa, on the other hand, held that a *walī* was not necessary if a woman concluded a marriage for herself with a man who was her equal and for a dowry that was not less than one appropriate for her. For the Hanafi position, see J. Schacht, A. Layish, R. Shaham, Ghaus Ansari, J. M. Otto, S. Pompe, J. Knappert and Jean Boyd, "Nikāḥ," in *Encyclopaedia of Islam, Second Edition*.

42. Ibn Abī Shayba, *al-Musannaf,* 7, 3:272, no.1.

43. Badr al-Dīn Abū ʿAbdullah Muḥammad b. ʿAbdullah b. Bahādur al-Zarkashī, *Zahr al-ʿarīsh fī tahrīm al-hashīsh,* study and verification by A. Faraj (Dār al-Wafā' wa al-Nashr wa al-Tawzī, 1970); Badr al-Dīn Abū ʿAbdullah Muḥammad b. ʿAbdullah b. Bahādur al-Zarkashī, *al-Ijāba li-īrādi mā istadrakathu ʿĀ'isha ʿala al-ṣahāba,* ed. Saʿīd al-Afghānī, 2nd ed. (Beirut: Al-Kutub al-Islāmī), 165. I am grateful to Omar Matadar of Qasid Institute in Amman, Jordan, for this reference. He was the first to mention this work to me, and he sent me the PDF. Later, I came across the amazing and much needed dissertation of Sofia Abdur Rehman from the University of Leeds.

44. Asma Sayeed, "Women and Ḥadīth Transmission: Two Case Studies from Mamluk Damascus," *Studia Islamica* 95 (2002): 71–94.

45. Herbert Berg, "The 'Isnād' and the Production of Cultural Memory: Ibn ʿAbbās as a Case Study," *Numen* 58, no. 2/3 (2011): 259–83.

46. Herbert Berg, *The Development of Exegesis in Early Islam: The Authenticity of Muslim Literature from the Formative Period* (New York: Routledge, 2000), 12–37, 173–218.

47. Claude Gilliot, "ʿAbdallāh b. ʿAbbās," in *Encyclopaedia of Islam, THREE.*

48. Andrew Rippin, "*Tafsīr Ibn ʿAbbās* and Criteria for Dating Early *Tafsīr* Texts," *Jerusalem* Studies *in Arabic and Islam* 18 (1994): 38–83.

49. Rippin, "*Tafsīr Ibn ʿAbbās,*" 40.

50. See Gilliot, "ʿAbdallāh b. ʿAbbās."

51. Andrew Rippin, "Ibn ʿAbbās's *al-Lughāt fī al-Qurʾān,*" *Bulletin of the School of Oriental and African Studies* 44, no. 1 (1981): 15–25.

52. Berg, *The Development of Exegesis*, 173–218.

53. Ibn ʿAbbās is one of ten Companions who are said to have a commentary. The others are the first four caliphs, Ibn Masʿūd, Ubayy b. Kaʿb, Zayd b. Thābit, Abū Mūsā al-Ashʿarī, and ʿAbd Allāh b. al-Zubayr; Jalāl al-Dīn al-Suyūṭī, *al-Itqan fī ʿulūm al-Qurʾān* (Beirut: Dār al-Kutub al- ʿIlmiyya, 1987), chapter 80, 4:233.

54. Muhammad Mustafa al-Azami, *Studies in Early Hadith Literature* (Indianapolis: American Trust Publications, 1978; originally published in Beirut: al-Maktab al-Islāmī, 1388/1968), 40–42.

55. G. H. A. Juynboll, *Muslim Tradition: Studies on Chronology, Provenance and Authorship of Early Ḥadīth* (Cambridge: Cambridge University Press, 1983).

56. The "skeptics" and "true believers" on the question of the "authenticity" of the hadith. On the one side, the most prominent scholars are Sprenger, Goldziher, Schact, and Wansbrough; on the opposing side are Abbott, Sezgin, al-Azami, and Motzki.

57. See Gilliot, "ʿAbdallāh b. ʿAbbās."

58. Al-Ṭabarī, who left the choice open by saying that both readings were grammatically possible, is sometimes accused of Shiʿism on account of this.

59. For a complete list, look at works attributed to Ibn ʿAbbās in Gilliot, "ʿAbdallāh b. ʿAbbās." For various relations between titles and texts, see Rippin, "*Tafsīr Ibn ʿAbbās.*"

60. ʿAbd Allāh Ibn ʿAbbās, *Tanwīr al-miqbās min tafsīr Ibn ʿAbbās* (Beirut: Dār al-Kutub al-ʿIlmiyya, 2000), 119–22.

61. Nūr al-Dīn ʿAlī b. Abī Bakr al-Haythamī, *Majmaʿ al-zawāʾid wa-manbaʿ al-fawāʾid* (Cairo: Dar al-Rayyan li-l-Turath, 1987), 4:486.

62. Al-Haythamī, *Majmaʿ al-zawāʾid,* 4:487–88.

63. Yeshayahu Goldfeld, "Pseudo Ibn ʿAbbās Responsa-Polemics against the Ghamiyya," *Arabica* 35, no. 3 (1988): 350–67.

64. See Abū ʿAbd Allāh al-Qurṭubī, *al-Jāmiʿ li-aḥkām al-Qurʾān wa-l-mubayyin li-mā taḍammana min al-sunna wa-āyāt al-furqān* (Beirut: al-Risāla Publishers, 2006), 3:116; see also W. Heffening, "Mutʿa," in *Encyclopaedia of Islam, Second Edition.*

65. See al-Qurṭubī, 3:116.

66. See Muslim Ibn al-Ḥajjāj, *al-Ṣaḥīḥ* (Cairo: n.p., 1374–75/1955–56), 9:182.

67. It is mentioned by al-Tirmidhī and others that something about the validity of *mutʿa* was reported in the name of Ibn ʿAbbās, then he recanted it because he was told that the Prophet Muhammad and most scholars commanded that it was forbidden. See Abū ʿĪsā Muḥammad al-Tirmidhī, *Ṣaḥīḥ* (Cairo: n.p., 1350–53/1931–34), 5:49.

68. Al-Haythamī, *Majmaʿ al-zawāʾid*, 4:487–88.

69. In general, see M. Plessner and Andrew Rippin, "Muḳātil b. Sulaymān," in *Encyclopaedia of Islam, Second Edition.*

70. Therefore, as to the basic issue of whether the oldest commentaries are actually the work of the scholars to whom they are ascribed, one would rather side with the pragmatism and positive attitude of J. Fick than with I. Goldziher's and J. Schacht's all-embracing negativism and accept the bibliographical information about the existence of books in Arabic as an expression of a very agile spiritual activity since the time of the Prophet Muhammad, as well as before his time; see Ignaz Goldziher, *Introduction to Islamic Theology and Law* (Princeton, NJ: Princeton University Press, 1981); Joseph Schacht, *An Introduction to Islamic Law* (Oxford: Oxford University Press, 1982). Andrew Rippin in particular accepts the ascription of this text to Muqātil, see "Al-Zukhrī, *Naskh al-Qurʾān* and the Problem of Early *Tafsīr* Texts," *Bulletin of the School of Oriental and African Studies* 47 (1984): 23.

71. This is one reason why John Wansbrough uses him and classifies it as haggadic, see *Quranic Studies* (London: Oxford University Press, 1977).

72. Feras Hamza, Sajjad Rizvi, and Farhana Mayer, eds., *On the Nature of the Divine*. Volume 1 of *An Anthology of Qur'anic Commentaries* (Oxford: Oxford University Press, 2010), 21–23.

73. Hamza, Rizvi, and Mayer, *On the Nature of the Divine,* 22.

74. Muqātil b. Sulaymān al-Balkhī, *Tafsīr*, ed. ʿAbd Allāh Maḥmūd Shiḥāta, 5 vols. (Cairo: al- Hayʾa al-Miṣriyya al-ʿĀmma li-l-Kitāb, 1979–89).

75. Q 59:7, "As for gains granted by God to His Messenger from the people of (other) lands, they are for God and the Messenger, his close relatives, orphans, the poor, and (needy) travellers so that the wealth may not merely circulate among your rich. Whatever the Messenger gives you, take it. And whatever he forbids you from, leave it. And fear God. Surely God is severe in punishment."

76. See C. E. Bosworth, "al-Ṭabarī," in *Encyclopaedia of Islam, Second Edition*; R. Paret, "al-Ṭabarī," in *Encyclopaedia of Islam, First Edition (1913–1936)*; and Hamza, Rizvi, and Mayer, *On the Nature of the Divine*, 28–29.

77. The history is titled *al-Rusul wa-l-mulūk* (The history of prophets and kings), and it marked the beginning of a type of history writing that was unprecedented among Muslims. For the first time there was a universal history that covered time from the beginning of creation up until the historian's own time. Al-Ṭabarī's commentary is *Jāmiʿ al-bayān fī taʾwīl al-Qurʾān.*

78. Despite originating from Tabaristan—which had not, in any case, in the early third/nineth century become closely identified with Zaydī Shiʿism—there is no evidence whatsoever of al-Ṭabarī having any inclination toward Shiʿism beyond an admiration for ʿAli as a person, which was often found in the staunchest of the Sunni.

79. Named after al-Ṭabarī's father.

80. Bosworth, "al-Ṭabarī."

81. Bosworth, "al-Ṭabarī."

82. Abū Jaʿfar Muḥammad b. Jarīr al-Ṭabarī, *Jāmiʿ al-bayān fī taʾwīl al-Qurʾān*, eds. Muḥammad Shākir and Aḥmad Shākir (Cairo: al-Hayʾa al-Miṣriyya al-ʿĀmma li-l-Kitāb, 1954), 8:60–68. All citations in from al-Ṭabarī in this section are from these pages.

83. Sunni exegetes mention the deviant version of the Qurʾanic verse on *mutʿa*, but not as proof of its legitimacy; on the contrary, since it contradicts the version found in the ʿUthmānic codex, it serves as further proof that it is not to be trusted.

84. Bosworth, "al-Ṭabarī."

85. See S. M. Stern, "Abū Ḥātim al-Rāzī," in *Encyclopaedia of Islam, Second Edition*; and Hamza, Rizvi, and Mayer, *On the Nature of the Divine*, 29–30.

86. See M. Canard, "Daʿwā," in *Encyclopaedia of Islam, Second Edition*; and Paul E. Walker, "Dāʿī (in Ismāʿīlī Islam)," in *Encyclopaedia of Islam, THREE.*

87. For further study, see Farhad Daftary, *The Isma'ilis: Their History and Doctrines* (Cambridge: Cambridge University Press, 1992).

88. Despite modern progress in Ismaʿili studies, wide gaps remain in our knowledge, especially concerning their early history and doctrines. The extant works of early thinkers, such as Abū Ḥātim al-Rāzī, Abū Yaʿqūb al- Sijistānī, Jaʿfar b. Manṣūr al-Yaman, and al-Qādi al-Nuʿmān, are not yet published. A considerable number of the published works are improperly and inadequately edited. Leaving aside the fact that most of the manuscripts are of Indian provenance, that is, they were transcribed during the tenth/sixteenth century and thereafter, very little textual history is available about the transmission of the corpus. In addition, we lack monographic studies about major thinkers and on important doctrinal aspects. Since this fundamental groundwork is yet to be undertaken, it is premature to formulate a definitive and authoritative statement of their doctrines.

89. Abū Ḥātim al-Rāzī, *Kitāb al-Iṣlāḥ*, eds. Hasan Minuchihr and Mahdi Muhaqqiq (Montreal: McGill Institute of Islamic Studies, 1998).

90. Abū Ḥātim al-Rāzī, *Aʿlam al-nubuwwa*, eds. Salah al-Sawi and Ghulam Rida Awani (Tehran: Imperial Academy of Philosophy, 1977).

91. For further study, see Wilferd Madelung, "Ḳarmaṭī," in *Encyclopaedia of Islam, Second Edition.*

92. Abū Ḥātim al-Rāzī, *Kitāb al-Zīna fī al-kalimāt al-ʿarabiyya al-Islamiyya*, ed. Ḥusayn b. Fayḍ Allāh al-Ḥamdānī, 2 vols. (Cairo: Dār al-Kitāb al-ʿArabī, 1957–58).

93. See B. Lewis, "al-ʿAyyāshī," in *Encyclopaedia of Islam, Second Edition*; Hamid Reza Fahimi and Matthew Melvin-Koushki, "al-ʿAyyāshī," in *Encyclopaedia Islamica*, eds. Wilferd Madelung and Farhad Daftary; Meir M. Bar-Asher, *Scripture and Exegesis in Early Imāmī Shiism* (Leiden: Brill, 1999), 58–62; and Hamza, Rizvi, and Mayer, *On the Nature of the Divine*, 26–27.

94. Lewis, "al-ʿAyyāshī."

95. Abū al-Naḍr Muḥammad b. Masʿūd al-Samarqandī al-ʿAyyāshī, *al-Tafsīr li-Abī al-Naḍr Muḥammad Ibn Masʿūd al-ʿAyyāshī*, 3 vols. (Qom: Maktabat al-Biʿtha, 2000).

Chapter Three

The Evolution of *Tafsīr*

Reaching New Heights

The previous chapter analyzed early *tafsīr* and interpretations of Q 4:24, showing how there was a lack of consensus among authoritative Sunni scholars regarding the permissibility of *mutʿa*. Among the Shiʿi exegetes the chapter covered, al-Ayyāshī was the only one who unequivocally permitted *mutʿa*. This early period was one of uncertainty, but now we will turn to the middle (medieval) period, when sectarian concerns became much more solidified and scholars engaged in exegesis to convey specific theological messages.

This chapter explores the medieval period and looks at how scholars greatly expanded the Islamic science of *tafsīr* by demarcating sectarian terminology as well as intermingling and incorporating different philosophical and theological schools. I focus on eight exegetical scholars, who come from different backgrounds and sectarian affiliations, including Sunni, Shiʿi, Muʿtazili, and Sufi. I begin with al-Thaʿlabī (d. 427/1035) for two reasons. First, his *al-Kashf wa-l-bayān ʿan tafsīr al-Qurʾān* is one of the most important medieval *tafsīr* works and provides an overview of works in this genre from the previous four centuries. Al-Thaʿlabī's aim was to review and critically analyze all prior *tafsīr* works and suggest improvements when he detects weaknesses.[1] Second, al-Thaʿlabī's *tafsīr* came at a critical moment in history: in the fourth/eleventh century, an entire school of Qurʾanic exegesis was established by three scholars from Nishapur, including al-Thaʿlabī, and this transformed the genre.[2]

AḤMAD B. MUḤAMMAD AL-THAʿLABĪ (D. 427/1035)

Abū Isḥāq Aḥmad b. Muḥammad b. Ibrāhīm al-Nīsāpūrī al-Thaʿlabī was a Sunni exegete who was born and died in Nishapur.[3] Nishapur fostered a rich and diverse intellectual environment, and as Muslim intellectual traditions matured and differentiated themselves from one another, this type of environment later became inconceivable.[4] The city was home to al-Ghazālī's teacher as well as the traditionalist and theologian Ibn Fārūq (d. 465/1072). The institution of the madrasa developed in Nishapur, and this was also where Abū Manṣūr Muḥammad al-Azharī (d. 370/980) compiled his magnum opus, *Tahdhīb al-lugha*, the most important lexicon in the Arabic language and the foundation for all later lexicographical works. Thus, Nishapur played a pivotal role in the consolidation of Sunni orthodoxy and was the environment in which al-Thaʿlabī developed and thrived.

He is famous for two works: *ʿArāʾis al-majālis fī qiṣaṣ al-anbiyāʾ*, his popular book on stories of the prophets, which was composed to provide historical information as well as entertainment, and *al-Kashf wa-l-bayān ʿan tafsīr al-Qurʾān*, a massive *tafsīr*. Recent scholarship has shown that al-Thaʿlabī's *al-Kashf* was widely known throughout the Muslim world; however, with the exception of a biographical introduction,[5] it remained unpublished until recently. There are two reasons for this delay: first, al-Thaʿlabī incorporated Shafiʿi, Shiʿi, and mystical material that his contemporaries frowned upon; second, his commentary revealed the influence of the heterodox Karrāmiyya.[6] These factors led to his intellectual conflict with Ibn Taymiyya (d. 728/1328)[7] and disqualified him from being recognized by most of Sunni orthodoxy.[8] Another reason *al-Kashf* may have remained unpublished for so long is because modern orthodoxy prefers ignoring such inclusive exegesis. However, a polyvalent pluralism existed within the classical Sunni *tafsīr* tradition, and al-Thaʿlabī, a Sunni exegete par excellence, drew upon the wide range of exegesis available at that time.[9]

There are four main interventions that al-Thaʿlabī introduced to the Islamic intellectual and religious conflicts of his time. The first was establishing philology as a tool for hermeneutics (a direct response to Muʿtazili intellectuals' assaults against Sunnis, which were far graver than many realize),[10] while simultaneously insisting this tool did not contradict the inherited interpretive traditions of Sunnism.[11] The second involved including mystics' Qurʾanic interpretations into mainstream Sunni Qurʾan commentary; al-Thaʿlabī made them acceptable and part of Sunnism and was the first to adopt a favorable attitude toward Sufi interpretation within Qurʾanic exegesis.[12] The third brought hadith literature into conversation with Qurʾan commentary. Al-Thaʿlabī's *tafsīr* contains a staggering amount of hadith, and after him, hadith began to flood exegesis in general. Pietistic Sunni sensibilities became allowed as well, since al-Thaʿlabī was not concerned with "authentic" hadith. He thus wove the entire corpus of the religious Islamic tradition into *tafsīr*. And finally, the fourth intervention entailed al-Thaʿlabī's willingness to give Shiʿi sensibility a far higher share of respect and attention than was customary in earlier Sunni Qurʾan commentaries.[13] The love of Prophet Muhammad's household was enshrined in his work, but on Sunni terms.[14] He preserved the Sunni hierarchy and inviolable sanctity of the Companions; therefore, the presence of Shiʿi material in *al-Kashf* was in fact a co-option of it.[15]

Al-Thaʿlabī strove to make *tafsīr* a medium that defined and defended Sunnism. However, his approach was not an exclusivist project; rather, it was an encyclopedic effort to make the *tafsīr* genre expansive, integrative, and inclusive of as many voices as possible from among the various Muslim sects.[16] Walid Saleh argues that al-Thaʿlabī represents the "intellectual victory" of Sunnism during a period when it was "weak but most culturally open."[17] Al-Thaʿlabī became a Sunni who was widely cited by Shiʿi exegetes and polemicists. He was a traditionalist who drew on Sufi commentary to demonstrate the polyvalent nature of the Qurʾan, a thinker interested in pre-Islamic religious writings, and a scholar who used seemingly pro-Shiʿi material to make anti-Shiʿi polemical points—this the case with the *mutʿa āya*.

Like scholars before him, al-Thaʿlabī starts his discussion of this *āya* by analyzing the term *muḥṣināt*.[18] He writes that the Arabs understood *al-iḥṣān* in four ways (which were mentioned in chapter 2): free women, Muslim women, chaste women, and married women. He then states that as Ibn ʿAbbās explained, the *āya* requires a man give the bride her *mahr*, dowry, as soon as he consummates the marriage, and this portion of the *āya* relates to *nikāḥ al-mutʿa*, *mutʿa* marriage. Al-Thaʿlabī is quick to note that Ibn Muṣīb states this practice was abrogated and says that we know *mutʿa* was practiced during the advent of Islam but was later "prohibited by the Prophet of God." He mentions *mutʿa* again when discussing the next section of the *āya*, "it is permissible to be mutually gracious regarding the set dowry." Al-Thaʿlabī says this line relates to increasing the amount of the dowry once the amount originally promised has been met. He adds that this section is said to refer to *mutʿa*, as it mentions the possibility of increasing the amount of payment or increasing the duration originally decided upon in the original *mutʿa* contract.

Al-Thaʿlabī's treatment of this *āya* illustrates his alignment with the mainstream Sunni opinion that *mutʿa* is forbidden; although he mentions the conflicting opinions, he presents the counterarguments with more force.

JĀR ALLĀH AL-ZAMAKHSHARĪ (D. 538/1144)

The Sunni exegete Abū al-Qāsim Jār Allāh Maḥmūd b. ʿUmar al-Zamakhsharī was born in Khwarazm[19] in 467/1075 and died there in 538/1144.[20] His father, who had very little means, wanted him to become a tailor, but he pressed his father to allow him to continue his studies and worked as a manuscript copier to support himself while studying. His original aspiration was to work as a government secretary, and his first job involved writing praise poems for Niẓām al-Mulk (d. 485/1092). He continued writing poems for dignitaries and traveling widely to study Arabic grammar and *tafsīr*. He later taught in Persian Transoxiana and is thought to be one of the last great Sunni Muʿtazili thinkers.[21]

Among his most famous works are a collection of Arabic proverbs and a book on grammar, *al-Mufaṣṣil fī al-naḥw*, an oft-quoted compendium that generated at least twenty-four known commentaries. What distinguishes this work from previous ones is the arrangement of the material;[22] instead of the classical division of syntax, morphology, and phonology, al-Zamakhsharī chose to divide his work according to the three parts of speech. He also wrote other grammatical texts; for example, one on syntax, another discussing grammatical controversies, and commentaries on other famous works of grammar, most notably on the work of Sībawayh.[23] He also wrote an Arabic thesaurus, *Asās al-balāgha*, and a bilingual Arabic-Persian dictionary, *Muqaddimāt al-adab*.

His *tafsīr*, *al-Kashshāf ʿan ḥaqāʾiq al-tanzīl wa-ʿuyūn al-aqāwīl* (The unveiling of the realities of revelation and essences of divine sayings), has a strong grammatical foundation and sets his Muʿtazili theology aside to offer an interesting treatment of syntax, morphology, and philology.[24] Al-Zamakhsharī believed God's message was deliberately delivered in Arabic. The language was essential to it rather than a coincidence; therefore, understanding the Qurʾanic sciences required knowledge of Arabic grammar. As a preeminent authority on grammar, al- Zamakhsharī's analysis of *āyāt* and his grammatical and philological exegesis have been quoted by a range of scholars from all types of theological persuasions, even from Zaydī and Twelver circles.

Al-Zamakhsharī starts his *tafsīr*[25] of Q 4:24 with the seemingly obligatory discussion of *muḥṣināt*. He claims the word is read with a *fatḥa* on the *ṣād* (i.e., *muḥṣanāt*), although many exegetes read it with a *kasra* here. According to al-Zamakhsharī, this word refers to married women, as marriage protects their private parts. Interestingly, he does not discuss the significance of *min al-nisāʾ*, among women, a curious, redundant phrase. Next, he indicates that *illā mā malakat imānakum* means "those women who have been captured in war." Like other exegetes, he says that sexual relations with these women is permissible, even if they are married.

He provides an intensive grammatical explanation of the rest of the *āya*, covering all possibilities for each word and their roles in the *āya*. He defines a *kitāb* as a book of God that prescribes what is permissible and what is prohibited so that we may act accordingly. This includes using our wealth in good conscience and not engaging in debauchery.

Regarding the part of the *āya* that reads *fa-mā istamta'tūm*, he claims it refers to women with whom one has formalized a marriage contract, had sex, or sat in a closed space, thus requiring the man to give them their due.[26] He then delves into a discussion of the particle *mā*, which will be discussed further in chapter 4. Al-Zamakhsharī questions the reasons for using *mā* in the *āya*, stating that the *mā* does not fit and does not make sense. He then lists the possible meanings and purposes for the *mā*. He writes that the *mā* could serve to distinguish a few women from the gender as a whole; it may function to set apart "those women you enjoy from all the women out there." He then addresses the next part of the *āya* and determines that if both parties agree, then they can increase the *mahr*, dowry.

Abruptly, and without any introductory preface or concluding commentary of his own, al- Zamakhsharī provides three *aḥādīth* that pertain to *mut'a*. He attests that *mut'a* was either permitted for three days or was permitted three times. During the occupation of Mecca, the Prophet Muhammad permitted *mut'a* for either a day, two days, one week, or two weeks, and then he prohibited it. Al-Zamakhsharī also provides evidence that 'Umar prohibited it, stating that 'Umar also declared that if he found a couple engaged in *mut'a*, he would stone them both. He then relays another narration from the Prophet Muhammad that states, "O people, I permitted *mut'a*, but now God has forbidden it until the end of time." He writes that it was permitted twice and forbidden twice, a construction that is not meant to be taken literally but rather to indicate several times. He then writes that Ibn 'Abbās permitted *mut'a*, since he read the verse with the addition of those you enjoy "for a prescribed time." However, he conveys that it is said that Ibn 'Abbās retracted his words when he was dying by saying, "May God forgive me for my words on *mut'a*." The section ends here, without al-Zamakhsharī giving his opinion or providing further analysis of the controversy. However, he presumably agrees with the Sunni consensus, since each narration of the permissibility of *mut'a* concludes with proof of its negation.

AL-FAḌL B. AL-ḤASAN AL-ṬABRISĪ (D. 548/1154)

Amīn al-Dīn (or Amīn al-Islām) Abū Al-Faḍl b. al-Ḥasan al-Ṭabrisī was a Shi'i exegete who was born in 470/1077–78, grew up in Khurasan in the village of Tabris, between Kashan and Isfahan,[27] and is buried in Mashhad, where he died in 548/1154. He wrote at least twenty works, and his theology was an example of a Shi'i modification of Mu'tazili thought initiated by al-Shaykh al-Mufīd (d. 413/1020) and al-Sharīf al-Murtaḍa (d. 436/1044). Al-Ṭabrisī had many well-known teachers; he was a student of the student of the leader of the Shi'i community in Baghdad, al-Shaykh Abū Ja'far al-Ṭūsī

(d. 460/1067).[28] He was also the most important Shiʿi figure of his time, writing two of the four most important books of hadith narrations.

His Muʿtazili *tafsīr*, *Kitāb Majmaʿ al-bayān li-ʿulūm al-Qurʾān* (or *Fī maʿānī al-Qurʾān fī tafsīr al-Qurʾān*), became the most authoritative and most quoted Shiʿi *tafsīr*. Because he studied with two famous Sunni scholars, Maḥmūd b. al-Ḥusayn al-Kiramānī (d. c. 500/1106–7) and ʿAbd al-Fatḥ ʿUbayd Allāh al-Qushayrī (d. 521/1127), he was familiar with Sunni methods of commentary, such as *bi-l-raʾy*, speculation, *bi-l-ishāra*, allusion and *bi-l-maʾthūr*, binding proof.[29] His *tafsīr* includes narrations from both Sunni and Shiʿi narrators,[30] as well as theological discussions, philological observations, and periphrastic remarks. It was influenced by the exegetical work of al-Zamakhsharī—al-Ṭabrisī wrote an abridgment of this text. Al-Ṭabrisī also acknowledges his debt to al-Ṭūsī's *al-Ṭibyān fī tafsīr al-Qurʾān* while simultaneously criticizing his use of unreliable material.

The overall structure of al-Ṭabrisī's *tafsīr* is fairly consistent and contains comprehensive explanations of all aspects of the *āyāt* studied.[31] For example, the formal consideration of the reading, syntax, and philology is presented alongside proofs for his argument. When possible, he also discusses the theological significance of the *āya*. He analyzes the language and gives copious examples from pre-Islamic poetry. Sometimes, al-Ṭabrisī discusses *asbāb al-nuzūl*, the occasions of revelation. These elements illustrate the three features that characterize his commentary: discussion of language, syntactical arrangement, and theological significance.

Al-Ṭabrisī begins his discussion of Q 4:24 by discussing the syntax of *muḥṣināt*; this differs from previous exegetes, who only discussed the meaning and pronunciation of it. He also gives us variations in the pronunciation of *uḥilla lakum* and says that the people of Kufa (except for Abū Bakr and Abū Jaʿfar) read it with a *kasra* on the *ḥāʾ*, while all other Arabic speakers read it with a *fatḥa* on the *hamza* and the *ḥāʾ*. He also gives us the meanings of *muḥṣināt* that were mentioned earlier. In the section on philology, he mentions the phrase *kitāb Allāh ʿalaykum* and says that it has a hidden verb, *kataba*, (i.e., *kataba kitāb Allāh ʿalaykum*, the book of God permits or prohibits for you).

Then, he discusses the phrase "lawful to you are all beyond these—as long as you seek them with your wealth" and gives four meanings. The first meaning is that you are permitted women not among those that are forbidden to you through familial and milk relations.[32] Second, you are permitted no more than four wives. Third, you are permitted what your right hand possesses, meaning slaves. And fourth, he writes that you are permitted to marry more than four women whom you seek with your money, whether through *nikāḥ*, marriage, or through the purchase of a slave, and this explanation, he writes, is best. He then says that there is no contradiction between this saying because it comes from Ibn ʿAbbās. He is of course referring to *mutʿa* here, since this marriage is not counted among the four marriages permitted.

The next section of his discussion is the lengthiest—about one half of the entire discussion of this *āya*—and focuses on the term *istamtaʿtūm*. He presents five arguments in favor of the interpretation of this *āya* as a proof text for the permissibility of *mutʿa*. First, he says that this *āya* refers to *mutʿa*, and we know this from the Companions Ibn ʿAbbās, al-Sīdī, Ibn Saʿīd, and others. He writes that the imams of the *ahl al-bayt*, People of the House, also permit it, and it was also practiced by their followers. His second argument is linguistic. He writes that this practice was known by the name *mutʿa* at the time of the Prophet Muhammad; therefore, there is no reason to ascribe a different meaning to this word. He explains that both Sunni and Shiʿi used *bi-ʿurf al-sharʿ*, examples of legal usage, to develop the term *istamtaʿtūm* to mean "a temporary marriage contract," which he says is the intended meaning of the *āya*. Furthermore, *istamtaʿtūm* cannot refer to pleasure in the sense of pleasure that is derived from marriage since the man must give the woman her *mahr*, dowry (or at least part of it), even if he receives no pleasure from the arrangement, as he must give her half the *mahr* even if he releases her before consummating the marriage. The third argument he gives is the variant reading, and he writes that Ibn ʿAbbās had a *muṣḥaf*, copy of the Qurʾan, featuring the variant "for a prescribed time" added to the *āya*. Next, he presents the argument that the *āya* was abrogated by the Prophet Muhammad and says this cannot be the case because we have evidence that *mutʿa* was practiced during the reigns of Abū Bakr, ʿUthmān, and ʿUmar until he prohibited its practice. His fifth and final piece of evidence is ʿUmar's hadith. He claims it makes it clear that ʿUmar prohibited *mutʿa* on his own, since we have a record of him saying that two types of *mutʿa* were permitted at the time of the Prophet Muhammad and he (ʿUmar) forbade both and would punish those who practiced either of them. He also gives us the hadith from ʿAli, which reads that had it not been for ʿUmar, no one but the wretched would have committed *zināʾ*, fornication.

He also discusses the word *ajr* and writes that Q 4:24 cannot refer to permanent marriage, since the continuation of the *āya* "and give them their *ajr*" is a command to give the *mutʿa* wife her entire *ajr* at the time of the contract. This, he says, is not a requirement for a permanent marriage. He ends his discussion by explaining the last section of the *āya*, saying that this line gives the two parties in a *mutʿa* permission to increase or decrease both the time and the *mahr*, dowry, and this can be decided upon after the original agreement has been fulfilled. Thus, al-Ṭabrisī does not entertain any doubt about what this *āya* means. His language is very direct and categorical: It means that *mutʿa* is allowed.

FAKHR AL-DĪN AL-RĀZĪ (D. 606/1209)

Abū ʿAbd Allāh Muḥammad b. ʿUmar b. al-Ḥusayn Fakhr al-Dīn al-Rāzī was one of the most influential medieval Sunni theologians.[33] He was an Ashʿarī philosopher who studied under Abū al-Qāsim al-Anṣārī, himself a student of the great Imam al-Ḥaramayn Abū al-Maʾalī al-Juwaynī (d. 477/1085), as well as with Majd al-Dīn al-Jīlī, the teacher of other luminaries from this period. Al-Rāzī wrote a major commentary on the work of Ibn Sīna (d. 428/1037), and this work is also one of the most important classical works outlining Sunni beliefs, *Mafātīḥ al-ghayb* (Keys to the unseen), otherwise known as *al-Tafsīr al-kabīr* (the great commentary). It is a compendium of philological, traditionalist, theological, and philosophical discussions on the *āyāt* of the Qurʾan, with commentary on each *āya* divided into sections and subsections, and various arguments and counterarguments are presented, evaluated, and accepted, rejected, or proposed. This is possibly the largest commentary from the medieval period, and it contains the longest discussion on the *mutʿa āya* (Q 4:24) from this five-hundred-year period.[34]

Al-Rāzī's discussion of this *āya* is the lengthiest and most systematic of all the ones discussed in this chapter, and it can also be labeled as polemical, since it sometimes seems like he ignores Shiʿi claims. He begins by admitting that some people use Q 4:24 as a proof text for the permissibility of *mutʿa*. He writes that all scholars agree that *mutʿa* was permitted at the time of the Prophet Muhammad. The disagreement lies in whether or not it was later prohibited. The discussion that follows systematically covers arguments or proofs presented by the Shiʿa and his responses to their arguments.

Those who maintain, by which he means the Shiʿa, that *mutʿa* is permitted, do so on the basis of *aḥādīth* related by Ibn ʿAbbās and Imran b. al-Husyan (d. 52/672). Al-Rāzī then presents three different *aḥādīth* from Ibn ʿAbbās; the first where he is thought to have permitted *mutʿa*, the second where he permitted *mutʿa* only under certain circumstances of hardship, and the third where he prohibited *mutʿa*. He also provides a hadith related from Imran maintaining that *mutʿa* was prohibited. Next, he turns his attention to *aḥādīth* by ʿAli, which he says the Shiʿa also use as a basis for the permissibility of *mutʿa*, and he provides counter *aḥādīth* where ʿAli is said to say *mutʿa* is prohibited. Thus, al-Rāzī counters the claim that *mutʿa* is legal according to the *sunna* by presenting *aḥādīth* in which the same people maintain that it was prohibited. He also writes that there are other *aḥādīth* that clearly state that *mutʿa* is prohibited.

He then turns his attention to ʿUmar's sermon. He writes that ʿUmar said, "I am prohibiting the two types of *mutʿa* practiced at the time of Prophet and will chastise anyone who practices it."[35] This declaration was made in front of a majority of the Companions, and no one rebuked him. This, al-Rāzī writes, leads us to three possible conclusions: The Companions knew of the prohibitions and agreed with ʿUmar, they knew it was permitted but kept silent, or that they neither knew it was permitted nor knew it was prohibited and thus refrained from saying anything. The second option, according to al-Rāzī, cannot be possible, since if they knew *mutʿa* was permissible and let ʿUmar prohibit it, this would make them infidels. The third possibility is also untenable because if *mutʿa* was lawful, then much like permanent marriage, everyone would have known the rules and regulations. This, al-Rāzī says, leaves us with the first possibility, which is that ʿUmar's sermon was predicated on prior knowledge that *mutʿa*'s permissibility had been abrogated.

After discussing the sunna and ʿUmar's sermon, he focuses on Q 4:24. His discussion of the *āya* and its various parts is several pages long and is intertwined with lengthy peripheral issues. He presents proofs employed by the Shiʿa and then provides his response to their evidence. He says that according to the Shiʿa, Q 4:24 articulates the permissibility of *mutʿa*. But, he follows this by stating that we should consider both possibilities: Q 4:24 either permits temporary marriage or speaks about permanent marriage.

Like other scholars, he provides a lengthy discussion on the word *muḥṣināt*; he writes that there are several issues, some mentioned by other exegetes and some discussed only by him. The first issue is the linguistic meaning of *iḥṣān*, which he defines as "protection." For example, he says that *iḥṣān* can be used to indicate a protected city or a shield that protects the shield bearer from getting hurt. He provides examples from the Qurʾan where the word is used with the same linguistic context: "We taught him the art of making body armour to protect you [*tuḥṣinakum*] in battle. Will you then be grateful?" (Q 21:80); and "Mary, the daughter of 'Imran, who guarded [*aḥṣanat*] her chastity" (Q 66:12). The term *muḥṣan* has a variety of connotations when it is used in the Qurʾan: a free person (Q 24:4);[36] chastity (Q 66:12);[37] Islam (Q 4:25),[38] or as some exegetes interpret it, "and when they become Muslims"[39]; and marriage (Q 4:24), as in "women who have spouses."[40] By way of a conclusion, he states that all four meanings revolve around the original meanings of "guarding" and "protection," and in this *āya*, *muḥṣināt* refers to married women.

Al-Rāzī then discusses the phrase *muḥṣināt min al-nisāʾ*, from which he says two meanings are possible. The first is "married women," and this means the *āya* implies: "so no married women is permitted to you unless you possess her through a new marriage, after clear proof that she is no more with her previous husband." The objective is to protect women from adultery or any sexual contact except through a new marriage—or, in the case of a slave woman, if she is possessed by a new owner. The only married women who are permitted with to engage in sexual activity outside of marriage are war captives, according to some scholars.

He writes that the Shiʿa claim that according to Q 4:24 the *āya* mandates payment for *istamta*ʿ, enjoyment, which in this case refers to enjoying a woman sexually through a temporary marriage because, in a permanent marriage, paying the dowry does not depend upon *istamta*ʿ but on the marital contract. This idea is substantiated by the Qurʾanic provision that even without sexual contact, the groom is obligated to pay half the dowry.[41] Al-Rāzī writes that this can be understood as differentiating permanent marriage from *istamta*ʿ. However, he responds to this claim by saying *istamta*ʿ means "enjoying benefit from something" and gives an example from the Qurʾan: "Our Lord! We *benefitted* from each other's company" (Q 6:128). He does not interpret *istamta*ʿ as sexual enjoyment; rather, he understands it as plain enjoyment and refers to other *āyāt* to explain this meaning. Further in his response, al-Rāzī writes that the preceding *āya* (Q 4:23)[42] discusses *maḥarmāt*, women one cannot marry, while Q 4:24 discusses women one can marry. Therefore, both *āyāt* refer to permanent marriage.

Next, he discusses *fa-mā istamtaʿtūm bihi min hunna*, which he says can be interpreted in two ways: First, offer the women you marry their reward for whatever benefit you enjoy (sexual or otherwise, as per his discussion above) from them. Second, the *mā* refers to women, and this can also be understood from the *mā*[43] in the *āya* before this,[44] which is translated as "all beyond these," referring to women other than those who are married. Al-Rāzī writes that the *min* in *min hunna* can means some (i.e., part) of the women. The pronoun in the clause *bihi* thus refers to *mā* because it is the only term in the expression that it could refer to. The word *ujūrahunna*, which appears a little later in the passage, refers to the dowry as is seen in the following *āya*. He then notes, with a strikingly modern sensibility, that God has referred to the dowry as *ajr*, dues, because it is something given in exchange for the benefit enjoyed rather than the usual sense of a sale of exchange (e.g., buying an animal for a fee).

The next section of al-Rāzī's exegesis provides Qurʾanic evidence for the abrogation of *mutʿa*. He writes that sexual intercourse is not permissible except with a spouse or slave, which is evident from Q 70:29.[45] It is undeniable that *mutʿa* is conducted with neither a real wife nor a slave. Three factors prove this: First, if she was considered a true wife, she would inherit as commanded in Q 4:12,[46] but she does not. Second, the Prophet Muhammad said, "The child belongs to the marriage bed,"[47] but a child born from *mutʿa* cannot be attributed to the husband. This is surprising, not only because no one before—or after—al-Rāzī had presented this argument but also because the Shiʿa use this same hadith to bolster the opposite argument, according to them a child born from *mutʿa* receives the father's name and inheritance. Finally, al-Rāzī argues that there is no *ʿidda*, waiting period, prescribed in the

Qur'an for the wife in a *mut'a* but there is one prescribed for a permanent wife in Q 2:234.[48] It cannot be fathomed that al-Rāzī did not know that the Shi'i response to this is that these *āyāt* came before the *mut'a āya* and therefore cannot abrogate it.

He then states that it is also possible that this *āya* only refers to *mut'a* and not permanent marriage, since we have a report from Ubayy b. Ka'b and Ibn 'Abbās that they used to read this *āya* with the addition, "those whom you enjoy *for a limited time*." Al-Rāzī does not simply present these readings; he responds by saying these arguments are negated by 'Umar's sermon, at which both Ibn 'Abbās and Ubayy were present.

Al-Rāzī treats Q 4:24 in detail. Although he does present both sides of the argument—that the *āya* either supports or refutes the practice of *mut'a*—he ultimately presents most of the arguments as evidence that *mut'a* is forbidden.

RASHĪD AL-DĪN MAYBUDĪ (FL. SIXTH/TWELFTH CENTURY)

We do not know much about the life of the Sufi exegete Maybudī.[49] What we do know is that he started to write his commentary on the Qur'an, *Kashf al-asrār wa-'uddat al-abrār* (The unveiling of secrets and the provision of the righteous), in 520/1126.[50] Since it is a lengthy work, it is likely to have taken several years to complete, and since it appear to be the work of a mature person, it can be safely assumed that he was born at the end of the fifth/eleventh century and died in the sixth/twelfth century. The name Maybudī indicates that he was from a town fifty kilometers from Yazd, and he likely received his early education in Yazd or somewhere else in the region, possibly Herat.

Kashf al-asrār is one of the earliest extant mystical commentaries, *tafasīr*, on the Qur'an in Persian. It has ten volumes in its printed edition.[51] One important feature of this *tafsīr* is its inclusion of both esoteric and exoteric interpretations of the Qur'an.[52] It also gives us an *āya*-by-*āya* translation. While the text of *Kashf al-asrār* does not yield any further data about Maybudī's life, it provides substantial data about his doctrines and interests. Like his self-proclaimed master, he was both a mystic and an ardent traditionalist.

Maybudī's *tafsīr* has an unusual format. First, he divides the Qur'an into manageable parts and then divides his commentary on each part into three sections. The first section consists of concise translations of the *āyāt* into Persian, and the second section contains the conventional commentary and mentions the usual elements, like *asbāb al-nuzūl*, the occasions of revelation, relevant *aḥādīth* and rulings, and so on. It consists of material drawn from previous Arabic *tafsīr* works, sometimes expanded with his own comments, and a surprisingly large amount of material is left untranslated and merely cited in Arabic. The third section consists of Maybudī's mystical commentary, thus its style and content are original. He does not, however, address all the *āyāt* here, having done so in the second section. He presents the commentary in order to present a mystical path that stems from the Qur'an more so than to explain the Qur'an.[53] Maybudī's *tafsīr* also has a uniquely accessible format, which means that it could be understood by more than just elite scholars, and thus it had popular appeal.[54]

Maybudī does not discuss Q 4:24. This indicates the issue of *mut'a* was not significant to him. Analyzing his discussion of Q 4:10,[55] the verses on polygamy, should reveal his thoughts on marriage, but he only mentions the importance of treating orphans fairly. In this discussion, he concludes with a story about Jesus passing by a graveyard and asking a young man buried there who he was and when he died. The young man gives his name and says that he died 2,700 years prior. Jesus next asks how his time has been since his death; the young man replies, "Pure torture." Jesus asks why, and the young man responds that he once stole a piece of silver from an orphan and he is still being made to repent.[56] Maybudī's discussion of the fair treatment of orphans rather than polygamy in this verse is also something emphasized by modern feminist scholars of the Qur'an.[57]

ABŪ 'ABD ALLĀH AL-QURṬUBĪ (D. 671/1272)

Abū 'Abd Allāh al-Qurṭubī or Abū 'Abd Allāh Muḥammad b. Aḥmad b. Abū Bakr al-Anṣārī al-Qurṭubī was a famous Sunni hadith exegete and scholar of Mālikī *fiqh*.[58] He is famous for his *tafsīr*. We do not know much about his life other than that he was born in Cordoba, Spain, and fled the city after it was captured by King Fernando I. He spent some time studying in different Muslim centers of knowledge and eventually settled down in Munyā Abī al-Khuṣayb, Egypt, where he died in 671/1272; a mausoleum was built there in his honor in 1971. In addition to being known as a superb scholar, he was also known for his piety and was said to have always appeared in public in the same outfit and greatly inclined toward asceticism. Among his works, his *tafsīr* on the Qur'an, *al-Jāmī' li-aḥkām al-Qur'ān wa-l-mubayyin li-mā taḍammana min al-sunna wa-āyāt al-furqān*, is well-known for its richness and utility.[59]

Al-Qurṭubī's work has four noteworthy characteristics. First, it includes a wealth of hadith, including some not mentioned by al-Ṭabarī, because al-Qurṭubī is interested in the *matn*, content or subject, and not the *isnād*, process or chain of transmission. Second, his commentary is designed to clarify the meaning and implications of law, and thus, his work closely resembles *uṣūl*, principles or roots, and *furū*ʿ, branches. Third, it is grounded in al-Qurṭubī's study of grammar and thereby serves as a philological commentary based on works of rhetoric and *adab*, literature. Finally, in contrast to the works of al-Ṭabarī and al-Rāzī, his work dramatically reduces the use of *isrāʾīliyyāt*, biblical narratives.

Al-Qurṭubī discusses the issue of *mutʿa* in considerable detail.[60] In his commentary, he goes to great lengths to prove that *mutʿa* has been abrogated by the Qurʾan, although it was permitted prior to that. And, he presents this argument after he quotes a tradition that indicates the *āya* in question cannot be understood to imply the validity of *mutʿa*, saying that "It is wrong to interpret the verse as permitting *mutʿa*, because God's Messenger, may God pray for him and give him peace, rejects *mutʿa* marriage and made it forbidden."[61] He then presents numerous traditions that testify to the abrogation of *mutʿa*, two of which go back to ʿAlī b. Abī Ṭālib, who is quoted as confirming the abrogation. In al-Qurṭubī's words,

> al-Dāraquṭnī related in the name of ʿAlī b. Abī Ṭālib, who said, "The Messenger of God, may God pray for him and bless him, forbade *mutʿa* marriage," and he added, "*Mutʿa* was meant for those who did not find a permanent wife. But when the matters of marriage, divorce, waiting period, and inheritance between husband and wife were revealed, *mutʿa* was abrogated." It is related in the name of ʿAlī, may God be pleased with him, that he said, "The first of Ramadan abrogated all other fasts, the charity of *zakāa* abrogated all other characteristics, and divorce, waiting period, and laws of inheritance abrogated *mutʿa* marriage."[62]

He then mentions the views of numerous Islamic scholars and jurists to put an end to the debate in a way that confirms the prohibition of *mutʿa*. He confirms the claim that the Sunni forbid it, although they admit it was permitted at a certain time in the past and was later abrogated.

ʿABD AL-RAZZĀQ AL-KĀSHĀNĪ (D. 736/1336)

Kamāl al-Dīn Abū al-Faḍl ʿAbd al-Razzāq b. Jamāl al-Dīn Abī al-Ghanāʾim Aḥmad (or Isḥāq) al-Kāshānī was a major Sufi figure who lived during the Ilkhanid period in Iran.[63] Not much is known about his life, and there is also confusion about the ascription of his *tafsīr* to Ibn ʿArabī (d. 638/1240). He was a student of a Shiʿi traditionalist in Shiraz, Aṣīl al-Dīn ʿAbd Allāh al-ʿAlawī (d. 685/1285), so he most likely had Shiʿi affiliations. The second most important scholar he studied under was a Sunni Sufi, Nūr al-Dīn ʿAbd al-Ṣamad al-Naṭanzī (d. 699/1299).

His *tafsīr*, which provides allegorical elucidation,[64] belongs to the genre of *tafsīr al-ishārī*, allusive commentary. "In particular, Kashani's tafsir is largely based on *tatbiq*—that is, the regular 'application' of macrocosmic references in the Qurʾan to the human microcosm."[65] It is an esoteric and mystical reading intended to guide the initiate along the path of spiritual realization through subtle, pedagogic allusions to the truth and inner self. This process of *taʿwīl*, hermeneutics, is "a systematic attempt at locating the experience of the text in the spiritual self and interrogating the world and recognizing the signs of God through His explicit revelation (the Qurʾan) and an implicit revelation (the lives of pious saints and the cosmos)."[66] Much Sufi teaching about the relationship between the word and the world is predicated upon three metaphysical realities: God, the macrocosmic world, and the microcosmic human. The "text" is a means of expressing each of these realities. Thus, Sufi *tafsīr* is not just an explanation, periphrasis, or interpretation of the Qurʾan on the linguistic, philosophical, dogmatic, and textual levels, it also expresses an understanding of reality both within and outside of the self. Therefore, it differs from the *bi-l-maʾthūr*, binding proof, and *bi-l-raʾy*, speculation, methods because it rarely contains transmitted narrations or considers different opinions. Al-Kāshānī, like Maybudī, does not discuss Q 4:24.[67]

ISMĀʿĪL ḤAQQĪ BURUṢĀWĪ (D. 1137/1725)

Shaykh Abū al-Fidāʾ Ismāʿīl b. Muṣṭafā Buruṣāwī Uskundarī was born in Aydos (Aitos, present-day Bulgaria) in 1063/1652.[68] He began his studies at home and then moved to Istanbul in 1084/1673 for further study. In Istanbul, he was initiated into the Khalwatiyya Sufi order by ʿUthmān Faḍlī. While there, he also developed an interest in Persian poetry, which had a marked effect on his later output. But he spent most of his life in Bursa and died there in 1137/1725. He was a true Ottoman man of letters, composing works in both Turkish and Arabic, and was well versed in a variety of disciplines. He was a prolific preacher and writer. Apart from his writings on poetry, he also wrote a history on his Sufi order, homiletics, collections of sermons, and a major work on Sufi metaphysics. Many of his works are available as autographed copies in his Sufi *tekke* in Bursa.

One of his most famous works is his Sufi *tafsīr* on the Qurʾan, *Rūḥ al-bayān* (Spirit of elucidation), which was influenced by Ibn ʿArabī and includes copious references to Sufi poetry. As the name of the work indicates, it is a work aimed at eliciting the essential message of the Qurʾan. He describes his methods as an attempt to elucidate the Qurʾan's mystical wisdom and subtle allusions, and it is grounded in his own mystical experience as a major Khalwatī shaykh. The work has been edited in ten volumes and is mainly in Arabic, with generous citations of Persian poetry and prose, as well as some sentences in Ottoman Turkish.

His exegesis on Q 4:24 is quite elaborate. He breaks the *āya* into parts, like other exegetes, and discusses the linguistic and grammatical relevance of each word or group of words.[69] We do not learn anything new from his *tafsīr*; however, one point worth mentioning is that when he comes to the word *istamta ʿtūm*, he barely writes one sentence: "which you enjoy by marriage or what is assumed when you are alone in a secluded space."[70] He neither acknowledges that there is another argument nor does he mention Ibn ʿAbbās, the Shiʿi perspective, or that some scholars have thought this *āya* refers to *mutʿa*. His discussion of the rest of the *āya* is more verbose. He gives a very thorough and comprehensive discussion of complicated words, such as *muḥṣanāt*, and provides extra information on the subject matter, for example, the types of women one cannot marry.

CONCLUSION

This chapter discussed seven exegetes from different Islamic traditions. Al-Thaʿlabī's exegesis states that the practice of *mutʿa* existed during the time of the Prophet Muhammad but was later abrogated. Although he mentions both positions, he advances the arguments that refute the permissibility of *mutʿa* more forcefully. Jār Allāh al-Zamakhsharī does the same, presenting arguments from both sides but concluding any presentation of the permissibility of *mutʿa* with a refutation. He affirms that there are *aḥādīth* from Ibn ʿAbbās allowing *mutʿa* but claims that he retracted this on his death bed.

Unlike the first two exegetes, al-Ṭabrisī is much more direct in his position that *mutʿa* is allowed. He presents "There will be no blame on you if [. . .] you agree mutually to vary it" as indicating the ability to alter both the duration and the *mahr*, dowry, of a *mutʿa* after the end of the initial contract.

Al-Rāzī provides extensive commentary on Q 4:24. Although he systematically discusses arguments supporting and opposing *mutʿa*, most of the arguments he presents seem to weigh in favor of *mutʿa* being impermissible.

Neither Maybudī nor the Sufi exegete al-Kāshānī discuss Q 4:24. This could either be because they did not find the issue important, or because the *āya* did not warrant discussion. However, in other places in the Qurʾan where polygamy is mentioned, Maybudī elaborates on the kind treatment of orphans instead of discussing either polygamy or *mutʿa*.

Abū ʿAbd Allāh al-Qurṭubī discusses *mutʿa* extensively, primarily to assert that the practice was abrogated by the Qurʾan. Although he admits that it was once permitted, he claims that the revelation of *āyāt* on issues such as *nikāḥ*, marriage, *ʿidda*, waiting period, *ṭalāq*, divorce, and marital inheritance, abrogated the practice; thus, Q 4:24 cannot be interpreted as authorizing *mutʿa*. He cites both the Prophet Muhammad's disapproval of the practice as well as narrations by ʿAlī b. Abī Ṭālib, perhaps a nod to the Shiʿi understanding of its permissibility.

Although Ismāʿīl Ḥaqqī Buruṣāwī elaborates on the entire *āya* in detail, including translations of words within it, he does not mention the variety of opinions on Q 4:24, particularly the understanding that it refers to *mutʿa*. It could be that at this time, Sunni scholars generally agreed on the meaning of the verse, and therefore, it did not warrant discussion.

In chapter 2, it was clear that the Sunni view, with its mutually contradictory traditions and lack of uniform views on whether and when *mutʿa* was abrogated, was a strong contrast to the clear Shiʿi consensus on the matter. In this chapter, it appeared that most Sunni exegetes not only refused to accept the *āya* as a proof text for *mutʿa*'s impermissibility but also did not bother to provide detailed defenses of this position. Shiʿi exegetes still maintained their consensus on this issue. In the medieval period, we begin to see the mention of (the Shiʿi) imams as authoritative figures, a trend that continues in later scholarship. In chapter 4, the discussion of modern scholars will illustrate how trends shifted in subtle ways due in large part to the influences of colonialism and modernity, and in this chapter will we also discuss the work of two female exegetes.

NOTES

1. Walid A. Saleh, *The Formation of the Classical Tafsīr Tradition: The Qurʾān Commentary of al-Thaʿlabī (d. 427/1035)* (Leiden: Brill, 2004), 77–99.

2. The influence of three scholars who are connected through an academic genealogy—Ibn Ḥabīb (d. 406/1015), his student Aḥmad b. Muḥammad al-Thaʿlabī (d. 427/1035), and al-Thaʿlabī's student ʿAlī b. Aḥmad al-Wāḥidī (d. 468/1076)—calls for a reassessment of the history of medieval Islamic exegesis. A close inspection of the genre of Qurʾanic exegesis clearly shows that al-Thaʿlabī and his student al-Wāḥidī played fundamental roles in shaping it. Most of Ibn Ḥabīb's works are lost, seemingly because he was a Karrāmī; see Saleh, *Formation of the Classical Tafsīr Tradition*, 45–48. We know that the Karrāmī sect ceased to be part of the Sunni community a century after Ibn Ḥabīb's death, and its members were ostracized.

3. Andrew Rippin, "al-T̲ h̲ aʿlabī," in *Encyclopaedia of Islam, Second Edition*, eds. P. Bearman, Th. Bianquis, C. E. Bosworth, E. van Donzel, and W. P. Heinrichs (Brill Online, 2012). See also C. Brockelmann, "al-T̲ h̲ aʿlabī," in *Encyclopaedia of Islam, First Edition (1913–1936)*, eds. M. Th. Houtsma, T. W. Arnold, R. Basset, and R. Hartmann (Brill Online).

4. Walid A. Saleh, "Exegesis viii. Nishapuri School of Quranic Exegesis," in *Encyclopedia Iranica*, January 1, 2020, http://www.iranicaonline.org/articles/exegesis-viii-nishapuri-school-quranic-exegesis; and Saleh, *Formation of the Classical Tafsīr Tradition*, 4, 49.

5. See Isaiah Goldfield, *Qur'ānic Commentary in the Eastern Islamic Tradition of the First Four Centuries of the Hijra: An Annotated Preface of al-Tha'labī's "Kitāb al-Kashf Wa l-Bayān 'an Tafsīr al-Qur'ān"* (Acre: Scrugy Printers and Publishers, 1984).

6. Founded by Abū 'Abdallāh Muḥammad b. Karrām, the Karrāmiyya movement arose out of the Hanafī school, though later it diverged from it, and was also influenced by the Murji'a theological school and relied heavily upon Prophetic tradition. It promoted anthropomorphism, interpreting God as having a literal body, as well as asceticism, and was the first movement to be associated with the institution of the *khānqāh*, a religious complex. For these reasons, they were increasingly criticized by their enemies, which included the Khurāsānian Malāmatiyya among others. See L. Berger, "al-Karrāmiyya," in *Encyclopaedia of Islam, THREE*, eds. Kate Fleet, Gudrun Krämer, Denis Matringe, John Nawas, and Everett Rowson (Brill Online).

7. The Ḥanbalī jurisconsult Ibn Taymiyya (d. 728/1328) mounted a concerted effort to undermine the reputation of both al-Tha'labī and al-Wāḥidī. The root of his displeasure was the ease with which their works were used by Shi'i polemicists. Though this attack could hardly matter at first, it would, however, gain traction as the reputation of Ibn Taymiyya was established in the early parts of the twentieth century. Soon his assessment of al-Tha'labī and al-Wāḥidī became the reason why both were neglected. The situation is now changing since Muslim universities are editing the classical corpus regardless of the theological biases of modern Muslims.

8. Saleh, *Formation of the Classical Tafsīr Tradition*, 229, fn 3. Saleh's book title reflects a desire to reorient the academic study of exegesis and recognize that medieval exegesis was neither closed nor exclusivist.

9. Saleh, *Formation of the Classical Tafsīr Tradition,* 77–99.

10. Moreover, the intellectual challenge posed by Mu'tazili theology and hermeneutics was profoundly unsettling to the Sunni intellectuals of Nishapur. Sunni hermeneutics fell short compared to the philologically based Mu'tazili hermeneutics. As such, the Sunni response was vigilantly intellectual, since it could not afford to be otherwise.

11. From this point onward, al-Zajjāj (d. 311/923) was included in works of exegesis, much like Ibn 'Abbās (d. 68/687), a figure familiar in post-Nishapuri literature but often overlooked as the outcome of the work of the Nishapuri school. *Al-Kashf* is thus a bewildering work; it is simultaneously a highly sophisticated piece of philology and an archaically mythologizing work, see Saleh, *Formation of the Classical Tafsīr Tradition*, 130–40.

12. Saleh, *Formation of the Classical Tafsīr Tradition*, 151–61.

13. If the Mu'tazili challenge was answered by giving philology serious attention, the Shi'i threat in a period when the Fatimids were at their zenith was dealt with by celebrating Shi'i pietism.

14. We find a consistent citation of *aḥādīth* that honored Imam ʿAli and gave his descendants the honor they deserve in his exegesis of certain Qurʾanic *āyāt*.

15. Saleh, *Formation of the Classical Tafsīr Tradition,* 178–91.

16. Saleh, *Formation of the Classical Tafsīr Tradition,* 178–91, 18–20.

17. Saleh, *Formation of the Classical Tafsīr Tradition,* 22

18. Aḥmad b. Muḥammad al-Thaʿlabī, *al-Kashf wa-l-bayān ʿan tafsīr al-Qurʾān,* ed. ʿAlī ʿĀshūr (Beirut: Dār Iḥyāʾ al-Turāth al-ʿArabī, 2002), 120–25. All subsequent passages from the *tafsīr* are from the section given in this citation.

19. Khwarazm was an ancient city in medieval Central Asia in present day Uzbekistan. It was one of the oldest civilizations present in Central Asia and was conquered by the Muslims in the first/seventh century. By al-Zamakhsharī's time, Khwarazm had become extremely prosperous and was a significant center of trade and learning. It was a powerful and prominent capital city. The city flourished until Timur destroyed its complex irrigation system, which was the source of much of its prosperity in the late eighth/fourteenth century. See C. E. Bosworth, "K͟hwārazm," in *Encyclopaedia of Islam, Second Edition.*

20. C. H. M. Versteegh, "al-Zamakhsharī" in *Encyclopaedia of Islam, Second Edition*; Wilferd Madelung, "al-Zamakhsharī" in *Encyclopaedia of Islam, Second Edition*; C. Brockelmann, "al-Zamakhsharī," *Encyclopaedia of Islam, First Edition (1913–1936).*

21. D. Gimaret, "Muʿtazila," in *Encyclopaedia of Islam, Second Edition.*

22. Feras Hamza, Sajjad Rizvi, and Farhana Mayer, *On the Nature of the Divine* vol. 1 of *An Anthology of Qurʾanic Commentaries* (Oxford: Oxford University Press, 2010), 35.

23. Sībawayh is one of the most famous Arabic grammarians. His *al-Kitāb fī an-naḥw* (The book on grammar) has been in use since its publication. For more, see "Sībawayh," in *Encyclopedia Britannica*, January 8, 2015, https://www.britannica.com/biography/Sibawayh.

24. For a more comprehensive study of this question, see Andrew J. Lane, *A Traditional Muʿtazilite Qurʾān Commentary: The Kashshāf of Jār Allāh al-Zamakhsharī (d. 538–1144),* (Leiden: E. J. Brill, 2006).

25. Jār Allāh Maḥmūd b. ʿUmar al-Zamakhsharī, *al-Kashshāf ʿan ḥaqāʾiq al-tanzīl wa-ʿuyūn al-aqāwīl fī wujūh al-taʾwīl* (Beirut: Dār al-Maʿrifa, 2009), 1:23. All subsequent passages from the *tafsīr* are from the section given in this citation.

26. If a couple has been alone together or, as it is stated in most texts on the subject, "whenever a door has been locked or a curtain drawn," intercourse is presumed to have taken place, and the woman must receive a dowry. The exception to this is a couple left alone at a time when intercourse is forbidden; during Ramadan, for example, or when the woman is menstruating, or when both parties are in a state of *iḥrām*. If one is fasting in any month other than Ramadan and is found alone with someone of the opposite sex, then participation in sexual intercourse is presumed. In these texts, every act of intercourse, lawful or not, requires a dowry.

27. See E. Kohlberg, "al-Ṭabrisī," in *Encyclopaedia of Islam, Second Edition*; and Hamza, Rizvi and Mayer, *On the Nature of the Divine,* 36–37.

28. Hamza, Rizvi, and Mayer, *On the Nature of the Divine*, 36.

29. Ibid.
30. He does not entertain the arguments of Sunni scholars in his *tafsīr*, however, but just presents his own.
31. Al-Faḍl b. al-Ḥasan al-Ṭabrisī (Ṭabarsī), *Majmaʿ al-bayān fī tafsīr al-Qurʾān* (Beirut: Dār al-Murtada, 2006), 3:48–51.
32. Milk relations is a category in Islamic law that makes the nurse and the suckling child relatives. This is relevant because a milk-relative child cannot marry the nurse's biological child.
33. G. C. Anawati, "Fakhr al-Dīn al-Rāzī," in *Encyclopaedia of Islam, Second Edition*.
34. Fakhr al-Dīn Muḥammad b. ʿUmar al-Rāzī, *Mafātīḥ al-ghayb aw al-tafsīr al-kabīr* (Beirut: Dār al-Fikr, 1981), 10:38–57.
35. Aḥmad Ibn Ḥanbal, *Musnad* (Cairo: n.p., 1971), 3:325, 356, 363.
36. Q 24:4, "Those who accuse chaste women (of adultery) and fail to produce four witnesses, give them eighty lashes (each). And do not ever accept any testimony from them—for they are indeed the rebellious."
37. Q 66:12, "(There is) also (the example of) Mary, the daughter of 'Imrân, who guarded her chastity, so We breathed into her (womb) through our angel (Gabriel). She testified to the words of her Lord and His Scriptures, and was one of the (sincerely) devout."
38. Q 4:25, "But if any of you cannot afford to marry a free believing woman, then (let him marry) a believing bondwoman possessed by one of you. God knows best (the state of) your faith (and theirs). You are from one another. So marry them with the permission of their owners, giving them their dowry in fairness, if they are chaste, neither promiscuous nor having secret affairs. If they commit indecency after marriage, they receive half the punishment of free women. This is for those of you who fear falling into sin. But if you are patient, it is better for you. And God is All-Forgiving, Most Merciful."
39. Al-Rāzī, *al-Tafsīr al-kabīr*, 10:38.
40. Ibid.
41. See Q 2:237.
42. Q 4:23, "Also forbidden to you for marriage are your mothers, your daughters, your sisters, your paternal and maternal aunts, your brother's daughters, your sister's daughters, your foster-mothers, your foster-sisters, your mothers-in-law, your stepdaughters under your guardianship if you have consummated marriage with their mothers—but if you have not, then you can marry them—nor the wives of your own sons, nor two sisters together at the same time—except what was done previously. Surely God is All-Forgiving, Most Merciful."
43. We will later see in Ṭabāṭabāʾī's discussion how he claims that the *mā* refers to an inanimate object (temporary marriage) rather than an animate object (women), unlike al-Rāzī.
44. See endnote 42.
45. Q 70:29, "[A]nd those who guard their chastity."
46. Q 4:12, "You will inherit half of what your wives leave if they are childless. But if they have children, then (your share is) one-fourth of the estate—after the

fulfilment of bequests and debts. And your wives will inherit one-fourth of what you leave if you are childless. But if you have children, then your wives will receive one-eighth of your estate—after the fulfilment of bequests and debts. And if a man or a woman leaves neither parents nor children but only a brother or a sister (from their mother's side), they will each inherit one-sixth, but if they are more than one, they (all) will share one-third of the estate—after the fulfilment of bequests and debts without harm (to the heirs). (This is) a commandment from God. And God is All-Knowing, Most Forbearing."

47. In Islamic law, this denotes that all children are legitimate.

48. Q 2:234, "As for those of you who die and leave widows behind, let them observe a waiting period of four months and ten days. When they have reached the end of this period, then you are not accountable for what they decide for themselves in a reasonable manner. And God is All-Aware of what you do."

49. C. E. Bosworth, "al-Maybudī," in *Encyclopaedia of Islam, Second Edition*; and Hamza, Rizvi, and Mayer, *On the Nature of the Divine*, 32–35.

50. Abū al-Faḍl Rashīd al-Dīn Maybudī, *Kashf al-asrār wa-ʿuddat al-abrār*, ed. ʿAlī Aṣghar Ḥikmat (Tehran: Tehran University Press, 1952–60), 2:23–29.

51. On Qurʾanic commentaries in Persian, see Annabel Keeler, "Exegesis iii, In Persian," in *Encyclopedia Iranica*, December 15, 1999, https://www.iranicaonline.org/articles/exegesis-iii.

52. For a study of the hermeneutics of Maybudī's *Kashf al-asrār*, see Annabel Keeler, *Sufi Hermeneutics: The Qurʾan Commentary of Rashīd al-Dīn Maybudī* (Oxford: Oxford University Press, 2006).

53. For this aspect of Maybudī's hermeneutics, see Annabel Keeler, "Ẓāhir and Bāṭin in Maybudī's *Kashf al-Asrār*" in *Proceedings of the Third European Conference of Iranian Studies, Part 2: Medieval and Modern Persian Studies*, ed. Charles Melville (Wiesbaden: Otto Harrassowitz, 1999), 167–78.

54. His work also influenced several later Persian mystical commentaries on the Qurʾan. On the development of Sufi exegesis, see Keeler, *Sufi Hermeneutics*.

55. Q 4:10, "Indeed, those who unjustly consume orphans' wealth (in fact) consume nothing but fire into their bellies. And they will be burned in a blazing Hell!"

56. *Isrāʾīliyyāt* are narratives that are thought to be borrowed from Jewish sources and found their way into Muslim works. For more, see G. Vajda, "Isrāʾīliyyāt," in *Encyclopaedia of Islam, Second Edition*.

57. For examples, see the work of Kecia Ali, Amina Wadud, Asma Barlas, and Aysha Hidayatullah, among others.

58. R. Y. Ebied and M. J. L. Young, "al-Ḳurṭubī," in *Encyclopaedia of Islam, Second Edition*; and "Ibn Ḥaiyān," in *Encyclopaedia of Islam, First Edition (1913–1936)*.

59. For example, in the preface to the second edition of this *tafsīr,* Aḥmad ʿAbd al-ʿAlīm al-Bardūnī wrote, "This work is such that the reader can almost dispend with the study of works of *fiqh*"; see Abū ʿAbd Allāh al-Qurṭubī, *al-Jāmiʿ li-aḥkām al-Qurʾān wa-l-mubayyin li-mā taḍammana min al-sunna wa-āyāt al-furqān* (Beirut: al-Risāla Publishers, 2006).

60. Al-Qurṭubī, *al-Jāmiʿ*, 3:114–16.

61. Ibid., 3:115.

62. Ibid., 3:116.
63. Macdonald, "ʿAbd al-Razzāḳ," in *Encyclopaedia of Islam, First Edition (1913–1936)*.
64. More generally, on this genre and Sufi *tafsīr*, see Alan Godlas, "Ṣūfism," in *The Wiley Blackwell Companion to the Qur'an*, eds. Jawid Mojaddedi and Andrew Rippin (Malden, MA: Wiley-Blackwell, 2006), 350–61.
65. Hamza, Rizvi, and Mayer, *On the Nature of the Divine*, 39.
66. *Taʾwīl* is a verbal noun whose root means "return to the origin." For more, see I. Poonawala, "Taʾwīl," in *Encyclopaedia of Islam, Second Edition*.
67. ʿAbd al-Razzāq Kāshānī, *Tafsīr al-Qurʾān al-karīm* [or *Taʾwīlāt al-Qurʾān*, popularly but erroneously known as *Tafsīr Ibn ʿArabī*] (Beirut: Dār al-Yaqẓa al-ʿArabiyya, 1968), 1:84–90.
68. Summarized from Günay Alpay Kut, "Ismāʿīl Ḥaḳḳī," in *Encyclopaedia of Islam, Second Edition*; and Hamza, Rizvi, and Mayer, *On the Nature of the Divine*, 45–46.
69. Ismāʿīl Ḥāqqī al-Burūsawī, *Tafsīr rūḥ al-bayān* (Beirut: Dār al-Fikr, n.d.) 4:44–48.
70. Al-Burūsawī, *Tafsīr rūḥ al-bayān*, 4:44–48.

Chapter Four

Tafsīr

The Modern Period

In the medieval period a general consensus was established regarding Q 4:24, and this took place along sectarian lines. This was a trend that continued as scholars produced *tafsīr* addressing contemporary issues. Then, in the modern period Muslim intellectuals were forced to deal with the various ruptures—geographic, intellectual, emotional, and spiritual—that colonialism created. Due to the anxiety produced by colonialism, modern Muslim intellectual thought has predominately been concerned with the formation and definition of a "Muslim identity," as well as "true" Islam, and how to live accordingly. This chapter addresses the work of postcolonial intellectuals in various parts of the Muslim world who were central figures in the Muslim debates around the reconstruction of knowledge. At the heart of revivalist Islamic politics are radical figures such as Abū al-Aʿlā Mawdūdī and revolutionaries like Faḍl Allāh. I also analyze the *tafāsīr* of the female scholars Farḥat Hāshmī and Nuṣrat Begum Amīn, the activist-scholars Muḥammad ʿAbduh and Muḥammad Rashīd Riḍā, the outlier scholar Ibn ʿĀshūr, and the Shiʿi intellectual and scholar Sayyid Muḥammad Ḥusayn Ṭabāṭabāʾī to illustrate how the *tafāsīr* of this period have competing responses to postcolonialism and modernity.

MUḤAMMAD ʿABDUH (D. 1323/1905) AND MUḤAMMAD RASHĪD RIḌĀ (D. 1354/1935)

Muḥammad ʿAbduh and his student Muḥammad Rashīd Riḍā were Sunni intellectuals and coauthors of the commentary *Tafsīr al-Manār* (Exegesis of the guiding light). They helped start a movement using an exegetical project and its namesake journal, *al-Manār* (The guiding light). Its goals were to reduce the legal and doctrinal differences between Sunni Muslims, to narrow the differences between Shiʿi and Sunni Muslims, and to reconcile differences among the Abrahamic faiths. And ʿAbduh had another major goal: to construct a scientific and rational understanding of the Divine Word.

Muḥammad ʿAbduh was born into a poor peasant family in Lower Egypt in 1227/1849.[1] He studied at a local Qurʾan school and then moved to Cairo to study at al-Azhar. There he gained solid grounding in the Sunni Islamic sciences. However, the most significant event that occurred in Cairo was his meeting with Sayyid Jamāl al-Dīn al-Afghānī (d. 1278/1897), a key intellectual force of his time who was well known for his political activism against British colonial forces and was thus forced to constantly relocate.[2] ʿAbduh's most important theological work is the *Risālat al-Tawhīd* (Epistle on the divine unity) of which there are two editions, an earlier Neo-Muʿtazili edition and a later reformist, revivalist Salafi edition. Intellectually, his thought leaned toward the Muʿtazili rationalist school, making him unpopular among some more traditional scholars.

Muḥammad Rashīd Ridā was born in Qalamoun, near Tripoli in northern Lebanon, in 1246/1865 to a *sayyid* family.[3] He had an early affiliation with the Naqshbandī Sufi order, though he later became critical of Sufi thought and practice. He moved to Cairo to lead the religious reform program with ʿAbduh. Once there, he traveled around the world to raise awareness of Islam's compatibility with modernity. He emphasized fresh reasoning and *ijtihād*, the independent exercise of judgment, in Islamic law and everyday life. After the dissolution of the Ottoman Empire, Ridā wrote *al-Khilāfa aw al-imāma al-ʿuzmā*, a treatise that outlines the ideals of "right leadership" of a Muslim country or society.[4] He exhibited bias in favor of Saudi Wahhabi thought and against Shiʿi thought, an unfortunate reversal from his previous stance that was in line with ʿAbduh's opinions. Nevertheless, he is respected for his scholarship and his writings remain popular, especially in the Arab world.

ʿAbduh began working on *Tafsīr al-manār*, his Qurʾanic commentary, with Ridā. The goals of the work were to rationalize the Word of God, make it more accessible, and create an impetus for action and reform. The work was originally a set of lectures given by ʿAbduh, which Ridā organized for publication. In some instances Ridā abridged the lectures and in others he expanded upon them. Unfortunately, ʿAbduh died without completing his commentary, which was published posthumously, twenty-six years later. Thus, *al-Manār* only covers the first twelve *sūrat*, about two-fifths of the Qurʾan. Still, his commentary remains one of the most widely read commentaries in the Arab world.

Two concepts are central to *al-Manār*.[5] The first is a set of divinely designed cosmological norms or laws according to which God has designed the universe. They create order and consistency in time and space, and humans must recognize that they are from God. The second concept is a set of divinely designed social norms that are the direct result of a human being's application of freedom of choice, which is given to them by God. From *al-Manār*'s perspective, this freedom should be neither too unrestricted—and eclipse God's norms—or too reduced—and lapse into determinism. Like other exegetical works we have analyzed, *al-Manār* discusses *mut'a.*

Like earlier exegetes, 'Abduh begins by discussing the meaning of *muḥṣanāt*. He states it is the plural of *muḥṣan*, married woman, and comes from the word *iḥṣān*, which comes from the root word *ḥiṣn*, meaning a castle or a place that is impregnable. Thus, by becoming a *muḥṣan*, the woman has become shielded, and marriage is the fortress that protects her. He says that her family protected her by giving her in marriage. 'Abduh then writes that the majority of jurisconsults state the meaning of *muḥṣanāt* is "married women," and some say it is "free women," while others say "all women." Rashīd Riḍā prefers the meaning "free, married women."

'Abduh then discusses the grammatical meaning of *muḥṣanāt* by analyzing the meaning of *iḥṣān*, which was determined by the pronunciation of the *ṣād* with a *fatḥa*, making it a passive participle. It can also be read with a *kasra*, as many readers have done. Reading it with a *kasra* makes it an active participle, meaning that women protect themselves instead of needing to be protected. He cites Ibn 'Arabī, who mentions three words that despite the fact they are pronounced with a *fatḥa*, which technically makes them passive participles, they remain active participles; one of these words is *aḥṣana*, which has the same root letters as *iḥṣān*: *ḥa*, *ṣād*, and *nūn*. They are *aḥṣana*, to be protected, *alfaja*, to become bankrupt, and *ashaba*, to be a chatterbox.

Interestingly, 'Abduh is one of the few exegetes to discuss the phrase *min al-nisā'*, expressing surprise that it is mentioned in the *āya* because it results in a redundancy—who else could men marry but women. According to him, some scholars believe that *min al-nisā'* is intended for emphasis.

In his discussion of the next section of the *āya*, 'Abduh says scholars are unanimous that *muḥṣanāt* does not include war captives, even if they were married in their respective lands, and he goes on to discuss just, permissible war in Islam. Returning to the subject of women, he discusses the conditions through which it become permissible to have sexual contact with women: when not menstruating; if previously married, then after the waiting period; and if pregnant, then after delivery. He defends the wisdom of polygamy as an institution to protect women, claiming that "the men of such women have probably died," that "it is out of the welfare of women because she needs someone to take care of her and provide her daily bread," and "she needs someone to protect her," thus Islam in its wisdom and justice provides for her.

He then analyzes the word *istamta'tūm*, stating that *istamtā'* means enjoying or benefiting from something, as in the *āya* "you enjoyed your part, as you enjoyed your share" (Q 9:69). According to ʿAbduh, some scholars say that the letters *sīn* and the *tāʾ* are for emphasis and do not connote the concept of seeking that is inherent in the verbal form *istafʿala*. The letters *sīn* and *tāʾ* are also significant when speaking of *mahr*, dowry, a set amount given in exchange for enjoyment in marriage. He is the first scholar to note the importance of the presence of the *sīn* and *tāʾ* in relation to the time that the *mahr* is due. ʿAbduh notes that if the word follows the verbal form *istafʿala*, then you can pay the *mahr* after the consummation of the marriage because the form means seeking. But if the verb does not contain the *sīn* and the *tāʾ*, then the *mahr* is paid before this. He states that the word *ajr* in the *āya* means a reward given in return for something, and here, it indicates *mahr*, as an earlier part of *Sūrat al-Nisāʾ* instructs men to give women a dowry as a compulsory gift. In defense of the idea of *mahr*, ʿAbduh addresses modern criticisms by suggesting that is not compensation for buying sexual access to women, but rather it is a gift, a payment offered to engender tranquility and love within the marriage. He also says the couple may change the amount without any duress as long as it is based on what they believe will produce mutual harmony and love.

He then addresses at length the Shiʿi claim that this *āya* permits *mutʿa*. He starts by defining *mutʿa* as marriage for a predetermined period of time. ʿAbduh mentions that there is some scholarship on a variant reading by Ibn ʿAbbās (discussed in earlier chapters) but notes that this variation has never been accepted. He also writes that the source hadith is weak because it only has a single narration. ʿAbduh later emphasizes that Ibn ʿAbbās's ruling only applies in cases of extreme hardship.

He next cites evidence from the Qurʾan, stating it repeatedly commands that individuals should protect their private parts from everyone except their spouses. This implies that the parties in a *mutʿa* are committing a grave sin—he does not, of course, consider the Shiʿi claim that *mutʿa* is a valid marriage and the people partaking in it are spouses. ʿAbduh writes that a *mutʿa* wife, even in Shiʿi Islam, is not one of the four permitted wives, as a Shiʿi man can have as many temporary wives as he pleases. This, according to ʿAbduh, is against the Qurʾan's explicit provision, enough of a reason to take issue with the institution. However, it should be noted that he does not problematize the notion that *mutʿa* allows a man to simultaneously enjoy as many women as he wants but only allows a woman to enjoy multiple men sequentially. Further commenting on the invalid nature of *mutʿa*, ʿAbduh says that the woman has no *nafaqa*, inheritance or support, nor must she complete *ʿidda*, the waiting period. Here though, he either is misinformed or purposefully ignores the fact that the Shiʿa do prescribe a waiting period for a *mutʿa* wife. He ends by saying that "the truth is that the Qurʾan is very far from this position," and there is no evidence in this *āya* (4:24), and no pseudo-evidence either.

Next, he acknowledges the historical existence of *mutʿa* in both Sunni and Shiʿi books. He gives two explanations for this. We have encountered the first one before, the permissibility of *mutʿa* was due to hardship and to avoid *zināʾ*, fornication, while the second explanation is new, *mutʿa* was allowed and disallowed more than once to remove such behavior from society gradually, much like the removal of drinking alcohol. He then writes that the Sunni do not permit *mutʿa* based on three arguments: the Qurʾan, the sunna, and ʿUmar's sermon.[6]

He then discusses the final argument the Shiʿa present: they have *aḥādīth* from the *ahl al-bayt*—literally "the people of the house," referring to the Prophet Muhammad's family—that are absolute and permit *mutʿa*. As much as ʿAbduh acknowledges that the Shiʿa have other sources that they rely on, he does not consider them and states that "we have not seen these narrations, or their chains of transmission," making a verdict impossible. This does not seem likely, since this information is easily available in any book on *mutʿa* from the Shiʿi corpus. As a final nail in the coffin, he states that ʿAli has said *mutʿa* is not allowed, and those who do not believe it are like those who do not accept ʿAli's sayings simply because they come from the adversary.

He ends this section by presenting a new argument, one not presented by earlier exegetes: *mutʿa,* because of its temporary nature, corrupts marriage, and Islam is thus weakened. ʿAbduh writes that jumping from one sexual desire to another is frowned upon in Islam. Marriage offers protection to men and women and helps establish a righteous house for the *umma*.

To summarize, *al-Manār* considers the Shiʿi position but responds to misinformed ideas—whether this is on purpose or by mistake is unclear. Finally, ʿAbduh, like Ridā, claims to be interested in *ijtihād*, the independent exercise of judgment, and Shiʿi-Sunni unity, but neither one is open to considering *mutʿa* as a new *ijtihād*, nor do they give any serious credence to the Shiʿi argument.

IBN ʿĀSHŪR (D. 1973/1394)

The Tunisian Muḥammad al-Ṭāhir b. Muḥammad al-Ṭāhir,[7] more commonly known as Ibn ʿĀshūr, is considered one of the greatest Islamic scholars of the twentieth century. He was born in 1296/1879 and died in 1394/1973 at the age of ninety-four. During his lifetime, he saw major political (the turbulence of colonization and its effects) and social (scientific development and its rationalistic push) changes, which greatly influenced his life and career, and a third influence was the reformist thought of ʿAbduh, whom we read about above. Ibn ʿĀshūr's legacy includes the important public and administrative roles he played as well as his staggering scholarly production. Most of his work still awaits critical study in western academia, which still has not sufficiently engaged with works and scholars from the peripheries of the Muslim world.

Ibn ʿĀshūr was born into a family we would refer to as the intellectual and social elite. His maternal and paternal grandparents were leading *ʿulamāʾ* and high-standing government officials. Ibn ʿĀshūr started his education at a traditional Tunisian *kuttāb* and eventually graduated from the prestigious Zaytūna University, where he studied with the most renowned scholars of his time. Three years after graduating, he become a professor at the same university at the young age of twenty-four. Just one year later, he was appointed state deputy there, and he worked to reform the university's education system—this became one of his lifelong projects. From 1908 to 1912 he was also a member of the official commission that dealt with reforming all levels of education in Tunisia. He served as the Shaykh of Zaytūna University, Mālikī Shaykh al-Islām, and the Grand Muftī of Tunisia. In sum, he had a long and illustrious career in both academia and government service.

Ibn ʿĀshūr was one of the most prolific writers of his time. He wrote more than forty books, a vast number of short essays, and unnumerable fatwas, all on diverse Islamic topics, and was also a poet and student of Arabic language and literature. Ibn Āshūr's main intellectual contributions are "four major works that deal with his vision of educational reform, his contribution to Islamic legal theory, his understanding of the nature of modern Islamic society, and his exegesis of the Qur'an."[8] What interests us here is his Qurʾanic exegesis, his thirty-volume opus magnum, which he wrote over a fourteen-year period at the end of his life. He started working on it in 1956 and completed it in 1970, three years before his death; it was his last publication. This exegetical work, *al-Taḥrīr wal-Tanwīr*[9] (The verification and enlightenment), "is the culmination of a long life of Islamic learning and involvement in Islamic education and public life, the judiciary and the mufti-dom."[10] According to Hadia Mubarak, Ibn ʿĀshūr

> viewed tafsīr as primarily an academic, scholarly endeavor. The primary function of tafsīr is not to serve as a pulpit from which one preaches to the layman, but it is to unearth the rich layers of meaning of the Qurʾan through the scholarly methodologies of an exegete highly trained in all the essential disciplines related to tafsīr, and most importantly, philology. His tafsīr is an attempt to revive the enshrined, but neglected methodologies that he believes constitute a proper tafsīr.[11]

Unlike some of the other exegetes we have looked at, Ibn ʿĀshūr does not start his exegesis of Q 4:24 by engaging with the debates on *mutʿa* presented in the premodern exegetical tradition. He spends several pages discussing the philology of different words and the grammar of different phrases in the *āya*. Most of this discussion is also covered in *tafāsīr* we discussed earlier, and some of the content will be mentioned in *tafāsīr* studied later in this chapter. Here I would like to focus on what is most unique about his exegesis. In the final paragraphs of his seven-page analysis of this *āya*, Ibn ʿĀshūr summarily and non-polemically permits *mutʿa*, albeit only in the case of dire need. He is the first Sunni *mufassir* to do so.

He starts out by discussing that *mutʿa* existed, was made permissible and impermissible several times, and that there is a disagreement regarding its impermissibility. He also discusses the fatwa of Ibn ʿAbbās, who permitted *mutʿa*, and the sermon of ʿUmar, who prohibited it. He writes, what we can gather from different historical texts is that *mutʿa* was permitted and disallowed two times by the Prophet Muhammad; this means it was not prohibited more than twice. The ruling of the permissibility of *mutʿa* is attached to circumstances (i.e., when there is a dire need). Then, he writes that it has been established that Muslims practiced *mutʿa* in the time of Abū Bakr and ʿUmar, and ʿUmar only forbade it at the end of his caliphate. He says that "what we basically gather from the different narrations is that the ruling of *mutʿa* is permissible provided there is a real, dire need for it. For example, if someone is in a foreign country traveling, or they are away from home for military expedition, [which are times] when a man's wife is not accompanying him."[12] Then he proceeds to describe what *mutʿa* is and what makes it valid. He writes that what is required is a *mahr*, dowry, witness, and *walī*, guardian. Here it is important to recall that the Shiʿa do not require a witness, and only require a *walī* in the case of a virgin, but many Shiʿi scholars do not allow a virgin to enter into a *mutʿa* marriage. He mentions that the wife ceases to be a wife at the end of the predetermined period of the *mutʿa*, there is no inheritance shared between them should one of them die while married, the *ʿidda*, waiting period, is one menstrual cycle, and the children are legitimate children. Interestingly, he writes that this *āya* is not a proof text for *mutʿa*, but it is possible that the word *istamtaʿtūm* is a general statement; therefore, we can have a general discussion about the pleasure derived from marriage. In relation to the legality of *mutʿa*, one should turn to history and look at what was historically practiced and permittable.

Ibn ʿĀshūr is the first (and in my knowledge only) Sunni *mufassir* to not unconditionally forbid *mutʿa*, but he only allows it under certain circumstances. More significantly, he does this in a unique way: He allows it because he does not consider its permissibility to have been abrogated. There are several noteworthy things to point out here. First, we might ask how it was possible for Ibn ʿĀshūr, a classically trained Sunni scholar, to hold this position. Walid A. Saleh gives us a partial explanation, writing that places like

Tunisia were autonomous from the "center" of the Muslim world (i.e., the established places of Sunni and Shiʿi learning in Egypt, Iran, Iraq, and Saudi Arabia), which meant that knowledge production in places such as Tunisia did not rely on the scholarly "conceptual vision" of the center, specifically in relation to the *tafsīr* genre, and therefore, the scholars in the "periphery" could be dynamic and unencumbered in their thinking.[13]

Second, Ibn ʿĀshūr is not polemical in his approach to *mutʿa.* The tone of his exegesis on this *āya* is tempered. It reveals no distress concerning the existence of *mutʿa* as an institution permitted only by the Shiʿa. Basheer Nafi writes, and I concur, that "al-Taḥrīr wal-Tanwi is one of the least ideologically constructed works of tafsīr in the twentieth century."[14] Ibn ʿĀshūr's comprehensive exegesis of Q 4:24 demonstrates this. It takes the varying opinions held by Sunni and Shiʿi scholars into account.

Third, Ibn ʿĀshūr, unlike most Shiʿi scholars, does not treat Q 4:24 as a proof text for *mutʿa.* He bases its permissibility on his historical understanding, which is that there was no final prohibition. Ibn ʿĀshūr deduces what he believed to be the purpose of the Qurʾanic injunction through an analysis of the historical reality of the practice. Ibn ʿĀshūr's *tafsīr* of Q 4:24 brings renewed life to legal and philological debates that were presumably exhausted in the Sunni exegetical world. Nafi captures this best when he says that Ibn ʿĀshūr's work "cannot always be attributed to a single madhhab or a school of thought, but they are there as a natural and logical outcome of the *bayan,* a *bayan* for which a formidable arsenal of linguistic erudition is utilized."[15]

Fourth, it is important that *al-Taḥrīr wal-Tanwīr* not be considered just another Sunni exegesis of the Qurʾan. As a learned *mufassir* in all areas of the Islamic religious sciences, Ibn ʿĀshūr represents not just the Sunni tradition but the entire Islamic scholarly tradition. For example, in his exegesis of this *āya,* he is not merely interested in delineating Sunni interpretive categories, but rather, through his philological methodology, which is continuous with the classical tradition but not restricted to discussing its positions, he puts forward original insights.[16] Not only is Ibn ʿĀshūr willing to include some of the sources found in Shiʿi *tafāsīr,* but he also includes opinions from Companions who are the subject of polemical critique in earlier Sunni works.

In conclusion, Ibn ʿĀshūr's approach to exegesis is a remarkably fresh and creative way of discovering the meanings of the Qurʾan. This openness in his method allows him to not discard other schools' and sects' interpretations. Rather, he painstakingly analyzes such works to help him reveal the true meaning of the Qurʾan while also engaging in his own hermeneutic method.

SAYYID ABŪ AL-AʿLĀ MAWDŪDĪ (D. 1399/1979)

Sayyid Abū al-Aʿlā Mawdūdī was a Sunni scholar and activist born on September 25, 1903, in Aurangabad, Deccan.[17] His family was well known, educated, affiliated with the Chishti Sufi order, and worked for the rulers of Hyderabad.[18] His initial education started at traditional madrasas in Deccan and Delhi. He became involved in Muslim politics at the end of World War I. He was involved with the Khilafat movement and then joined the Jamʿiyyat-i-ʿUlamaʾ-i Hind. He also gained journalistic experience and became a formidable writer. In 1941, he formed the Jamaʿat-i Islamī, a political party that became influential throughout the Indian subcontinent.

Mawdūdī was one of the first intellectuals to call for an independent Muslim state.[19] After the creation of Pakistan, he constantly found himself at odds with the new government and was in and out of prison; however, he played a significant role in drafting the "Objective Resolution" in March 1949, which lay down the Islamic principles of the constitution. After a long career of political activism, he died at the age of seventy-four while undergoing medical treatment on September 17, 1979 in Buffalo, New York. His funeral was held in Lahore and only attended by several friends and followers.

He was a prolific writer and published more than 150 books and short tracts that addressed the social and political issues Muslims faced because of colonialism.[20] Mawdūdī viewed the Qurʾan as a divinely guided program that addresses all spheres of life. If Muslims properly examined the Qurʾan, they could find solutions to all their problems, communal and individual.[21]

His *tafsīr*, *Tafhīm al-Qurʾān* (*Towards Understanding the Qurʾān*) took thirty years to write and is arguably the most read *tafsīr* in Urdu.[22] It was also translated into English and gathered a wider, international audience.[23] The title reveals his approach and aim. Mawdūdī did not believe a grammatical or philological approach to the Qurʾan offered useful guidance. He saw the Qurʾan as a dynamic text that should be used to answer everyday problems and felt that it serves as a call to action; only through answering this call can Muslims heal all that ails them and retain their sense of identity and pride in the face of colonization.

Mawdūdī starts each chapter of his *tafsīr* with a detailed discussion of *asbāb al-nuzūl*, the occasions of revelation. He writes that *Sūrat al-Nisāʾ* contains *āyāt* revealed in Medina between the latter part of the period between 3/624, 4/625, and 5/626. Although it is difficult to say which *āyāt* were revealed when, several of them contain allusions to certain injunctions or events whose dates are known; therefore, the date of revelation can be approximated accordingly.

When Mawdūdī discusses Q 4:24, he employs an interesting strategy. He does not acknowledge how Shiʿi scholars have historically used the *āya* to permit *mutʿa* nor that there is any confusion about it in exegetical literature. This is intriguing, particularly since he engages in a lengthy discussion on the permissibility of sexual relations with a slave girl or captive and covers issues like *ʿidda*, the waiting period, *nafaqa*, inheritance, and sexual enjoyment, which are relevant to discussions about *mutʿa*. His analysis of these subjects indicates that at minimum, his failure to discuss *mutʿa* was predicated upon an understanding of *mutʿa* as antiquated and thus unworthy of analysis—or it was a complete erasure of Shiʿi scholarship.

SAYYID MUḤAMMAD ḤUSAYN FAḌL ALLĀH (D. 1330/2010)

Sayyid Muḥammad Ḥusayn Faḍl Allāh was a Shiʿi scholar and cleric born on November 16, 1935 in the Iraqi shrine city of Najaf.[24] Faḍl Allāh pursued his early studies in Najaf, and after completing his education under prominent scholars there, he moved to Lebanon in 1966 and lived and worked in Nabaʿa in East Beirut. He organized cultural seminars, delivered sermons, and held discussions on social issues, but his main focus was his academic work. He established a school called the Islamic Shariʿa School, and leading religious scholars of the region graduated from it. He also established a public library, a women's cultural center, a medical clinic, public religious schools, and several orphanages.

Faḍl Allāh was a scholar who took strong (even notorious) positions on policy issues and was also known for his relatively liberal views on women, whom he viewed and spoke of as equal to men. He believed they have the same societal responsibilities and should model good behavior for both men and women. In his view, the hijab helps women appear as human beings—as opposed to just sexual objects—in men's eyes. Faḍl Allāh was vocal about physical and social violence against women. His rulings reaffirmed a woman's right to work outside and at home without threat and categorically stated that Islam provides women with legal rights that no man can take away. He also gave fatwas against female circumcision and honor killings and permitted abortion if carrying the baby to term would endanger a woman's life.

In Faḍl Allāh's *tafsīr*, *Min wahy al-Qurʾān* (From the revelation of the Qurʾan),[25] he divides his discussion on Q 4:24 into three parts. The first part discusses the *āya*, and the other two parts are responses to arguments presented against *mutʿa*.

The first section opens with a modern discussion of *mahr*, dowry, where he emphatically states that it is not the price of the woman or access to her but rather is a gift of love for the enjoyment a spouse receives. God intended marriage to engender love, compassion, and spirituality between the couple; however, the language of buying belittles the institution of marriage, demeans women's humanity, and takes away from their nobility.

He then discusses the meaning of *istamtaʿtūm*, pointing out that other exegetes have not devoted enough attention to this word. According to him, the term refers to *mutʿa*, a marriage lasting for a predetermined time and conducted for a predetermined amount of remuneration, as well as following several other rules, some (but not all) of which agree with the rules of permanent marriage; thus, he makes parallels between *mutʿa* and permanent marriage. He directly quotes Ṭabāṭabāʾī's *tafsīr*, *al-Mizān*, which will be discussed in detail later in this chapter. Faḍl Allāh states there is no doubt that *istamtaʿtūm* signifies *mutʿa* because this type of marriage existed, was practiced at the time of the Prophet Muhammad, and was known by this name.

The next section purports to discuss the arguments presented by other scholars against *mutʿa*. Faḍl Allāh starts by acknowledging that Muslim jurists and exegetes have disagreed on *mutʿa*'s permissibility. Some say it was abrogated, some that it was prohibited according to *ijmāʿ*, scholarly consensus, and others deny both of these claims. He presents three different arguments for why this *āya* could not have been abrogated: first, due to the principle of the general versus the particular (*mutʿa* is a particular example of the general concept of marriage). Second, the *āyāt* that are said to abrogate *mutʿa* were revealed before the one thought to permit it. Third, those who believe the *āya* had been abrogated present certain *aḥādīth* that Faḍl Allāh finds unreliable. He writes that the *aḥādīth* used for this argument, which he incidentally fails to provide, are from a single narration, thus rendering them weak and incapable of abrogating an *āya*.

Finally, like ʿAbduh, he responds to the idea that ʿUmar's sermon abrogated the practice. Faḍl Allāh states, without providing evidence, that ʿUmar prohibited *mutʿa* without attributing the decision to the Prophet Muhammad. Thus, this prohibition is an administrative prohibition issued only on ʿUmar's *ijtihād*, independent exercise of judgment, making it nonbinding. He further elaborates that this is why the Companions practiced *mutʿa* before and after ʿUmar's edict, as well as why the imams are unanimous in their approval of *mutʿa*, encouraging it so that it can remain current in the lives of the *umma*.

The final section of Faḍl Allāh's analysis of Q 4:24 is a discussion of some social concerns pertaining to sexuality. He starts by mentioning that (unnamed) scholars say the Prophet Muhammad permitted *mutʿa* because it served a need, which still exists today. If this need convinced scholars to permit *mutʿa* in that era, then it is only logical that *mutʿa* be permitted in the modern era. He continues, writing that because *zināʾ*, fornication, has been a consistent problem throughout history, we cannot think of it only as depravity and disobedience. Permanent marriage has not resolved this problem; thus, a different solution is required, namely *mut'a*. The words of ʿAli, "Had ʿUmar not prohibited *mut'a* marriage, none but a few would do *zinā'*," or in other narrations, "no one but the depraved would do *zinā'*," are also used to arrive at the same conclusion.

Faḍl Allāh ends the discussion on *mut'a* here and moves on to the final section of the *āya*, saying that it refers to two people freely increasing or decreasing a *mahr*, dowry, after it had already been decided.

FARḤAT HĀSHMĪ (B. 1471/1957)

Farḥat Hāshmī, a Sunni scholar and preacher, was born in Sargodha in 1957. She was the eldest of twelve children,[26] and her father, ʿAbd al-Raḥman Hāshmī, the local leader of Jamaʿat-i Islamī, taught his children the Qur'an and the basic teaching of Islam at home. Farḥat Hāshmī credits her father for her success and love of Islam. She attended college in Sargodha, where she was involved in college politics and led the Jamāʿat's student wing, and then earned a master's in Arabic from the University of Punjab. She married a fellow student, and they were both awarded teaching positions at the International Islamic University in Islamabad. The couple then moved to Glasgow, where they both obtained doctorates in Islamic studies from the University of Glasgow and traveled across the Muslim world to meet key Islamic scholars. Farḥat Hāshmī's journey from a small town in Sargodha to Lahore, Islamabad, and eventually Glasgow was quite extraordinary at the time, particularly for a woman.

Shortly after her return from Glasgow, Farḥat Hāshmī converted the informal Qur'an lessons she had given to women in her home into a formal institute, al-Huda, and now offers year-long structured courses and diplomas. As the institute's popularity increased, her husband and children also became involved. Their first school opened in 1994 in Islamabad, and soon after, they added branches in Karachi and Lahore, eventually growing to a total of seventy locations in urban areas all over Pakistan. Al-Huda also runs programs in North America, Europe, and East Asia, where there are large South Asian diasporic communities. Farḥat Hāshmī's lectures attract thousands of women, and her teachings are available through audio cassettes, CDs, books, and pamphlets. She often appears on television programs and radio shows and has a website where her lectures can be searched and downloaded.[27]

Al-Huda's curriculum focuses on the text of the Qur'an and *aḥādīth*, encourages learning Arabic, and is marked by an understanding of Islam broadly identified as the Ahl-e Ḥadīth branch of Sunni Islam in South Asia. This school of thought is quite puritanical in its self-understanding, privileged texts, and rejects all cultural renderings of lived Islam. The curriculum teaches women not just to understand the canonical texts but also to apply them to their daily lives, reform themselves, and then teach others. The schools have attracted urban educated women from Pakistan's upper middle classes, and Farḥat Hāshmī increased their appeal by stating her goal was to reinterpret issues in a modern way while staying within the parameters of the Qur'an.[28] However, after examining the content of her message, Dr. Riffat Hassan found Farḥat Hāshmī's ideological stance to be "still very markedly right-wing."[29]

Her *tafsīr* of *Sūrat al-Nisā'* is available online in audio format.[30] She begins by reciting the *āya* in precise Arabic, translating it word by word into Urdu. Much like in her writing, her discussion weaves in and out of various subjects. She says that God created man and created in him many desires; one is the desire for sex. These *āyāt*, she says, discuss the permissibility of sex—with whom it is permissible—and sexual satisfaction as accepted and valid in Islam. Of note here is that she does not think women and men have the same sexual needs. At the end of this session, a woman in the lecture asks her, "Why is it that women are not allowed to marry several men?" Farḥat Hāshmī laughs and says that women can hardly satisfy one man, let alone several. Also, she says that for a woman, marriage is not just about sexual relations; it is also about support, family, community, and society. Therefore, women are willing to sacrifice their need for sexual satisfaction to maintain the ties of marriage for the sake of family and society.

After extensive commentary on the permissibility of sexual relations with various kinds of women, including war captives and slaves, Farḥat Hāshmī rushes through a discussion of key vocabulary in Q 4:24. She defines *muḥṣināt* as married, free, pure, and/or Muslim women and claims that here it means pure women, suggesting to her audience that it "should be clear to you in your head" which of the four meanings is being used here.[31]

Then she translates *fa-mā istamta'tūm bihi min hunna* as "whatever enjoyment you gained from these women" and *fa-'ātūhunna ujūrahunna* as "then give them their *mahr*," which is *farīza*, a compulsory act, not a choice. The women can forgive her *mahr*, dowry, as there is no harm for you, *wa-lā junāḥ 'alaykum*, if together you agree to increase or decrease it. She further emphasizes the importance of *mahr* to validate a marriage but, astonishingly, does not acknowledge the relevance of *mut'a* at all. Her claims lack references, and she moves quickly between topics to avoid complicating the exegesis for her listeners. The lack of attention to *mut'a* represents a noticeable gap in her exegesis. It is worth noting here that she and Mawdūdī, who are both South Asian—and Sunni—do not even hint at the idea that this *āya* has been historically used as a proof text for *mut'a*. By reading them, or at least if only reading them, the reader would not learn about *mut'a*.

ĀYATULLĀH SAYYID MUḤAMMAD ḤUSAYN ṬABĀṬABĀ'Ī (D. 1400/1981)

Sayyid Muḥammad Ḥusayn Ṭabāṭabā'ī, a Shiʿi scholar and cleric, was born in 1282/1903 in Tabriz.[32] Under the care of his paternal uncle, he began his education in Tabriz, memorizing the Qur'an and studying the works of the Persian poet Sadʿī, prior to commencing his schooling in Islamic studies around the age of nineteen.[33] Ṭabāṭabā'ī then moved to Najaf to pursue advance studies, reaching the highest level of *ijtihād*, the independent exercise of judgment, and later returning to Tabriz in 1935 to start teaching.[34] At the end of World War II, he moved to Tehran and then Qom. While in Qom, he devoted himself to teaching and scholarship and died there in 1981 at the age of seventy-nine.

Ṭabāṭabā'ī was renowned in Iran and among the international community and was respected as an international authority on Shiʿism. From 1958 to 1977, he engaged in weekly meetings with scholars, such as the French philosopher Henri Corbin and the Islamic studies scholar Seyyed Hossein Nasr.[35] He was honored even after his death; in Iran he had a university named after him and his works continue to enjoy great popularity. He wrote prolifically in both Persian and Arabic on religious and philosophical topics. Among his religious works, the most famous are *Qur'an dar Islām* (*The Qur'an in Islam*) and *Shiʿa dar Islām* (*Shiʿite Islam*), both of which have been translated into English.[36] His most relevant work here is his commentary on the Qur'an, *al-Mizān fī tafsīr al-Qur'ān* (The scales of Qur'anic exegesis). He wrote it over the course of almost two decades (1954–72) using a methodology committed to explaining all passages in the Qur'an using only other Qur'anic passages. In his opinion, this approach guarantees that no external factors influence the exegete's understanding of God's Word. Prior to interpreting a passage, Ṭabāṭabā'ī considers classical as well as recent Qur'anic commentaries written by both Sunni and Shiʿi scholars. His *tafsīr* is widely acknowledged as the most authoritative Shiʿi commentary of this century.

Ṭabāṭabā'ī begins by translating Q 4:24 into Persian.[37] Next, he gives a general introduction to explain why he chose to discuss Q 4:23–28 as a continuous unit. He explains that these *āyāt* have a clear thematic connection; however, he aims to show that what is unclear is that the phrase "forbidden to you" in Q 4:23 refers to marriage. Thus, by addressing this portion of his discussion to a Sunni audience, Ṭabāṭabā'ī assumes a defensive position. He takes the existing contentious history of *mutʿa* as his starting point, rather than starting with the *āya*.

Ṭabāṭabā'ī emphasizes that these *āyāt* are addressed to men, not women, since it is in men's nature to seek and propose marriage. This assumption blatantly disregards Khadīja's proposal to the Prophet Muhammad.[38] He then lists the women with whom marriage is unambiguously prohibited, without noting any conditions or exceptions.

Next, he explains the use of the plural *muḥṣināt* in Q 4:24, saying it implies any woman a man is forbidden to marry. Other scholars, as previously noted, also analyze its meaning, but they discuss whether the word is active or passive in the verse and the potential implications of each. Ṭabāṭabāʾī treats it as passive participle and gives no indication that it could also be used as an active participle. He then gives a detailed list of the word's three possible meanings. He says it comes from *ḥiṣn*, a protected fortress, and gives three possible connotations: the women are chaste, as in Q 66:12; the women are married and therefore protected by marriage; or, the women are free and keep away from illicit sexual relations. He says that in this *āya*, the word can only refer to married women.

There is no problem, he declares, with marrying someone who is not chaste or who is a slave. He writes that we know from history that masters can take married slaves away from their husbands, have them observe the prescribed waiting period to make sure they are not pregnant, and then have sexual relations with them. Therefore, the clause, "women except for what your right-hand possesses (slaves)," excludes married slave women. This is a point of great consternation with Muslim feminists, and the Muslim community needs to seriously reckon with it.

Ṭabāṭabāʾī says the next part of the *āya*, "what is besides that," *mā wa rāʾa dhālikum*, requires careful consideration. He appears to use grammar to illustrate that the *mā*, a relative pronoun usually translated as "what," refers to inanimate objects, and therefore, *mā*/what refers to *mutʿa* here, but the way he does this is ingenious. It is hard to imagine that he is not sufficiently well versed in classical grammar to know that *mā,* which he claims refers to "un-rational" things, also classically refers to rational beings. For instance, in the previous chapter we saw how al-Rāzī uses it to indicate women (i.e., rational beings). Ṭabāṭabāʾī then writes that the demonstrative pronoun *dhālikum*, that, refers to a masculine singular object, man, and states that this section of the *āya* has the meaning of "lawful to you," which refers to *mutʿa*. He is the first exegete in this study to use the *mā* for an inanimate object: *mutʿa*.

After this, he presents counter explanation presented by other, unnamed exegetes, who can safely be considered to be Sunni exegetes. He elaborates how some Muslim scholars apply the relative pronoun *mā* to rational beings (like we saw al-Rāzī do), but there can be no justification for it since the relative pronoun *mā* and the demonstrative pronoun *dhālikum* both refer to the same object, which is implied by the opening word of Q 4:23, *ḥurrimat*, forbidden, which refers to a type of sexual intercourse, for him and the Shiʿa it is *mutʿa*. He writes that this means sexual intercourse is lawful with women other than those that fall under the fifteen forbidden categories. Additionally, the appositional substantive phrase "[provided] that you seek them [women] with your wealth, with chastity, not fornication" make sense when the rest of the sentence is read this way.

He explains that the next section of the *āya*, "[provided] that you seek them [women] with your wealth, with chastity, not fornication," refers to the lawful way to approach women for sex. The *āya* attaches importance to seeking them by means of one's wealth. Ṭabāṭabāʾī explains that by "wealth," he means dowry in the case of marriage and sale price in the case of slavery. He goes on to write that sexual enjoyment is what man, by his nature, seeks; it is unclear here if by man he intends humankind or men in particular. This idea of *mutʿa* fulfilling a sexual need, primarily for men, is as we noted in chapter 1, is the new packaging used to present *mutʿa* in the contemporary period. In this discussion, he writes quite extensively on how chastity and fornication in this part of the *āya* do not refer to either "masturbation"—he uses the phrase "spilling of the seed"—or sexual intercourse only for the sake of procreation. He writes that both are incorrect, since they would make the marriage of an infertile couple, or being married to a menopausal woman, or intercourse without ejaculation unlawful, and they are not.

Next, he discusses, "So, such of them with whom you have *mutʿa* give them their wages as settled," *fa-mā istamtaʿtūm bihi min hunna fa-ʾātūhunna ujūrahunna*. He starts his commentary by discussing the grammar of this section. One explanation is that *mā* is a relative pronoun and the verb "you have *mutʿa*" its antecedent; thus, the section would read "then as to such of the women with whom you have *mutʿa*." A second possible grammatical explanation is that the pronoun *bihi* refers to cohabitation, which changes the meaning to "then whenever you seek to enjoy sexually with any of them, give them their wages as settled." He also says that in this rendering, *mā* would then denote time, as in "whenever," and the words "of them" would be connected to the verb *istamtaʿtūm*.

He next discusses the *fa*, or "so," at the start of this section of the *āya*; among the *tafāsīr* we have looked, he is the first exegete to do this. He states that the *fa* grammatically proves that this part of the *āya* is the conclusion reached by the previous words. Therefore, this section—"So, such of them with whom you have *mutʿa* give them their wages as settled"—is either part of the previous subject or an example of it because of the use of *fa*. Since the previous section deals with different kinds of permissible sexual relations, by marriage or through slave ownership, it can be concluded that this section of the *āya* is providing us with another type of marriage, one that was not mentioned earlier; this type that requires a man to pay *ajr* to his wife (i.e., it is referring to *mutʿa*).

Further on, Ṭabāṭabā'ī categorically states that there is no doubt that the word *istimtā'*, lit. "to enjoy," in this *āya* refers to *mut'a*. He also elaborates on the *āya*'s *asbāb al-nuzūl*, occasions of revelation. He writes that it is Medinan: This part of *Sūrat al-Nisā'* was revealed in the first half of the Prophet Muhammad's life in Medina. He claims there was no doubt that *mut'a* was a common practice and prevalent among Muslims during this period. He also writes, but without providing further evidence, that no other word was used to describe this type of marriage. Therefore, he writes, one must apply the historical meaning of this type of marriage to this Qur'anic clause because it was known by this name when the *āya* was revealed. Prophet Muhammad introduced some new uses of words into the *shari'a* (e.g., *ṣalāa*, prayer, *ṣawm*, fasting, *zakāt*, alms), which came to be understood to denote their technical meaning, and were not necessarily part of their dictionary meaning.[39] Hence, according to him, *istimtā'* can only mean *mut'a* because it was a term used to refer to *mut'a* during that time period, and there is no justification for using its literal meaning (which translates as "seeking pleasure in marriage" according to the Sunnis). This explanation is also furthered to counter some exegetes' presentation of *istimtā'* to actually means *tamatta'tum*, where the *sīn* and *tā'* have been added for emphasis and therefore do not indicate the seeking of something.

Next, Ṭabāṭabā'ī discusses in some detail what some scholars say about these *āyāt*. Here, similar to the rest of his discussion, he does not use names, nor does he say these are Sunni scholars. However, he is referring to the *āyāt* that Sunni scholars say abrogate *mut'a*—*āyāt* on inheritance (Q 4:12),[40] *'idda* (Q 65:1,[41] Q 2:228[42]), paternity (Q 33:5),[43] the limit of four wives (Q 4:3),[44] and marriage (Q 23:5,[45] Q 4:23[46])—which are Meccan *āyāt*, whereas the *āya* that permits *mut'a* is Medinan, and a Meccan *āya* cannot abrogate a Medinan one that came after it. He also writes the relationship between these *āyāt* is not abrogation but rather of the relationship that exists between the general and the particular, or the unrestricted and the restricted. Take the example of inheritance, it is general and covers all wives, both permanent and temporary, but then the tradition makes it particular and removes groups from it; for example, a slave woman does not inherit, someone who has killed her husband does not inherit, a Jewish or Christian wife does not inherit, and in Shi'i *fiqh* a *mut'a* wife does not inherit.

Although Ṭabāṭabā'ī claims to perform exegesis through the Qur'an, and using grammar, he does so clearly with a Shi'i outlook. His case for the permissibility of *mut'a* relies to a large extent on the *mā* referring to an inanimate object (*mut'a*), when the *mā* can and has been used to represent animate objects (in this case possibly women), and the *fa* helps us see that another type of marriage, *mut'a*, is being mentioned, which was not mentioned previously.

NUṢRAT BEGUM AMĪN (D. 1403/1983)

Nuṣrat Amīn, a Shiʿi exegetical scholar, was born in Isfahan to a merchant family and spent most of her life there.[47] It is thought that she leaned toward a religious education because she had many examples of religiously trained female elders in her family, most notably her paternal aunt, who was a *mujtahida*, a female jurist qualified to practice *ijtihād*, the independent exercise of judgment.[48] Her religious education started by studying the Qurʾan and Persian literature; after getting married at fifteen, she went on to continue her education in Arabic, Islamic jurisprudence, and philosophy, among other subjects, under the guidance of Āyatullāh Mir Sayyid ʿAli Najafabādī.[49] It was her father, not her husband, who paid for her studies after marriage.[50] Her first book, *al-Arbaʿīn al-hāshimīyyah*, is a commentary on forty *aḥādīth*. Various *ʿulamāʾ* began posing questions to test her knowledge as a scholar because of the text's popularity,[51] and her meticulous answers led to her reputation as a leading *mujtahida*.[52]

Nuṣrat Amīn did not just study the religious tradition; she also created opportunities for other women to study Islam. She started an all-girls Qurʾan academy in Isfahan in the 1960s. Later, she opened an introductory Islamic seminary for women called *Maktab-i-Fatemah*. Her stance on gender is not as straightforward as one might imagine for a scholar who strove to ensure that women from all walks of life could acquire higher Islamic knowledge. For example, in her book *Rayesh-e-khoshbakhti* (Paths to happiness), she outlines the characteristics of a pious woman and emphasizes her domestic role: Women are mainly responsible for the home and their children's education. Although Nuṣrat Amīn created a school and a seminary, women were not allowed to acquire advanced degrees. They were only trained at a junior level and not able to acquire higher levels of training; thus, these women could not actually play any meaningful role in the scholarly community.

Nuṣrat Amīn is considered one of the most outstanding twentieth-century female jurists from Iran. Other than being an expert in the fields of hadith and *fiqh*, she was also revered as a mystic and ethicist.[53] Despite her level of training and education, she refused to be considered a *marjaʿ-e taqlīd*,[54] a Shiʿi title reserved for individuals whose interpretations of religion and law are followed by the people. She has published more than nine major works, in Arabic and Persian, including a sixteen-volume *tafsīr*. The first volume of the *tafsīr* is titled *Makhzan al-ʿirfān dar ʿolūm-e Qurʾān* (Source of knowledge: Interpretations of the Qurʾan).[55] This *tafsīr* was used as a key text in introductory courses on Islamic law at University of Tehran prior to the 1979 revolution.[56] Unfortunately, no scholarly commentaries have been written on her *tafsīr* and it has not been genuinely engaged with inside or outside Iran.[57]

She starts her *tafsīr* of Q 4:24 by discussing the word *muḥṣināt*, stating that it refers to women who are married. She mentions that the word is related to the previous *āya* and is a continuation of the prohibition found in it. Next, she cites the exception: if married women are captives of war, their marital status does not preclude them from becoming concubines or being chosen for marriage. She goes on to state that "what is other than that" in the *āya* means that other than married women, all women are permissible to you provided you seek it with your wealth and not in lust. When she mentions *fa-mā istamta'tūm,* she says this means when a woman partakes in *mut'a*; interestingly, she puts the agency on women. Then she describes *mut'a*, calling it a *nikāḥ*, marriage, that lasts for a set period of time and a set dowry. She uses *mut'a* and *nikāḥ* interchangeably.

In the next paragraph, she mentions that this *āya* is a proof text of *mut'a*'s permissibility for *ahl al-bayt*, the People of the House. Ibn 'Abbās and other Companions believed this *āya* should be read with the addition of "for a limited time" (i.e., those whom you enjoy for a limited time).

To make her thesis statement about this *āya* stronger in the next section, she discusses that one can increase or decrease the predetermined duration of the temporary marriage. She does not discuss that one can increase or decrease the predetermined amount of the dowry that is decided on at the outset of the temporary marriage.

She includes a special note with a heading claiming that 'Ali said *mut'a al-nisā'* and *mut'a al-ḥajj* were halal until 'Umar made them prohibited. Under this heading, she cites three *aḥādīth* in Arabic and their discussions in Persian without providing references. Two of them are generally common in such discussions, while one is relatively new. The first hadith is from 'Ali; it is worth noting that she puts 'Ali first, saying that had 'Umar not prohibited *mut'a*, only a few would commit *zinā'*. Then she writes that it is well known among both the Shi'a and the Sunni that 'Umar said the two types of *mut'a* were allowed during the life of the Prophet Muhammad and he forbade both, punishing anyone who practiced them. Without further clarification, she presents this hadith as evidence that 'Umar cannot forbid something that the Prophet Muhammad allowed, and his words are evidence of his admission that the Prophet Muhammad allowed *mut'a* while he disallowed it on his own authority. Then she provides a counter hadith, claiming that it is obvious from this evidence that *mut'a* is permissible. She concludes her discussion with a polemical saying, "What Muḥammad has made halal is halal until the end of time, and what Muḥammad has made *ḥarām* is *ḥarām* until the end of time." Her *tafsīr* is not elaborate; it also does not speak to or acknowledge modern feminist sensibilities—something one might expect from a female exegete.

CONCLUSION

In this chapter, I examined six exegetical works by seven scholars. Muḥammad ʿAbduh and Rashīd Riḍā wrote the *tafsīr al-Manār*; however, ʿAbduh is the one who discusses Q 4:24. He denies the validity of *mutʿa* by using some interesting strategies. First, he acknowledges it was once allowed and then asserts that it was allowed and forbidden on a few occasions to facilitate its ban gradually. Despite advocating Shiʿi-Sunni unity, he claimed to not have seen any of the narrations that the Shiʿa state permit *mutʿa*, which appears unlikely given their popularity. ʿAbduh also presents an argument related to social norms, asserting that *mutʿa* corrupts marriage, an institution that often serves as the foundation for key human relationships.

Ibn ʿĀshūr is the only Sunni exegete to my knowledge who, without resorting to polemical arguments, permits *mutʿa,* provided there is dire need for it. Further, unlike Shiʿi scholars, he does not permit it by using Q 4:24 as a proof text. Rather, he does so using evidence of its historical practice and claiming that *mutʿa* was never abrogated. He is a scholar par excellence known for his openness, his erudite scholarly skills, and his unwavering focus on discovering the meaning of the Qurʾan and not being bogged down by sectarian issues, and his exegesis of this *āya* is a testament to this.

Sayyid Abū al-Aʿlā Mawdūdī simply ignores the existence of *mutʿa*, while still acknowledging issues related to the *āya*, like sexual relations with slave women, *nafaqa*, inheritance, and *ʿidda*, waiting period.

Sayyid Muḥammad Ḥusayn Faḍl Allāh presents a multifaceted argument to invalidate arguments that claim Q 4:24 was abrogated and to present claims that justify the practice of *mutʿa*. These arguments cite Islamic legal principles, the reliability of *aḥādīth* used to support the claim, and the history of the Qurʾanic revelation, and they also mention that the *āyāt* thought to abrogate the practice were revealed before the *āya* said to allow it. For these reasons, ʿUmar's sermon alone cannot prohibit the practice. Faḍl Allāh also uses modern sensibilities to validate the practice. He asserts that *mutʿa* serves a particular need and solves a problem that has existed since the time of the Prophet Muhammad, the problem of sexual needs; this makes it even more necessary to allow the practice in modern times.

Farḥat Hāshmī discusses the rules around sexual relations and their permissibility. She defines key terms in the *āya* and acknowledges the importance of a *mahr*, dowry, but fails to discuss *mutʿa* in her exegesis of Q 4:24.

Sayyid Muḥammad Ḥusayn Ṭabāṭabāʾī's exegesis involves explanations and translations of each word in Q 4:24. He provides *asbāb al-nuzūl*, the occasions of revelation, to clarify that the *āya* can only refer to *mutʿa*—it was a prevalent form of marriage among Muslims at the time the *āya* was revealed in Medina. His exegesis is also predominantly a grammatical analysis of the verse.

Nuṣrat Amīn supports the use of Q 4:24 to validate the practice of *mutʿa* and argues that it was forbidden due to ʿUmar's sermon. She asserts that ʿUmar cannot forbid what the Prophet Muhammad allowed.

Modern exegetes interacted with and adopted a variety of new genres for their *tafāsīr*. For example, they engaged in postcolonial discourse—illustrated most clearly in the works of Muḥammad ʿAbduh and Rashīd Riḍā. ʿAbduh and Riḍā also respond to feminist critiques of Islam to varying degrees. Interestingly, neither Nuṣrat Amīn nor Farḥat Hāshmī toe the feminist line or apologize for failing to do so. Although ʿAbduh and Riḍā advocated pan-Islamic unity, the *tafsīr al-Manār* only half-heartedly considers the Shiʿi position; the ideas it takes into account are misrepresented as indicative of the Shiʿi opinion. Shiʿi exegetes like Faḍl Allāh, Amīn, and Ṭabāṭabāʾī often speak of human sexual needs, albeit in a gendered manner.

The scholars implement various strategies. Both Faḍl Allāh and ʿAbduh cite ʿUmar's sermon to support or deny the validity of the practice of *mutʿa* respectively. Nuṣrat Amīn also mentions ʿUmar's prohibition of *mutʿa* as invalid, despite failing to provide a detailed exegesis of the *āya* itself. Most of the scholars defend *mahr*, dowry, which is predicated upon their understanding of feminist critique, but they do not acknowledge this in their writings. Some scholars employ a strategy of what could be deemed feigned ignorance: They make no mention of the *āya*'s relationship with *mutʿa* nor acknowledge any debate surrounding it in exegetical literature. Mawdūdī and Hāshmī, both South Asian scholars, do not acknowledge the existence of *mutʿa* or the historical use of Q 4:24 to refer to it. Most significantly, all scholars discuss this verse from their already established communitarian identities and work within those boundaries without taking the other sects' claims seriously or accurately except for Ibn ʿĀshūr, who despite being Sunni allows for the practice of *mutʿa,* provided there is dire need. These scholars responded to contemporary issues and movements. In chapter 5, I will examine how *mutʿa* continues to be a relevant issue in modern times.

NOTES

1. A. C. Niemeijer, "Khilāfa," in *Encyclopaedia of Islam, Second Edition*, eds. P. Bearman, Th. Bianquis, C. E. Bosworth, E. van Donzel, and W. P. Heinrichs (Brill Online, 2012); Anke von Kügelgen, "ʿAbduh, Muḥammad," in *Encyclopaedia of Islam, THREE*, eds. Kate Fleet, Gudrun Krämer, Denis Matringe, John Nawas, and Everett Rowson (Brill Online).

2. As a result, he traveled around the Muslim world and even to France, Russia, and England. Al-Afghānī wrote important works on philosophy, most famously his discussion with Ernest Renan. These texts are considered especially important for the revival of Islamic thought.

3. W. Ende, "Rashīd Riḍā," in *Encyclopaedia of Islam, Second Edition*.

4. For more on this, see Niemeijer, "K̲h̲ilāfa."

5. Muḥammad ʿAbduh and Muḥammad Rashīd Riḍā, *Tafsīr al-Qurʾān al-ḥakīm al-mashhūr bi-tafsīr al-manār*, ed. Ibrāhīm Shams al-Dīn (Beirut: Dār al-Kutub al-ʿIlmiyya, 1999), 5:2–17. All references to the discussion of Q 4:24 that follow are from this section of their *tafsīr*. And all subsequent discussions of the *tafāsīr* of the exegetes discussed in this chapter follow this format: A citation with bibliographic information is given at the beginning of the discussion, and all subsequent citations are from the section given in the first citation.

6. The details of these three arguments can be found in chapter 1.

7. For a short family biography, see M. Talbi, "Ibn ʿĀshūr," in *Encyclopaedia of Islam, Second Edition*. For a longer discussion, especially of his *tafsīr*, see Basheer Nafi, "Ṭāhir Ibn ʿĀshūr: The Career and Thought of a Modern Reformist *ʿālim*, with Special Reference to His Work of *Tafsīr*," *Journal of Qurʾanic Studies* 7, no. 1 (2005): 1–32. And Hadia Mubarak, "Intersections: Modernity, Gender, and Qurʾanic Exegesis" (Phd diss., Georgetown University, 2014), 45–53. For a discussion of his legal theory, see Basheer Nafi, "The Rise of Islamic Reformist Thought and Its Challenge to Traditional Islam," in *Islamic Thought in the Twentieth Century*, eds. Suha Taji-Farouki and Basheer Nafi (London, New York: I. B. Tauris, 2004), 28–60. And Muḥammad El-Mesawi, *Treatise on Maqāsid al-Shariah* (Herndon, VA: International Institute of Islamic Thought, 2006). For a commentary on the methodology found in his tafsir and its meaning, see Walid A. Saleh, "Marginalia and Peripheries: A Tunisian Historian and the History of Qurʾanic Exegesis," *Numen* 58, no. 2/3 (2011): 284–313, http://www.jstor.org/stable/23046263.

8. Nafi, "Ṭāhir Ibn ʿĀshūr," 13.

9. Muḥammad al-Ṭāhir Ibn ʿAshūr, *Al-Taḥrīr wal-Tanwīr* (Tunis: al-Dār al-Tūnisiyya lil-Nashr, 1984), 5:7–12.

10. Nafi, "Ṭāhir Ibn ʿĀshūr," 17.

11. Mubarak, "Intersections," 78–79.

12. Ibn ʿAshūr, *Al-Taḥrīr wal-Tanwīr*, 5:12.

13. Saleh, "Marginalia and Peripheries," 287.

14. Nafi, "Ṭāhir Ibn ʿĀshūr," 20.

15. Ibid., 21.

16. Hadia Mubarak, "Change through Continuity: A Case Study of Q. 4:34 in Ibn ʿĀshūr's *al-Taḥrīr wa'l-tanwīr*," *Journal of Qur'anic Studies* 20, no. 1 (2018): 2.

17. There is quite a large body of literature on Mawdūdī. See F. C. R. Robinson, "Mawdūdī," in *Encyclopaedia of Islam, Second Edition*; Kalim Bahadur, *The Jamaʿat-i-Islami of Pakistan: Political Thought and Political Action* (New Delhi: Chetana, 1977); Leonard Binder, *Religion and Politics in Pakistan* (Berkeley: University of California Press, 1961); Maryam Jameelah, *Who is Maudoodi?* (Lahore:

Mohammad Yusuf Khan, 1973); and Khalid bin Sayeed, "The Jamaat-i-Islami Movement in Pakistan," *Pacific Affairs* 30, no. 1 (1957): 59–68.

18. Feras Hamza, Sajjad Rizvi, and Farhana Mayer, *On the Nature of the Divine*, vol. 1 of *An Anthology of Qur'anic Commentaries* (Oxford: Oxford University Press, 2010), 65, fn 270.

19. This refers to the partition of Pakistan as an independent state.

20. A list of these works can be found in Khurshid Ahmad and Zafar Ishaq Ansari, eds., *Islamic Perspectives: Studies in Honour of Mawlana Sayyid Abul A'la Mawdudi* (Leicester: Islamic Foundation, 1979), 3–14.

21. He presented a large portion of his program of reform and renewal—which was rooted in the Qur'an—in the magazine *Tarjumān al-Qur'ān*, which he acquired in 1932 and continued to run for most of his life.

22. Sayyid Abū al-Aʿlā Mawdūdī, *Tafhīm al-Qur'ān* (Lahore: Idāra-i Tarjumān al-Qur'ān, 2000), 2:27–30.

23. Sayyid Abū al-Aʿlā Mawdūdī, *Towards Understanding the Qur'ān: Abridged Version of Tafhīm al-Qur'ān*, trans. and ed. Zafar Ishaq Ansari (Leicester, UK: The Islamic Foundation, 1988).

24. See Morgan Clarke, "Neo-Calligraphy: Religious Authority and Media Technology in Contemporary Shiite Islam," *Comparative Studies in Society and History* 52, no. 2 (2010): 351–83; As'ad Abu Khalil, "Ideology and Practice of Hizballah in Lebanon: Islamization of Leninist Organizational Principles," *Middle Eastern Studies* 27, no. 3 (1991): 390–403; and Hamza, Rizvi, and Mayer, *On the Nature of the Divine*, 52.

25. Sayyid Muḥammad Ḥusayn Faḍl Allāh, *Min waḥy al-Qur'ān* (Beirut: Dar al-Malak, 1998), 8:21–23.

26. See Sumayya Kassamali, "A Politics of Submission: Conditional Agents and Canadian Threats at the Al-Huda Institute of Islamic Education for Women" (master's thesis, University of Toronto, 2009); Khanum Shaikh, "Gender, Religious Agency, and the Subject of Al-Huda International," *Meridians* 11, no. 2 (2011): 62–90; Faiza Mushtaq, "A Day with Al-Huda," *Contexts* 6, no. 2 (2007): 60–61; and Afiya Shehrbano Zia, "The Reinvention of Feminism in Pakistan," *Feminist Review* 91 (2009): 29–46.

27. Mumtaz Ahmad, "Media-Based Preachers and the Creation of New Muslim Publics in Pakistan," in *Who Speaks for Islam? Muslim Grassroots Leaders and Popular Preachers in South Asia*, eds. Mumtaz Ahmad, Dietrich Reetz and Thomas Johnson (Washington DC: The National Bureau of Asian Research, 2010), Special Report number 22.

28. Riffat Hassan, "Islam and Human Rights," Dawn, Review (November 14, 2002), 18. Available online at: http://www.columbia.edu/itc/mealac/pritchett/00islamlinks/txt_riffat_hasan/txt_riffat_hasan.htm.

29. Hassan, "Islam and Human Rights," 18.

30. See Farhat Hashmi, "Women: خواتین," in *Quran for All: In Every Hand, In Every Heart*, available online at https://www.farhathashmi.com/assorted-section/women/ (accessed August 5, 2020). I used this audio *tafsīr* to analyze Hāshmī's interpretation of the *āya*.

31. She goes on to mention that women may not engage in friendship with any man, even if you consider him a brother, as Islam does not have a conception of boyfriend and girlfriend. This friendship does not mean that you are physical. She proceeds to give an example from the Qur'an where God says to not call yourself pure. She does not give us an *āya* number. Further on she says, even after engagement, girls and boys are not allowed to speak to one another. All such conversations are *zinā'*, fornication. There is *zinā'* if they hear, see, or touch each other. Again, she provides no evidence for this.

32. See Seyyed Hossein Nasr, "Ṭabāṭabā'ī, Muḥammad Ḥusayn," in *The Oxford Encyclopaedia of the Modern Islamic World*, ed. John L. Esposito (Oxford Islamic Studies Online), http://www.oxfordislamicstudies.com/article/opr/t236MIW/e0771 (accessed November 22, 2021); and ʿAllama Sayyid Muḥammad Muḥammad Ḥusayn Ṭabāṭabā'ī, *Shi'ite Islam*, trans. Seyyed Hossein Nasr (Albany, NY: SUNY Press, 1977). This latter work includes the author's biography and a bibliography of his works.

33. Hamid Algar, "'Allama Sayyid Muhammad Husayn Tabataba'i: Philosopher, Exegete, and Gnostic," *Journal of Islamic Studies* 17, no. 3 (2006): 327.

34. Algar, "Allama Sayyid," 332.

35. Ibid., 341.

36. Ṭabāṭabā'ī, Shi'ite *Islam*; see also, Muḥammad Ḥusayn Ṭabāṭabā'ī, *The Quran in Islam: Its Impact and Influence in the Life of Muslims*, trans. A. Yates (London: Zahra, 1987).

37. ʿAllāma Ḥusayn Mudarrissī Ṭabāṭabā'ī, *al-Mizān fī tafsīr al-Qur'ān*, 20 vols. (Beirut: Mu'assasat al-Aʿlamī li-l-Maṭbūʿāt, 1973–74); and the English translation *Al-Mizān: An Exegesis of the Qur'ān*, trans. Sayyid Saʿīd Akhtar Rizwī (Tehran: World Organization for Islamic Services, 1983–92), 8:69–105.

38. This is mentioned in any major book on the life of the Prophet Muhammad. For example, Martin Lings, *Muhammad: His Life Based on the Earliest Sources* (New York: Inner Traditions, 2006).

39. For example, he says, the word *ḥajj* in the Qur'an only means pilgrimage, and not trade, interest, or profit, which are some of the word's literal meanings.

40. Q 4:12, "You will inherit half of what your wives leave if they are childless. But if they have children, then (your share is) one-fourth of the estate—after the fulfilment of bequests and debts. And your wives will inherit one-fourth of what you leave if you are childless. But if you have children, then your wives will receive one-eighth of your estate—after the fulfilment of bequests and debts. And if a man or a woman leaves neither parents nor children but only a brother or a sister (from their mother's side), they will each inherit one-sixth, but if they are more than one, they (all) will share one-third of the estate—after the fulfilment of bequests and debts without harm (to the heirs). (This is) a commandment from God. And God is All-Knowing, Most Forbearing."

41. Q 65:1, "O Prophet! (Instruct the believers:) When you (intend to) divorce women, then divorce them with concern for their waiting period, and count it accurately. And fear God, your Lord."

42. Q 2:228, "Divorced women must wait three monthly cycles (before they can re-marry). It is not lawful for them to conceal what God has created in their wombs, if they (truly) believe in God and the Last Day. And their husbands reserve the right to take them back within that period if they desire reconciliation. Women have rights similar to those of men equitably, although men have a degree (of responsibility) above them. And God is Almighty, All-Wise."

43. Q 33:5, "Let your adopted children keep their family names. That is more just in the sight of God. But if you do not know their fathers, then they are (simply) your fellow believers and close associates. There is no blame on you for what you do by mistake, but (only) for what you do intentionally. And God is All-Forgiving, Most Merciful."

44. Q 4:3, "Of you fear you might fail to give orphan women their (due) rights (if you were to marry them), then marry other women of your choice—two, three, or four. But if you are afraid you will fail to maintain justice, then (content yourselves with) one or those (bondwomen) in your possession. This way you are less likely to commit injustice."

45. Q 23:5, "[T]hose who guard their chastity."

46. Q 4:23, "(Also) forbidden to you for marriage are your mothers, your daughters, your sisters, your paternal and maternal aunts, your brother's daughters, your sister's daughters, your foster-mothers, your foster-sisters, your mother-in-law, your stepdaughters under your guardianship if you have consummated marriage with their mothers—but if you have not, then you can marry them—nor the wives of your own sons, nor two sisters together at the same time—except what was done previously. Surely God is All-Forgiving, Most Merciful."

47. See Maryam Rutner, "Religious Authority, Gendered Recognition, and Instrumentalization of Nusrat Amin in Life and after Death," *Journal of Middle East Women's Studies* 11, no. 1 (2015): 24–41; Mirjam Künkler and Roja Fazaeli, "The Life of Two *Mujtahidah*s: Female Religious Authority in Twentieth-Century Iran," in *Women, Leadership, and Mosques: Changes in Contemporary Islamic Authority*, eds. Masooda Bano and Hilary Kalmbach (Leiden: Brill, 2012), 127–60; and Tayyebeh Cheraghi, "Lady Nusrat Begum Amin," trans. Seyyeda Zahra Mirtendereski, *Message of Thaqlain* 14, no. 3 (2012): 109–29.

48. *Mujtahida* is the feminine form of *mujtahid*. In the contemporary, technical sense, it is used for someone who can perform *ijtihād* due to their training in the Islamic sciences. For further study, see J. Calmard, "Mud̲j̲tahid," in *Encyclopaedia of Islam, Second Edition*.

49. Künkler and Fazaeli, "The Life of Two *Mujtahidahs*," 132.

50. Ibid., 133.

51. Ibid.

52. Ibid., 134.

53. Ibid., 132.

54. J. Calmard, "Mard̲j̲aʿ-i Taḳlīd," in *Encyclopaedia of Islam, Second Edition*.

55. Nuṣrat Khānum, *Makhzan al-ʿirfān dar tafsīr-i Qurʾān* (Anjuman-i Ḥimāyat az Khānavādah'hā-yi Bī'sarparast-i Īrānī: Iṣfahān, 1990), 4:210–14.

56. Künkler and Fazaeli, "The Life of Two *Mujtahidah*s," 140.

57. There is only evidence of two MA dissertations on her *tafsīr* that were recently defended at Islamic Azad University.

Chapter Five

Rethinking Marital and Sexual Ethics in Islamic Law

When mentioning *ijtihād*, the independent exercise of judgment, Muslim scholars often quote the famous Prophetic hadith:[1]

> When the Prophet intended to send Muʿādh ibn Jabal to Yemen he asked: How will you judge when the occasion of deciding a case arises? He replied: I shall judge in accordance with Allah's book. Then the Prophet asked: What will you do if you do not find guidance in Allah's book? He replied: I shall act in accordance with the sunnah of the Prophet. The Prophet again asked: What will you do if you do not find guidance in the sunnah and the book. He replied: I shall do my best to form an opinion and spare no pains. The Prophet patted him and said: Praise be to Allah who helped the Prophet to find a thing which pleases him.[2]

I take succor from this hadith, and while the first four chapters of this book are dedicated to tracing and understanding the history of discussions of *mutʿa*, temporary marriage, in classical texts, this chapter presents a new interpretive path to Islamic law that seeks "a more viable and equitable ethics of sex."[3]

In her groundbreaking book, *Sexual Ethics in Islam*, Kecia Ali calls on lay Muslims and scholars alike to construct an "egalitarian sexual ethics" by "exposing reductive and misogynist understandings of the Qur'an and hadith [and] refusing to see medieval interpretations as coextensive with revelation."[4] And in *Sexual Violation in Islamic Law*, Hina Azam writes that questions related to gender and sexuality are also historical questions "oriented toward the potential: what can a study of [the] divergent ways in which Islamic doctrine evolved—and the very human ways in which jurists pursued the various lines of reasoning to which they committed—tell us about lines of reasoning not taken, about other directions in which these doctrines could yet develop?"[5] Ebrahim Moosa, commenting on ethics in Islamic law, discusses other lines of reasoning that can be taken:

> [o]ne way forward in Muslim norm-making today is to think of Islamic law as an enterprise in ethics. In ethical thinking, there are values that can be harnessed from the legal tradition which are often framed in a utilitarian idiom of interests (*masalih*). However, the legal and moral, as well as spiritual and philosophical, traditions of Islam also deliberate about the ethical as the essential imperatives that underpin the good life. Ultimately, this is about human flourishing and living a virtuous life.[6]

This chapter is my attempt to do the same, and it responds to all these calls.

The call to incorporate ethics is not limited to present-day scholars. Two pre-modern scholars also make similar calls. Abū al-Ḥasan al-Māwardī (d.1058), a Basra-born jurist and philosopher, recommended "finding solutions by drawing on multiple intellectual and disciplinary traditions"[7] alongside the Qurʾan and *aḥādīth*. Similarly, al-Māwardī "drew on the parables found in the writings of philosophers and the literary insights found in the work of the rhetoricians and poets."[8] In his famous book, *The Jurist's Primer*, the jurist and philosopher Ibn Rushd (d. 1198), known as Averroes in the west, wrote that the purpose of Islamic law is to cultivate *al-faḍāʾil al-nafsaniyya*, the virtues of the soul, alongside *ʿibadāt*, ritual practices, and what he called *al-sunan al-karamiyya*, "the norms of dignity." Moosa writes that Ibn Rushd "pushed us to contemplate what he called the norms of dignity and brought the conversation about Islamic law back to ethics and morality."[9]

In the spirit of our historical elders and our present elders, this book represents my ongoing engagement with two questions that have theoretical significance and real consequences for Muslims, particularly women. The first question is whether or not the use of Q 4:24 as a proof text for *mutʿa* can be hermeneutically justified. To answer this question, we must turn to hermeneutics and various methods of interpretation. As chapters 2, 3, and 4 have illustrated, the Qurʾan and *aḥādīth* have multiple levels of meaning and interpretive possibilities. We must consider the power that historical context and sectarian influences have over exegesis. These three chapters challenge the assumption that Qurʾanic commentaries transcended—and thus were not products of—their historical contexts. The *tafāsīr* on Q 4:24 studied in the earlier chapters illustrated the polysemy of Qurʾanic *āyāt* by tracing the intellectual history of exegesis. This *āya* (Q 4:24) and the arguments based on it do not provide a cohesive, conclusive argument regarding whether or not *mutʿa* is permissible. Exegetes and legal scholars decided if the practice of *mutʿa* was permissible—or not—by privileging certain aspects of the debates and choosing what material from among the available sources should be considered authentic and unproblematic.

The second question, which is intimately related to the first one, is the topic of this chapter: How can we determine whether *mutʿa* is permissible or not if the *āya* (Q 4:24) cannot give us a definitive answer? And related to this are additional questions: Is it possible to do this while constructing our arguments from within the Islamic legal tradition *and* centering marital and sexual ethics? Through their studies on sexual ethics and sexual violation in classical Islamic law, both Ali and Azam show that in the minds of jurists, sexual access was the single most important right a husband acquired after marrying a woman.[10] Legal understandings of sexual access as the key right granted through marriage certainly has implications for marital ethics and sexual ethics. The issue of sexual access is also foundational to debates about *mutʿa*. What are the consequences of *mutʿa* for Muslim women, children, and the family structure? Does permitting sex outside of permanent marriage change the nature of Muslim marriage and the Muslim sexual landscape?

In this chapter focusing on sexual and marital ethics, I argue that the question of the permissibility of *mutʿa* cannot be answered by looking solely at Q 4:24 and related classical texts. We must consider other factors when analyzing this issue. Scholars of Islamic legal studies, including feminists, conventionally have had a myopic focus on the hermeneutical traditions—based on the Qurʾan, hadith, legal texts, and gender theory—that pertain to Islamic law and have often lacked a multifaceted approach.

Indulge me then, as I pose as a tentative Imāmī feminist *mujtāhida* (jurist)[11] and utilize the *maqāṣid* (purposive) tools of the juristic process, developed by the contemporary Shiʿi scholar, Muḥammad Taqī al-Mudarrisī (b. 1945).[12] At its core, *maqāṣid*-based *ijtihād* as the independent exercise of judgment, rethinks individual juristic positions in light of new realities. Mudarrisī developed his *maqāṣid al-sharīʿa* (purposes or objectives of *sharīʿa*) to be a practical tool in the hand of jurists who could then adapt Islamic law to the interests of people, and I utilize his methodology as such. His *maqāṣid al-sharīʿa* framework provides, both a theory of understanding religion, as well as a method for improving the law.[13] I generate a four-part interrelated methodology using the *maqāṣidī* tools provided by Mudarrisī. The four divisions are interrelated in such a way that each one affects the other. One distinctive feature of Mudarrisī's *maqāṣid* is the role of non-scriptural sources[14]—which for me are Muslim feminist methodology, legal ethnography, moral philosophy, and the science of sexuality—alongside scriptural sources, Qurʾan and hadith. Therefore, my interrelated and multidisciplinary methodology is in line with Mudarrisī, who argues "that there should be several methods, which collectively reflect different aspects and dimensions of reality in order to achieve coherence and equilibrium."[15] I actualize his *maqāṣid* in questions and a set of actionable recommendations under each suggested four-part methodology, which when answered would provide a path to a new ruling on temporary marriage. These four parts do not in themselves lead to a new ruling on *mutʿa* because the *maqāṣid*, as a discipline, does not offer *fiqh*, and is therefore beyond the scope of this study. Further, the suggested four-part methodology and the questions posed within each section are by no means intended to be the final word. Here, questions and recommendations are intended as a platform from which further deliberations can emerge and develop. It is only by using such comprehensive and innovative methodologies that carefully consider *mutʿa*'s multivalent practice, will its implications—for better or for worse—become clear.

In essence, the fundamental purpose of *maqāṣid al-sharīʿa* is to bring forth benefit while ensuring that harm is avoided. During the twentieth century, Shiʿi and Sunni legal scholars interested in adapting Islamic law to new realities considered *maqāṣid al-sharīʿa* as an approach to the law through which the main purposes or objectives of the law are (re)considered in order to derive new legal rulings. Not surprisingly then, *maqāṣid al-sharīʿa* is a useful tool for discussing issues that pertain to the reinterpretation of *mutʿa* marriage. I have chosen Mudarrisī because he has a "flexible epistemology [that] allows the jurist to be ambitious and active by virtue of the wide scope that [S/]he[They] can interact with."[16] More specifically, he creates space for non-scriptural understanding as an important condition for the validity of legal rulings.[17] Another one of his contributions is opening up the possibility of establishing legal rulings based on less stringent forms of certainty.[18] Therefore, at least according to my reading, his approach to *maqāṣid* opens the door and allows us to seek different methods that can lead to a reasonable level of acceptable knowledge from which to derive legal rulings. Mudarrisī's *maqāṣid al-sharīʿa* paradigm is characterized by utilizing intellect, revelation, and reality as sources of value within moral and legal discussions.[19]

In my attempt at *maqāṣid*-based *ijtihād*, I outline the possible questions for each of the four methods presented, thereby attempting to illustrate what is expected in the process.[20] The current chapter then presents the final step of this book's methodological intervention. Like any monumental task, this chapter provides preliminary research that points out areas for further study and questions for interpretating *mutʿa* in a way that addresses sexual and marital ethics and their related concerns. It is not within the scope of this book to definitively answer the questions posed in this chapter or to present a comprehensive picture of what *mutʿa* might look like after such a comprehensive study takes place; rather, the chapter's aim is to direct future scholarship toward new methodologies. Here, I will explore the possible contributions and benefits of studies from various fields, including feminist interventions in Islamic studies, ethnography, moral philosophy, and scientific research on sexuality, and what these potential collaborative studies might look like. By answering Ali's call for just sexual ethics, this chapter argues it is necessary to reinterpret the permissibility of *mutʿa* within Islamic law and proposes four interlinking theoretical frameworks for doing this: (1) Muslim feminist methodological interventions; (2) legal ethnographic study; (3) moral philosophy; and (4) the science of sexuality.

MUSLIM FEMINIST METHODOLOGICAL INTERVENTIONS

In earlier chapters, we looked at some Muslim exegetes and their quests to understand the meaning of Q 4:24 using various methods, such as *ʿilm al-qiraʾat*, the science of variant readings, *asbāb al-nuzūl*, occasions of revelation, *nāsikh wa mansūkhuhu*, abrogation, and *naḥu*, grammar, as well as cultural practices, in order to understand the meaning of particular words in the *āya*. These chapters showed us that there is both ambiguity *and* polysemy in Q 4:24, which allows us to rethink Islamic law while centering marital and sexual ethics in the context of *mutʿa*.

An essential part of Mudarrisī's *maqāṣid* theory is *tadabbur* (deep reflection) on the Qurʾan. He defines *tadabbur* as "neither a professional exegetic process nor a simple thinking about the Qur'anic content," rather it is "a deep, concentrating and systematic reflection on the Qur'an through which the reader is not only able to understand the apparent Qur'anic content, but also to understand its deeper meaning and be able to apply it in practice."[21] Additionally, Mudarrisī, as a part of the Shiʿi reformist school of thought, was open to Sunni scholarship in order to benefit from it and adapt it within Shiʿi establishments.[22] Therefore, it is fair to assume that he would also be open to understanding, investigating, and incorporating Muslim feminist methodology as a form of *tadabbur* to generate a new exegesis of Q 4:24.

This chapter, and especially this section, is an attempt to come up with a textual methodology that could lead us toward ethical sexual intimacy, and this section illustrates how multiple Muslim feminists[23] have presented various methodological interventions. I want to make it clear that I am in no way saying that the Qurʾan, *aḥādīth*, and the classical tradition are to be done away with or that they are not to be taken seriously. Such a move on my part would at the least be akin to hubris and at the most, be blasphemous, not to mention that it would result in epistemological violence—not treating my or other Muslim believers' scholastic productions seriously.[24] I acknowledge that some scholars have come to the conclusion that patriarchy is rooted in the Qurʾan in such a way that makes it next to impossible to develop a truly egalitarian and feminist theology or methodology.[25] In contrast, I have faith in divine justice, and I accept that my idea of justice might not be God's idea of justice. The Muslim conception of the Qur᾽an is that it both transcends history and responds to the minutia of history as it happens—in every time and every place—and hence it is important to turn to it.

Muslim feminist works are based on the premise that gender equality is an ideal that is consistent with the higher aims of Islamic ethics and the Qur᾽an and that we need to critically engage Islamic traditions from within. Muslim feminists have a long history of presenting intellectually rigorous methodology in order to advance gender equality from within the tradition.[26] I will engage with some of their works that are often rendered invisible. This engagement is an important corrective to the emphasis on elite male intellectual production within Islamic and most other systems of knowledge. There are other works that could also be included in this conversation, but expanding this conversation is work for future scholarship.

The first methodological intervention is to think robustly about the intratextuality of the Qur᾽an. The second is intertextuality, by which I mean the critical analysis of *aḥādīth* and sharpening the tools already used in *tafāsīr*, such as rethinking the role and purpose of *asbāb al-nuzūl*. The third is considering some of the foundational assumptions of *fiqh* related to marriage. Finally, I discuss works that study genres other than the Qur᾽an and *fiqh*, for example Sufi texts and philosophical texts.

Muslim feminists recommend an exegetical strategy that can be defined as a call to read the Qur᾽an intratextually.[27] What does intratextuality mean? Taking inspiration from Fazlur Rahman's work, most contemporary Muslim feminist scholars have pointed out that an *āya*-by-*āya* explanation of the Qur᾽an cannot give us "[i]nsight into the cohesive outlook on the universe and life which the Qur'an undoubtedly possesses."[28] All the *tafāsīr* we have looked at in this book were the products of a mostly atomistic exegetical process, which leads to a limited or narrow understanding of the Qur᾽an. Ayesha Hidayatullah, borrowing from Amina Wadud, writes that intratextuality involves "comparing related Qur'anic verses and terms to one another instead of reading them in isolation, as well as reading verses in light of what the exegetes have identified as the Qur'an's overall movement towards advocating justice and equality for all humans."[29]

In the previous three chapters, we saw how some of the exegetes used the interpretive method that is classically understood as *tafsīr al-Qur᾽ān bi-l-Qur᾽ān*, the method of interpreting the Qur᾽an using other *āyāt* as explanative tools. This is method is based on the understanding that the Qur᾽an is the primary source for understanding its own meaning. It is important to note that *tafsīr al-Qur᾽ān bi-l-Qur᾽ān* is not what Muslim feminists are calling for per se. For example, as we saw in chapter 4, Sayyid Muḥammad Ḥusayn Ṭabāṭabā᾽ī explicitly follows this classical method, but it does not give us a holistic understanding of what marriage is in the Qur᾽an, or what sexual ethics are according to the Qur'anic worldview. The idea of *nazm,* the cohesion of the Qur'an, is closer to what Muslim feminists are calling for.

What would Qur'anic intratextuality look like in the context of our analysis? Looking at a group of *āyāt* collectively could help us develop a new exegesis of Q 4:24.[30] Some of the *āyāt* I will be looking at include: 2:187,[31] 2:222,[32] 2:223,[33] 4:1,[34] 4:3,[35] 4:34,[36] 4:128,[37] 4:129,[38] 9:71,[39] and 30:21;[40] related to human coupling, which is pertinent to our topic of marital and sexual ethics, 7:189,[41] 39:6,[42] and 51:49;[43] and on the creation of human beings from an initial pair, 49:13[44] and 75:39.[45] Feminist Muslim scholars have utilized intratextuality to further varying arguments around sexual rights, sexuality, and egalitarianism in the Qur'an. According to Wadud, the Qur'an "promotes male sexuality,"[46] particularly in *āyāt* 4:3 and 2:223. In response, Asma Barlas has argued that the Qur'an does not give men absolute rights in connection to sexual access and asks men to respect women's rights.[47] Celene Ibrahim's work also presents a new and unique type of intratextuality. She looks at sexuality in the Qur'an through a comprehensive analysis of narratives involving female figures.[48] Other similar attempts include Rawand Osman's book,[49] which studies female figures in Shi'i *aḥādīth*, exegesis, and biographical literature. These two works provide us with an invaluable female-centric lens through which to understand the Qur'an intratextually. A deeper analysis and fresh understanding of the meaning of the depiction of Zulaykhā's powerful sexuality in the Qur'an is also in order. After all, it is the only explicit mention of sexuality in the Qur'an, and the protagonist is a woman. Barlas also presents a psychoanalysis of several female figures who are present in the Qur'an and *aḥādīth*.[50]Another example of the use of intratextuality appears in Hadia Mubarak's forthcoming book,[51] where she discusses the issue of *nushūz*, rebellion, in Q 4:34 and Q 4:128—both male and female. It remains to be seen how she engages with Kecia Ali's critique that no current intratextual analysis of this *āya* addresses the fact that it outlines different treatment for men and women. From the standpoint of a literal reading of the *āya*, men receive preferential treatment, and the consequences "do not merely differ in the interpretation of the exegetes but are clearly differentiated in the text of the Qur'an itself."[52] From this brief discussion, we can already see that this is a complicated issue and needs extensive, thoughtful analysis.

The second feminist methodological intervention we will cover here is intertextuality. Intertextuality in this regard is evaluating the Qur'an in light of *aḥādīth* and sunnah, particularly the marital relationships of the prophet Muhammad. As I mentioned in chapter 1, the *aḥādīth* that pertain to *mut'a* must be studied closely, hence why the method of intertextuality is recommended Hidayatullah writes that "the uneven use and scrutiny of the Hadith demonstrated a methodological inconsistency across the collective body of feminist tafsir works."[53] Fatema Mernissi is generally considered the first contemporary Muslim feminist to investigate the authenticity and authority of *aḥādīth* attributed to the Prophet Muhammad about the issue of woman's leadership, thereby refuting a narrative by Abū Bakr.[54] Another example is Sa'diyya Shaikh, who studies the construction of gender in *aḥādīth* discussing women's knowledge and sexuality.[55] Historians and lay Muslims alike know that ʿA'isha, the Prophet Muhammad's wife, questioned early narrators' claims about what they heard from the Prophet Muhammad; questioning *aḥādīth,* therefore, is a long-standing Islamic tradition.[56] Hidayatullah captures the issue best when she writes: "thus, the field of feminist tafsir awaits the development of more consistent standards for utilizing the Hadith and a thorough examination of source difficulties to strengthen the use of the historical contextualization method in feminist readings of the Qur'an."[57] It is important to state that this is not a call to torch the hadith corpus, something some modernist Muslim scholars have called for;[58] it is instead a call to critically and systematically look at *aḥādīth* and bring change to our understanding of marital and sexual ethics from within this Islamic framework.

I would also add that there is a set of *aḥādīth* that have not been considered seriously in discussions about marital and sexual ethics. For example, in one hadith, the Prophet Muhammad refused to allow his son-in-law, ʿAlī b. Abī Ṭālib, to be in a polygynous relationship and marry another wife unless he first divorced his daughter Fāṭima.[59] What does this tell us about the feelings of a father for his daughter? The feelings of the daughter and wife? Significantly, this happened at a time when polygyny was a cultural norm (as shown in chapter 1). How should we interpret this?

Considering the Prophet Muhammad's marital relationships as examples to help develop marital and sexual ethics is warranted because the Qur'an (Q 33:21)[60] assigns him the role of *uswa ḥasana,* a beautiful example of perfect conduct. Muslim feminist scholars have argued that not enough attention has been paid to his behavior within marriage, and no consistent framework, nor even a positive model, has been developed from it;[61] however, Muslim scholars have used his marriages to derive several legal rulings.[62] In her study of the Prophet Muhammad as a husband, Ali makes an important distinction between the sunna of the Prophet Muhammad, which she describes as his personal conduct, and *aḥādīth,* which are various recordings of his supposed actual sayings. She argues that a way forward is to "focus our attention on those elements of legal, exegetic, and historical sources in our tradition that describe the conduct of the Prophet (peace be on him) himself in his own marital relationships"[63] or to focus on his sunnah and not necessarily *aḥādīth* because some of them are extremely problematic.[64] We find that his conduct toward his wives[65] was kind and not harsh: he was compassionate and loving;

he helped with household chores; he was gentle and never physically abusive; he divorced a woman who did not want to be married to him; and he did not allow his son-in-law to take a second wife.[66] Muslims, Ali argues, "can choose to treat this conduct as exemplary—the emulation of which is required of other Muslim husbands—rather than as exceptional, and specific to the Prophet (peace be on him) himself."[67] This methodological approach could produce a better system for evaluating sexual and marital ethics.

Rahemtulla and Ababneh further the discussion on the Prophet Muhammad's marital life by asking "what can we, as Muslim feminists committed to gender egalitarian partnerships in our own context, learn from this [Khadīja and the Prophet's] premodern marriage, and how can we reclaim it as model for contemporary Muslim masculinities?"[68] And, I would add, how might it affect our understanding of marital and sexual ethics? These scholars attempt a feminist reclaiming of Khadīja's twenty-five-year monogamous marriage with the Prophet Muhammad. Khadīja was independently wealthy and a career trader who was fifteen years older than the Prophet Muhammad. She employed him, proposed to him, and then he went to live in her house, and after their marriage, she supported his mission financially and emotionally and helped him understand his prophetic role. They lived harmoniously together for twenty-five years; however, it would be erroneous to claim that this was a marriage of equals. The Prophet Muhammad was dependent on her in many regards, and she was the more powerful partner. As Rahemtulla and Ababneh put it, "What we have in their example is a nonpatriarchal—indeed, acutely matriarchal—relation of power."[69] This gives us a model for conceptualizing a feminist masculinity with a "twofold objective: to challenge the existing patriarchal construction of normative (read hegemonic) masculinity, and, in its place, to envision alternative normative constructions committed to feminist values of gender equality and inclusion."[70] This framing of the relationship between Khadīja and the Prophet Muhammad gives us a lot to reflect on and is a source for future thinking and discussions on marital and sexual ethics.

Another reason the method of intertextuality is recommended here is in order to rethink the role of *asbāb al-nuzūl*, the context of revelation. Although the exegetes we discussed were aware that the context of revelation was important, they did not capture the full import of it. For example, Sonbol writes that the *asbāb al-nuzūl* of Q 4:3, which is considered a proof text for the permissibility of polygyny, was revealed during a particular event, the Battle of Uḥud, where the war widows and orphans became the responsibility of those who survived; thus, "it does not seem [to] have establish[ed] a general rule"[71] about the permissibility of polygyny. Sonbol wrote this in 2001, when polygyny was thought to be socially regressive; this idea has since been questioned.[72] Additionally, Sonbol's effort to complicate the understanding of *asbāb al-nuzūl* does not account for the historical reality that the Prophet Muhammad and the Companions all partook in polygyny. This notwithstanding, the significance of *asbāb al-nuzūl* has not been properly realized[73] and is another area for future research that could lead to better methodology and analysis.

The third methodological intervention by Muslim feminists considers issues of fiqh around marriage. An example of this can be found in the insights of Hina Azam, who finds Islamic law to have two competing and sometimes overlapping concerns when it comes to sexual ethics: one is "propriety" and the other is "theocentric" concerns.[74] Like Kecia Ali in the case of the marriage contract,[75] she finds that in the case of rape, the propriety framework makes it so that a woman's sexuality is treated like a commodity, and rape in this system is treated as theft and subject to monetary compensation alongside other retributions. Within the theocentric understanding of sexual ethics, illicit sex is immoral and considered a human sin in God's eyes. The proprietary elements of the Qurʾanic *mahr*, dowry, as in Q 4:24, conceptualized by jurists as *thaman al-buḍʿ*, "the vulva's price," need not be ascribed to the Qurʾan but rather to the jurists themselves and can be seen as simply a gift to the bride at the time of marriage. We still have to contend with the Qurʾan seemingly granting men permission to have intercourse with the enslaved, but bracketing this issue for the time being, let us ask: What might a sexual ethics that privileges theocentric concerns look like?

The fourth and final methodological intervention addressed in this section involves texts outside of Qur'an and fiqh, namely Sufi and philosophical texts. Unlike the Muslim feminist interventions discussed above that focus on the Qurʾan, hadith, and *fiqh,* Zahra Ayubi provides us with a brilliant analysis of the construction of a gender hierarchy in philosophical texts that deal with *akhlāq,* cultivation of personal virtue.[76] Her book is an essential and long-awaited corrective to the disproportionate attention that hermeneutics and legal discussions have received in feminist works. According to the ethicists[77] she studied, women[78] and nonelite men, though still human, are inferior to elite men and serve as tools for the elite men's self-refinement. The study of this genre is crucial for comprehending Islamic understandings of gender in the past, how this understanding informs the present, and for forming a different understanding of gender ethics in the future. In her closing chapter, the most original part of the book, Ayubi addresses the potential of *akhlāq* as a resource for contemporary Muslim feminist thought by guiding us to reexamine the tradition of *akhlāq* and suggesting we focus on revitalizing its professed metaphysical commitment to divine justice and human equality, thus providing us with another methodological tool for reimagining marital and sexual ethics.

Significantly, Ayubi's work is premised on the fundamental question of what it means to be a good human being. Sa'diyya Shaikh too grapples with this question in her landmark study looking at the scholarly production of the thirteenth-century Andalusian Muslim scholar and Sufi saint, Ibn ʿArabī (d. 1240).[79] Shaikh presents a cautious case for how Sufi metaphysics could help Muslim feminists develop an alternative understanding of gender. She does this by showing us how Sufism can challenge the divide between spiritual and social existence and thus open up a space for overturning existing gender hierarchies because, in Sufism, moral standing is determined entirely through submission to the divine and through moral acts, and this is true for all human beings—regardless of their gender. Hence, she provides us with a hermeneutically valid and historically grounded new normative register based on spiritual attainment and gender justice, which we can utilize for marital and sexual ethics.

Finally, as a cautionary note, our broader context and historical moment must be mentioned. It is not controversial to claim that premodern exegetes did not possess the concepts of historicity, gender, and sexual and marital ethics as we know and understand them today. They likely did not understand their works of exegesis to be time-bound endeavors; they did not consider that their interpretations were historically situated, which is what we analyzed in the last three chapters. We should also acknowledge our own historicity, which requires recognizing our colonial history and the role of western hegemony—none of us can conceptualize feminism[80] or egalitarianism completely free from these discourses and parameters. And we also have to contend with secular modernity, which affects us and shapes our ethics regarding what we think is just and fair. Put another way, western-educated Muslim feminists are disrupting ideas about "authority" and what is "authoritative" in traditional Islam. Even though the western context allows Muslims to rethink and reimagine our faith, this also contains the very real danger of western encroachment, ultimately raising questions about Muslim feminists' role in Islamic religious reform. The choice of one particular approach to the Qurʾan over another is linked to specific visions of religion and society. Secular modernity and western academia erase the transcendent from "sacred texts," as well as from their social and communal functions. Once the specific role of Muslim feminist Qurʾanic scholarship[81] is understood, we can better understand the obstacles to and opportunities for new intratextual and intertextual interpretations of the Qurʾan. Examining the *āya* on *mutʿa* considering intratextuality of other Qur'anic verses and intertextuality of *aḥādīth*, sunna, *asbāb al-nuzūl*, an egalitarian conception of *fiqh* and philosophical and Sufi texts will give us a broader perspective of sexual and marital ethics and a new interpretation of the *āya* 4.24. The next key to understanding the role of *mutʿa* is the actual lives of Muslim women and men.

ETHNOGRAPHIC STUDY

Mudarrisī suggests seeking the "spirit of the people." This describes the idea that "a certain society at a particular time and in a specific place passes through a socio-historical moment that requires specific needs, plans, and policies, and therefore the law has to be an expression of this collective 'spirit.' Mudarrisī deems this sort of 'spirit' as a framework that needs a rational method through which it should be studied."[82] Here, I present the method as legal ethnography. I propose conducting legal ethnographic studies among Muslim men, women, and children while treating their voices as a critical source for the law that reflects the "spirit of the people." By acknowledging and approaching *mutʿa* as a living Muslim practice, this interpretive schema presents Islamic legal scholars with a new path forward by suggesting we utilize ethnography alongside textual analysis when rethinking marital and sexual ethics.

Ethnographic studies on *mutʿa* have been conducted in the past. The most prominent one was conducted in postrevolutionary Iran by Shahla Haeri, a cultural anthropologist and the granddaughter of Ayatollah Haeri of Iran and was first published in 1989.[83] She is not interested in textual analysis but in Iranian women's lived experiences of *mutʿa*. Being an Ayatollah's granddaughter granted her easier access to certain places and people, and this gave her the opportunity to speak to both men and women who were practicing *mutʿa*. Her book details their thoughts and experiences. Haeri emphasizes the differences between *mutʿa* and prostitution but also does not downplay the shared aspects. She discovered that some women use *mutʿa* to benefit financially and/or sexually while also staying within the bounds of the law. To the surprise of many, she shows that *mutʿa* has liberatory potential for women—at least for women who have the same social standing vis-à-vis men.

Another major work on *mutʿa* is Linda S. Walbridge's 1991 study of the Shiʿi population in Dearborn, Michigan, which has the largest population of Arab Muslims in the United States, the majority of whom are Lebanese Shiʿa.[84] Walbridge focuses on the tension between religion and popular culture, theorizing that the Dearborn Islamic community's reactions to this tension reveal their attitudes toward religion, women, and marriage. She tests this hypothesis by studying the community's thoughts on *mutʿa* and finds that communal views are diverse but have some shared themes. Women overwhelmingly expressed dislike for the practice, and many female interviewees asserted that *mutʿa* runs counter to their religious beliefs. Conversely, the men in her study tended to accept the practice as justified, despite no significant praise for the practice. According to Walbridge, the consensus of the community is that *mutʿa*, though legally permissible, is not morally acceptable.

Despite the value of these studies, I argue that both scholars fail to ask their interlocutors certain key questions and thus miss the opportunity to gain a deeper understanding of the effects of *mutʿa* and its societal meaning. The first question that comes to mind is to ask the interviewees about their perceptions of the double standards that exist within the practice of *mutʿa*. For example, married men may partake in the practice, but not married women, a woman can initiate *mutʿa* legally, but she cannot pay for it, and a man can be in multiple *mutʿa* relationships simultaneously, but a woman can only be in one. Such rulings are representative of the environment they were produced in: one that struggled to even consider that men, too, might become disenfranchised enough to want to sell their bodies for money to provide for their families or that women, too, might be interested in multiple sexual partners. Questions about revoking rulings that do not allow *mutʿa* on equal terms for both genders (since DNA testing eliminates uncertainty about paternity, the main concern of legal scholars) allow us to understand *mutʿa* in a new light, one that has been hindered by the double standards of the past. This might tell us if this tradition has survived because of patriarchy, whereas, without gender discrimination, a different ruling might come to the fore.

As we saw in the previous chapters, *mutʿa* is often praised by Shiʿi exegetes as an institution that decreases adultery, and the subjects of ethnographic research on *mutʿa* must be asked how they define adultery. In English, adultery generally signifies extramarital sex. Sunni and Shiʿi *fiqh* allow for men to engage in polygyny and concubinage, while Shiʿi *fiqh* also allows married men to engage in *mutʿa*. Therefore, historically these sexual encounters have not been considered adultery in the Islamic context. However, having sex with someone a Muslim male is not married to is adultery—the one exception is if the person is enslaved. However, in the context of contemporary society, we need to ask if a *mutʿa* contracted by a married man is adultery? And why or why not?

There are other questions to bear in mind when considering the ethical implications of *mutʿa*. Sex outside of marriage exhibits a lack of self-restraint and control over desire, and the Qurʾan has instructed Muslims to control their desires. From an ethical preceptive, married men marrying other women fails to show respect and consideration toward those the demand to be monogamous is placed on (i.e., women). Another question is whether this undisciplined and inconsiderate behavior places needless strain on the marital relationship, threatening to destroy not just the marriage but also, by extension, the institution's social value.

Our next question to our interlocutors could be an extension of the double standard question, but this time in the context of adultery, and it goes something like this: Suppose we have a scenario in which the double standards and restrictions on married women have been removed and both spouses have agreed in advance that extramarital sex is acceptable behavior for each partner, provided everyone is acting justly.[85] Theoretically, such a declaration or understanding would be in line with the Qur'anic edict to treat all parties equally. Suppose that as a result no injustice—whether material, physical, or emotional—occurs. Thus, the conclusion reached might be that adultery in such a situation is simply not a problem. It is crucial that we ask whether these suppositions are actually plausible for a large segment of the population or only theoretically possible. Islamic jurists have answered this question in the positive, allowing the practice of polygyny. A related question is whether or not it is possible to judge if equitable circumstances do indeed exist in a variety of such cases. Islamic jurists leave this judgment to every individual man's conscience. However, if we are centering marital and sexual ethics, can we allow it to remain this way? Finally, even if things start out as equitable between all parties, is that any guarantee that down the road all parties will feel the same way. The answers to these questions collectively start to weave a picture about *mutʿa* that might not have been obvious earlier.

Moving away from married individuals to questions about single individuals, an ethnographic study should also ask Muslim interlocutors about their understanding of and views on promiscuity and casual sex. According to normative social judgment, promiscuity is casual sex that defies the traditional connection between sex and permanent marriage. Like adultery, promiscuity may be judged as problematic on the grounds that it endangers one of society's central institutions: permanent marriage. We saw Sunni exegetes argue that *mutʿa*, by allowing people to achieve sexual gratification while escaping long-term commitment, undermines marriage in such a way that it threatens the stability of society. This argument rests on two assumptions: first, promiscuity has adverse effects on permanent marriage; and second, permanent marriage is a socially superior alternative to other kinds of coupling. It is important to discuss these assumptions and what they mean within the Islamic worldview.

In defense of casual sex, we can imagine some of our interviewees' might present the argument that a sexual language is learned through interactions with multiple partners over time, and casual sex provides individuals with opportunities to acquire this language. Perhaps substantially more good than harm would come from sexual enjoyment being encouraged for its own sake. Further, some interlocutors might say that sex is an activity that can be enjoyed in a variety of suitable settings, with a variety of suitable partners. Another interlocutor might comment that Q 24:30–31 asks us to "guard" our private parts and "lower our gaze," limiting when and with whom sexual relations can occur and say that this is "purer" for us[86] and therefore sexual intimacy should be reserved for those with whom one has a legal connection (i.e., marriage). The mistake, another interlocutor might say, lies in believing that a typical adult will only have these feelings for one other adult during their lifetime, or even for only one other adult at a time. An adult ought to be able to love numerous adults without that love being different from the love experienced in traditional monogamous marriages, specifically since these traditional monogamous marriages are less and less common in this day and age, as shown in chapter 1. Our young interlocutors might say individuals in casual relationships can experience fulfilling sexual intimacy and that freeing sex from the monopoly of marriage—through *mutʿa*, for example—could lead to new forms of social existence that might satisfy the emotional and physical needs of individuals more effectively (as we saw contemporary Shiʿi scholars argue in chapter 1). It might also open up more personal freedom and initiate the creation of new lifestyles, particularly for those not interested in procreation or long-term relationships. The Qurʾan uses various words for kinship—Q 2:83,[87] Q 2:177,[88] Q 4:36[89]—to speak about family relations, which indicates the importance of family within the Qurʾanic worldview.[90] Alongside the reality of the changing marital landscape, these words, *āyāt*, and ethical concepts need to be incorporated into our collective thinking on the issue. Our interview would have to foreground the complexity of the issue by looking at both the positive and negative sides of casual sex and promiscuity.

Another significant question that has not been seriously considered in the context of *mutʿa* marriage: How does having sexual relations with multiple adults affect the children of these adults? How do children factor into this equation? How are children affected? Positively? Negatively? And who determines this? The father? The mother? The children themselves? A child psychologist? Further, what, if anything, do these adults owe their children? Thinking holistically, we must also think about the meaning of the Prophetic saying, "Surely, the best of you is he who is best to his family,"[91] which counsels us to consider the feelings of our family members and do what is best for them.

Further, we must seriously consider motherhood as distinct from a single female and think about what is ethically owed to mothers. Kecia Ali comments on Mary's pregnancy, labor, and delivery and states that the Qurʾan "affirms the sacredness and power of biologically female and specifically maternal experience; it invests childbearing with value."[92] The Arabic word for womb, *raḥim*, comes from the same root as the words for mercy, *raḥmān*, and compassion, *raḥīm*, which are two of God's divine names, *al-Raḥmān* and *al-Raḥīm*, and so, childbearing and mothers are connected to God's merciful and compassionate nature.[93] We must therefore think intentionally about mothers (and parenthood[94]) in our deliberations. Can, for example, a recent father partake in *mutʿa* marriage? Is it fair to the mother? What do we owe mothers?

The questions presented above only scratch the surface of the types of inquiries ethnographic research should attempt. Other questions include: Can there be just power dynamics in such multiple relationships? What is prostitution? Is consensual sex for money—like in *mutʿa*—prostitution? What is rape? Studies have shown that some individuals who enter a *mutʿa* do not have the ability to refuse. Would this be considered rape? Even if they receive money in exchange? It is also important to use ethnographic research to attempt to understand what marriage means in Islam and what meaning marriage should have for a society. For what reasons is marriage a morally desirable and just institution? Because marriage is loosely structured in both Islamic societies and *fiqh*, and since Muslim jurists have allowed other forms of marriage, like polygyny and *mutʿa*, and other sexual relations, like concubinage, these are complicated questions to answer. What about polygamy? Polygyny? *Mutʿa*? Why or why not monogamy? Do we owe children, whether they are the product of a monogamous marriage or *mutʿa*, anything? Should we consider whether and how it might affect them if the adults around them are in multiple relationships? What does *mutʿa* and sexual gratification outside of a traditional marriage mean for the permanent wife? What connects sexual intercourse, love, marriage, and other activities we find valuable? Finally, is not a fair and just monogamous relationship already an uphill, near impossible task? Is more than this asking for the impossible? These questions indicate the difficulty and complexity of the issues at hand and are only some of the questions that a legal ethnography should attempt to answer using a broad spectrum—age, class, gender, geographical location, sexual attitudes, and so on—of Muslim interlocutors. These questions also indicate the complicated and sometimes murky nature of what is considered moral or immoral from a sociological perspective. We then turn our attention to moral deliberations needed to evaluate sexual and marital ethics in the next section.

MORAL AND SOCIO-MORAL QUESTIONS

Many legal historians and scholars have argued that moral considerations inform Islamic law and cannot be discussed independent of it.[95] According to Mudarrisī, "engaging in broad moral discussion is necessary, not only for establishing a legal, moral theory but also for answering essential human existential questions."[96] Mudarrisī discusses the questions pertaining to moral and legal philosophy in the third volume of *al-Tashrīʿ al-Islāmī*. According to him, moral philosophy has three main values: love, justice, and life.[97] Mudarrisī argues that theology, morality, and law are one regenerating body where each one supports the other in turn.[98] In this section, I raise questions that aim to create links between moral philosophy and various legal implications. Although some of the moral considerations that underlined early *fiqh* do not fit our own modern sensibilities, here I try to speak directly to some contemporary moral considerations. I must begin this section by mentioning that I am not trained as a moral philosopher. My shortcomings notwithstanding, I advocate that in the context of debates regarding the permissibility of *mutʿa*, moral and socio-moral questions should be addressed alongside concerns related to marital and sexual ethics. Here I present *some* of the many questions we can and must consider in order to start this conversation.

The answers classical Muslim jurists provided to questions about sex and morality contain profound contradictions that are resolved using a variety of legal structures. Jurists allowed concubinage or extramarital sex with an enslaved woman, which was, in most cases, presumably nonconsensual, while simultaneously punishing adultery and rape; the Shiʿa allow *mutʿa* while prohibiting casual sex and prostitution. Some of these contradictions survive because, historically, the male elite have controlled the law- and value-making process.[99] However, this is not the case anymore, and the system bears rethinking.

The question of the permissibility of *mutʿa* is entangled with important moral questions. Although there are several questions and my list is not exhaustive, I will address seven key questions of morality in this section. First, is sexual activity connected to a Muslim's spiritual well-being? Posing this question allows us to consider the spiritual impact the body has on the soul, as opposed to conventional frameworks that examine the soul's impact on the body. If the answer is yes, then it seems reasonable to conclude that sexual activity should not be bought or sold the way it is in *mutʿa*. But if sexual activity does not have spiritual significance—if it is similar to being a sales clerk or typist, who both get paid for their services—then *mutʿa* may be faultless. While we know that nakedness during sexual intercourse is physical, psychological, and emotional, is it also spiritual? In other words, can humans sell, buy, or voluntarily partake in sexual activity without it affecting their spiritual being? Is transactional sexual intimacy somehow different from situations where we sell our labor as part of an economic transaction? Studying sexual objectification is an important development within sexual ethics,[100] and it acknowledges that the bodily nature of sex is morally significant. We should continue the trend and develop a richer understanding of the bodily experience of sex and its spiritual significance.

The second moral question relates to the concept of consent and sex. As shown in chapter 1, Muslim jurists deem a marriage legal when *ijab,* consent, is given by both the man and woman. Feminism and moral philosophy have long tried to complicate our understanding of consent, "its nature, when it is present and absent, and its ultimate moral force."[101] In many cases, some individuals cannot give consent; therefore, it is too simplistic to only refer to consent when dealing with questions related to sex and morality. Other factors might play an essential role, and other deliberations must be considered. Basically, we need to move beyond the legal idea of consent—a "yes" or "no"—and look at the moral question of *if* and *when* consent is possible. For example, moral philosophy tells us it is more important to ascertain when "yes" actually means "yes" then when "no" means "no" because ascertaining a no does not provide us with information about situations when a yes is given.[102] We have some indication that the Qurʾan acknowledges that not everyone can give consent: Q 24:32[103] commands those with power over enslaved women to not force them into the act of adultery with other men (for the sake of the slave owner making money off the sexual transaction).[104] Therefore, we need to think of consent as a moral question and not just a legal one. Feminists further the discussion of consent by adding that our thinking needs to incorporate at least two factors: coercion, both direct and indirect, and competence.[105] Why? First, because consensual (but unwanted) sex often harms a woman's autonomy in more subtle ways than rape, assault, or harassment.[106] Second, sex can be misleading because some of the physical actions of sex appear to convey trust, affection, care, and sensitivity alongside enjoyment and pleasure,[107] and this is morally consequential. For example, are war widows and financially strapped poor divorcees—without any coercion, including monetary—able to give consent to *mutʾa*? If the state provided for them, would they partake in this type of marriage? However, when asking these questions, I do not want to undermine their need or desire for sex and the satisfaction and pleasure associated with it. Moving on to thinking about competence: Are young women who might not be aware of the physiological effect of sexual intercourse on their physical and spiritual being able to give consent? This, alongside moral and feminist interventions, can be our entry point in thinking about consent and developing a morally strong standard for it.

The third moral question looks at the ethical questions around casual sex and the associated value of abstinence. Casual sex in the west largely escapes moral notice, nor does it raise much, if any, disapproval. The position that *mutʾa* is permissible matches up well with the casual sex model; the intentionality behind most temporary marriages is generally directed toward the pursuit of casual sex. A recent article from the "Modern Love" series in the *New York Times* presents the story of a white mother who approves of the *mutʾa* between her thirteen-year-old sexually precocious daughter and a Muslim boy from a religious family because it allows the boy to have sex with her daughter in a way his Muslim parents found acceptable.[108] This article highlights something Muslim scholars have mentioned in reference to *mutʾa*: It allows Muslims to engage in casual sex while feeling like they are still abiding by the moral dictates of Islam. Muslims—and almost anyone with access to western media—are confronted with images and discussions of casual sex in popular culture in a manner that undermines any notion of the virtue of abstinence or sexual restraint. Behind this is the role of what feminists have called the presence of "compulsory sexuality"[109] in society, and some problematize the easy formula of sexual activity equaling liberation.[110] In chapter 1, we saw that some Muslim feminists approve of *mut'a* because it takes away the stigma of virginity, and religiously sanctioning sexual exploration has liberatory potential. However, moral philosophy challenges the idea that the manifestation of positive feminism is the enjoyment of multiple sexual partners, and that sexual empowerment is synonymous with empowerment in general, arguing that the concept of compulsory sexuality helps us pay attention to the limitations of viewing sexuality as a path to liberation.[111]

Just as the concept of sexual empowerment is debated, abstinence is certainly one of the most maligned and misunderstood virtues in contemporary culture.[112] The word often evokes connotations of inhibition and prudery, but abstinence does not eliminate one's appetites or passions; it moderates them, enabling them to be informed by prudence and in this way used for the true good of the person.[113] If one has to be sexually active to realize ones' full personhood, then abstinence appears perverse and any form of sexual restraint suspect.[114] This is especially true in a culture that views sexual expression and pleasure as integral to personal health, happiness, and fulfillment. And if sexual expression is not necessarily limited to marital relationships for it to be seen as good, then even the notion of abstinence can be seen as arbitrary and oppressive.[115] As we read earlier and will discuss later in this chapter, sex indelibly affects individuals. Two people might look at casual sex as a passing indulgence, but its consequences are unpredictable; neither knows what reactions it might produce, what desires it might arouse, what needs it might reveal, and what harm it might cause—especially in the case of women, who have a different physiological experience of sex than men. And so, what was intended only as momentary gratification may prove to have unforeseen emotional repercussions and cause unexpected suffering or unhappiness.

Although sex should be enjoyable, it does not exist solely for the sake of pleasure. The obsessive focus on bodily pleasure often spirals into blank effacement of all things spiritual and noble. Søren Kierkegaard notes that despite the novelty achieved from experiencing an array of partners through casual sex, life ultimately succumbs to a cycle of sameness.[116] A good sex life cannot be achieved solely through physical gratification from multiple sexual partners; it must be wrung from the mundane nature of life and marriage. Multiple partners should not be shied away from simply because of a diminishing return of satisfaction. Even if it is enjoyable and relatively satisfying to engage in casual sex with multiple partners, it nevertheless might be morally problematic. Satisfaction can also be gained from refusing to jeopardize another person's moral and emotional security.

A secondary problem casual sex creates is the erosion of the discipline to be faithful within a marriage. Having never practiced abstinence, an individual might miss the variety of sexual partners or have difficulty remaining faithful to just one partner and the type of life monogamous marriage affords, creating a whole host of other problems.[117] Morally speaking, casual sex is altogether too much of a risk, especially since it is merely for occasional, momentary satisfaction. This is one of the strongest moral arguments in favor of abstinence.

The fourth moral consideration tries to focus on children's rights and child welfare issues stemming from the effects of multiple intimate relationships within family spaces.[118] There are two types of children that require our moral consideration: first, the children who exist within permanent marriages whose fathers (mothers cannot engage in *mut'a* while in a permanent marriage, a double standard addressed in the previous section) are partaking in temporary marriage(s); second, children conceived through temporary marriage. I regard it as a given that parents have a duty to protect their children from abuse and neglect, both physical and emotional. I also recognize that what counts as abuse or neglect can be different in the moral and legal spheres (legally a man is allowed to partake in *mut'a* while being married and having children), is sometimes difficult to determine (the age and gender of the child might make a difference), and may even change from context to context (for example, familial or geographical contexts may be a factor in determining abuse or neglect). Also, I assume that if parents fail to promote a child's interests, harm—sometimes lasting a lifetime—is caused. Questions about how *mut'a* affects children and what kind of moral neglect takes place due to it have never been formally considered, but to help us determine the permissibility of *mut'a*, they need to be addressed. One factor that separates *mut'a* from prostitution is that children produced through these marriages are considered legitimate—historically an important consideration within Muslim societies—and they have inheritance rights. As mentioned in chapter 1, no formal legal set up exists to make sure these children do receive their inheritances, nor is there a legal set up for monthly child support. Does the father participate in any childrearing activities when there is no formal legal requirement and how does such an absence affect the children? Here I am concerned with the moral responsibility of caring for the emotional well-being of children produced through permanent and temporary marriages. We must seriously consider actions that might place innocent children at risk of harm or neglect. Keeping children safe from harm is not simply a matter of physical safety; unless children are given continuous and positive attention, they will be harmed. This stewardship conception of parenting places a complex moral status onto the parents. This status involves two main factors: the rights of children and the needs of children. Parenting is thought of as a relation of care, advocacy, protection, and much more. Will we find that *mut'a* leads to parents being less caring and insensitive to the dependency and vulnerability of their children? Given the importance of what is at stake, both for the lives of our children and for society at large, the protection of children in our care is a matter of much moral significance. Therefore, I suggest thinking about our relationship with our children as a moral one and not just biological, encouraging a kind of appreciation for the moral meaning associated with bringing children into the world and the role of the family.

Marriage is a complex institution with layers of moral, social, and legal relations. Our fifth moral question asks if there is a morally ideal form of marriage? Is it monogamous? Polygynous? Polygamous? Polyandry? Temporary? and so on. In the American context, some Black Muslims see polygyny as a way of preserving the Black community.[119] Distorted gender ratios due to male incarceration, discriminatory educational structures, and underemployment have detrimentally affected Black marriages, and polygyny represents a practical way of providing women with husbands and fathers for their children.[120] Similarly, Saba Mahmood has shown how, in the Egyptian context, some women choose polygynous setups and find it fruitful. In contrast, India and China have more men than women due to large scale selective abortion of female fetuses, but this has not led to the invention of a tradition where one woman is allowed to marry several men or where several men choose to marry one woman.[121] I mention this to point out the role of patriarchy and gender discrimination in making it easy to see some purpose or usefeulness in polygyny; more often than not, contemporary polygyny is accompanied by sexist culture and theology, hierarchical power relations, and significant poverty. For our purposes then, traditionally conceived polygyny is morally objectionable when it precludes genuine equality between spouses. The genuine equality I mention is not just a present-day ethical ideal for marriage but something the Qur'an requires for polygynous marriages—and poignantly points out is most unlikely to be achieved.[122] The most obvious issues with polygyny are: gender discrimination, whereby men may marry multiple women but women may not marry multiple men; possible child neglect; and sometimes the coercion of women. Even if women are not physically forced into polygynous marriages, they might feel familial, religious, or economic pressure to enter them. I recognize that these faults are not necessarily specific to polygyny—some of them can and do exist in monogamous marriage—but here, my concern is temporary marriage, which is a type of polygynous marriage. The correlation between polygyny, discrimination, and abuse is seriously troubling, but the underlying causes are difficult to define. Instead, my core argument is that traditional polygyny perpetuates an inequality that directly affects women and children. However, I am also uncomfortable with accepting that, by default, lifelong monogamous marriage is the institution that can be best adapted to serve the interests of society, families, romantic partners, and children—and this is in part because of its association with Christianity. At the very least, we can attempt to move beyond framing the polygyny question as good versus bad and engage in a pragmatic assessment of whether polygyny might be regulated to be consistent with contemporary conceptions of equality and fairness in family life. Rethinking Islamic law in this context can ameliorate the power and bargaining disparities multiple marriages engender.

Our sixth moral question stems from thinking about the feelings of women in polygynous relationships. What are the moral implications of the negative feelings women in such relationships might have about each other, and about themselves, because they are co-wives? Indeed, there are some polygynous relationships where the women involved love each other and are like sisters, and others where the women are bothered by each other and so are negatively affected. Here I want to ask how ideas about the other wife's (or wives') desirability, beauty, strength, success, or a host of other things can unnerve these women. In particular, some of the feelings I want us to think about are envy, jealousy, passive or active rivalry, anger, maternal jealousy, and sexual jealousy and rivalry, among others. These feelings are produced in women and caused by men when they simultaneously marry multiple women. What is the moral weight of these negative emotions? Who should be held accountable for this moral weight and suffering? And how should we account for the complex emotional life polygyny produces? Should questions about the effects this type of marriage has on the emotional lives of women also enter into conversations about the moral acceptability of temporary marriage? Some people might criticize me for essentializing or adhering to stereotypes about women, but I am not claiming that all women necessarily feel this way. We do know that the Prophet Muhammad's wives ended up dealing with some of these emotions. So, given that for Muslims, he is a perfect example of a human being, we must seriously consider that if the Prophet Muhammad was not able to have a tranquil household without jealousy and strife between his wives, then we are likely not able to do so either. We must account for the grief, misery, strife, and a lack of well-being felt by these women. I do not necessarily want to promote monogamy here because I do not think it is perfect and without flaw; rather, I simply want to point out the moral issues related to polygyny. Monogamy is by no means perfect, but morally speaking, it is less treacherous, and it is simpler to work toward justice and equality within it.

Finally, our last moral question under consideration: Is a Muslim's body at their own disposal, and can they to do with it as they see fit? We can sell our kidneys or livers, but is this the same as selling sexual services? Is it morally permissible to profit by allowing one's body to be used to satisfy someone else's sexual desire, like in most *mut'a* marriages? In other words, is it morally permissible to make oneself an object that someone else can use to satisfy their sexual appetite, just as one satisfies their hunger with a burger? A narrow and traditional conceptualization of *mut'a* views it as one person (a woman) surrendering to another (a man) solely for the satisfaction of his sexual desire. When a person is used as an object to fulfill a desire, that desire is directed toward sex, not toward the person *as a human being*. The *mut'a* contract deals with the enjoyment of a part, not with the entire being, of a person. However, there is another way to view *mut'a*: through mutual desire and consent. Perhaps both persons are satisfying their desires (i.e., it is mutual), and there is no idea of gain; this "relationship" is only to fulfill the desire for (mutual) sexual satisfaction. Except for the question related to moral harm, there appears to be nothing morally contemptible about contracting a *mut'a* if there is reciprocity and consent. But one consideration remains: whether this is disliked by God because our bodies are ultimately vessels God created and should be treated with care. This is similar to the Kantian view that even if there is consent between two individuals, this sexual activity is not morally permissible if they are using each other as means and not as ends.[123] If giving in to sexual desire does not involve immorality, then anyone can engage in sexual intercourse and make whatever use they want of their body. If sex outside of marriage is unobjectionable—Muslim scholars allowed concubinage—then there is no harm in *mut'a*. But if extramarital sex is objectionable and violates moral dictates, it follows that there should be conditions outlining when sex is not in line with morality. There must be a moral principle that serves as the foundation for restraining our freedom to exercise our sexual impulses and restricting the use of our bodies.

Regardless of whether or not the arguments in this section are properly deemed moral arguments, arguments about the permissibility of *mut'a* ought not to fully convince anyone until questions like these are answered. And although I was unable to fully trace the ever-shifting and amorphous boundaries of the moral discussion of sexual morality and marriage, I hope at least to have advanced the discussion here, if only by encouraging others to further develop it. I suggest starting this discussion by being brave enough to concede the worst, namely that "human sexual interaction is essentially manipulative—physically, psychologically, emotionally, and even intellectually."[124] By admitting the worst (even as I recognize that sexual activity has positive value as an expression of love and commitment), we can be more judicious and can avoid easy justifications of certain types of sexual activity. Maybe the problem is not that *mut'a*, or adultery, prostitution, or casual sex, do not provide satisfaction or cannot be argued for from various modern contexts, but that they are morally problematic and must be thought about in a morally systematic way. Furthermore, considering the ways in which these acts may be morally problematic requires a greater understanding of sex and sexuality.

SCIENCE OF SEXUALITY

Mudarrisī accepts that the way to make legal rulings more consistent with the current times and to achieve the *maqāṣid* of the law "is through interaction with modern fields, especially those which relate to societal issues, such as relevant scientific expertise."[125] He posits that there is room for technical-scientific experts to play a significant role in legal thinking.[126] As an extension of his thinking, I propose taking the science of sexuality seriously in order to reevaluate gendered sexuality in Muslim legal scholarship.

Although there is no simple definition of sexuality, the 2014 *APA Handbook of Sexuality and Psychology* argues:

> Sexuality cannot be distilled down to one essential element but is composed of many; sexuality can also be understood as fundamentally relational, not a "something" at all, produced interplay within or among individuals, interpersonal interactions, or institutions. Sexuality can be understood as a laundry list of individual and social experiences and attributes, including desire, behaviors, identities, fantasies, preferences, orientations, and identities at the individual level and incorporating both mind and body, as well as sexual mores, laws, standards, communities, institutions, and cultures, at the social level. These intersecting dimensions coalesce and disaggregate to form a dynamic and changing system.[127]

In other words, sexuality is multidimensional, a primary aspect of identity, and a core part of a person's health and psychological well-being.

I am aware that the assumption of a universal sexual subjectivity can lead to an Orientalist understanding of sexuality.[128] I am not proposing such an understanding of sexuality, rather I am recommending further sophisticated investigation. The Qur'an is not explicit about sexuality in general (as mentioned earlier), and the only mention of it is Zulaykhā's sexual overtures to Yūsuf. However, it does addresses men about women's sexuality. It "affirms female sexuality and encourages men to value women's experiences of intimacy."[129]

In general, Muslim scholars claim that male sexuality is different from female sexuality; the former is virile, demands variety, and therefore requires provisions like *mut'a*.[130] Most Islamic laws that deal with sexuality are based on this understanding. Scientific research reveals that we are at the brink of a revolutionary new understanding of female sexuality,[131] and this has profound implications, not only in the social realm but also in the Islamico-legal realm. Groundbreaking research on human sexuality complicates the simplistic understanding of female sexuality presented by most Muslim scholars. Muslim scholars have failed to consider new theoretical developments and technologies and their implications for Islamic law. In this section, I call attention to the areas that require the consideration of Islamic scholars in order to move towards a equitable sexual and marital ethics: understanding of female anatomy, physiological changes that occur during female orgasm and its ethical implications, new research on sexual fluidity, knowledge of sex drive, an understanding of the scope of intercourse and pleasure beyond orgasm, as well as familiarity with technological advances. Muslim scholars must deliberate upon these areas in order to advance the field and make it just.[132]

Surprisingly, knowledge of female sexual anatomy is a relatively recent development. The first page of the *Huffington Post* site *Cliteracy* has three statements: "We put a man on the moon in 1969. We developed the Internet in 1982. We discovered the full anatomy of the clitoris in 1998."[133] These statements use irony to succinctly illustrate the gendered nature of research on female sexuality. Information on the clitoris is available in select medical journals but still invisible in daily discourse. This is the consequence of an extensive history of male-dominated sciences ignoring the importance of the clitoris. Sigmund Freud, in his work on psychosexual development, wrote that a clitoral orgasm is an immature and infantile orgasm, while a vaginal orgasm is a mature one: "Elimination of clitoral sexuality is a necessary precondition for the development of femininity [. . .] since it is immature and masculine in its nature."[134] This false conclusion is still largely accepted in the western world and has hold of the public imagination. Dr. Charles Mayo Goss, former editor of *Gray's Anatomy*, removed the anatomical drawing of the clitoris from the book in 1947.[135] This erasure raises two questions: one about the significance of gender issues (related to ideas about sex, the body, and medical treatment) and the other about our belief in the objectivity of science.

It was only in 1998 that Australian urologist Helen O'Connell captured the entire anatomy of the clitoris for the first time; this challenged every description of the clitoris to date. She demonstrated not only its immense size, spanning from the front of the body to the back, but also the number of nerves it has—8,000, two times more than the penis. Other studies have since shown that the size of the clitoris increases as women grow older, which increases the likelihood of orgasm for women as they age, unlike men, who suffer from pain, erectile dysfunction, and a decrease in orgasms. The point of mentioning this research is twofold: first, the most basic aspect of the clitoris, its anatomy, was unknown until 1998, illustrating the gendered bias when it comes to female sexuality. Second, how could scholars, including Muslim scholars, understand female sexuality when even its anatomy was not understood until recently? So, how does this knowledge change the way we address marital and sexual ethics?

Much like the absence of knowledge about the form and function of the female clitoris, not much has been written on or even considered regarding the physiological changes that take place during the female orgasm or its implications for sexual ethics.[136] During orgasm, the hormone oxytocin is released.[137] Oxytocin is perhaps best known for its role in female reproduction. It is released in large amounts during labor and aids childbirth; indeed, one of the oldest applications of the drug oxytocin is as a therapeutic agent during labor and delivery.[138] It is also released after stimulating the nipples during nursing and facilitates breastfeeding and mother-infant bonding.[139] However, recent studies have started investigating oxytocin's role in various other contexts, including orgasm, social recognition, bonding, and maternal behavior.[140] Oxytocin is often called the "love hormone" or the "cuddle hormone" because it heightens feelings of trust and intimacy, even among complete strangers. For example, a recent study published in *Nature* demonstrated that when strangers were asked to play a game in teams, an oxytocin nasal spray raised trust among team members.[141] It logically follows then that the hormone would further increase levels of trust between sexual partners. Research has established that oxytocin is released into the female brain during sexual activity and is considered crucial in forming a monogamous bond with her sexual partner.[142] The relationship between oxytocin and its role in trust building and social bonding should be taken into account when considering the permissibility of *mutʿa*. Separation from a partner with whom a woman has experienced orgasm could be a physiologically painful experience for her, given that her hormones have created a bond with this person, while the man has not formed a similar bond with her. Therefore, should *mutʿa* be allowed since the wife forms a bond with the husband upon achieving orgasm during sexual intercourse? In light of this, how should we proceed if we want to keep gender justice and sexual ethics at the forefront of our consideration?

Another factor to consider within the field of sexuality is Lisa M. Diamond's concept of sexual fluidity, which was influenced by the findings related to erotic plasticity and elaborated on in one of the most important recent works on female sexuality.[143] Diamond followed 100 women over the course of ten years, conducting interviews every two years.[144] Her research method differs from typical surveys or experiments on human sexuality because it is longitudinal, while other studies are often cross-sectional. Her thesis is that women, more so than men, have situation-dependent sexuality.[145] Although women, like men, appear to be born with a predetermined sexual orientation, women may experience variation as they enter different stages of their lives or different situations. For example, a woman with an exclusively heterosexual past can suddenly identify as a lesbian, or the reverse.[146] Diamond illustrates how the defining feature of female sexuality is fluidity; women's sexual responsiveness (and desire for either men or women) depends upon certain circumstances and is not fixed.[147] If Muslim scholars incorporated the idea of erotic sexual fluidity into their understandings of female sexuality, this could result in changes to their interpretations of Islamic law. Or, at the very least, it could debunk their understanding of male and female sexual desire.

In her most recent work on sexual diversity, Diamond suggests that we consider a new framework for studying sexuality.[148] She recommends an approach that accounts for *time* and *change*, since the most distinctive character of female sexuality is its variability over time. She advocates for the use of a dynamic system of models, which treats a woman's capacity for variability as a central rather than a peripheral phenomenon, and therefore seeks to understand both change and stability within female sexuality.[149] One major contribution of Diamond's new work is her argument that women's sexuality might be fundamentally different from that of men, and therefore, for various historical and contextual reasons, research has been too fixated on explaining sexual behaviors and orientations through a fixed male lens. This has also been the case with Islamic law, and it needs reconceptualization in light of current research.

Another area that requires greater attention within the field of sexuality studies concerns the sex drive.[150] The sex drive refers to sexual motivation, including frequency and intensity of sexual desires. It may be measured in numerous ways, including sexual thoughts, fantasies, desired frequency of intercourse, number of partners, and masturbation. Muslim scholars have held contradictory views of the female sex drive. They state that women have either a low sex drive or such a high sex drive that their sexuality is a danger to society. Looking outside of Muslim legal discourse, for example, the earliest extant erotic compendium in Arabic, *Encyclopedia of Pleasure* (*Jawami' al-ladha*), we find stories of hyper-sexed women. These narratives reinforce the common notion that women are closer to nature and therefore have greater libidos than men,[151] a notion that Pernilla Myrne confirmed was indeed found throughout various authorities in late antiquity and the early medieval world.[152] However, Islamic law has enshrined the opposite notion: women have a low sex drive, men are virile, and therefore men need multiple partners to fulfill their "natural" sex drive through polygyny and *mut'a*. The idea of a naturally low sex drive is based on an idea that emphasizes traits as biologically innate rather than socially constructed or shaped. Muslim scholars who are currently researching sexual and marital ethics need to seriously study this distinction. The perpetuation of the assumption that women have a naturally low sex drive is also due to women's lack of education about their own sexuality. Sex education for women focuses more on reproduction than sexual pleasure, leaving women uninformed about their bodies in relation to sexuality. The idea that women have lower sex drives is not limited to Muslim scholars; most cultures perpetuate this. However, the perpetuation of the assumption that women have low sex drives has changed slightly over time.

What role does masturbation—which is available to most everyone, except maybe some individuals who might have a physical disability that prohibits them from being able to physically perform it—play in our understanding of sexuality and sexual desire? Masturbation leads to orgasm, for both sexes, almost every time, while sex with a partner can be more complicated and may or may not lead to orgasm, especially for individuals who are biologically female. Most schools of Islamic law frown upon masturbation, allowing it in cases where something worse, like *zinā'*, fornication, might be the other alternative. Is it time that we incorporate the role masturbation plays when we think about sexual satisfaction? Additionally, if one can self-satisfy, then what does this mean for our understanding of sex? What does this mean for the permissibility of *mut'a*?

Another problem is that some circles define sex as exclusively penile-vaginal intercourse. Further, when it comes to heterosexual partnered sex, sexual activities such as oral sex or manual simulation, which typically imitate intercourse, are not included in studies on orgasm. Muslim scholars, like secular ones, have an erroneous view of the female sex drive and the orgasm gap. Acknowledging this misconception, while also incorporating advances in the field, could result in a more complex and nuanced picture of female sexuality. The idea of pleasure beyond orgasm is also missing in public discourse. Sexual education should be reformed to encourage less gender-differentiated sex socialization and to educate youth about human sexuality—without the type of heterosexual male bias present in discourses on *mut'a*. One example of pleasure beyond orgasm can be found in the book *Finding Your Sexual Voice: Celebrating Female Sexuality*.[153] The authors posit that sexuality is intimate and interactive, with a range of roles, meanings, and outcomes, and they present the "Good Enough Sex" (GES) model, which emphasizes sexuality as a process of giving and receiving pleasure-oriented touch. According to the authors, sexuality involves sensual, playful, and erotic touch in addition to penetration.[154] Most men stop being sexually active at fifty, sixty, or even as young as forty, turning to erection medications, penile injections, testosterone, and other medical interventions. Despite these treatments, few men return to having predictable erections. In time, when sexual encounters do not lead to intercourse, McCarthy and McCarthy suggest transitioning to an alternative erotic or sensual scenario of GES. GES promotes enjoying and receiving erotic stimulation rather than being obsessed with intercourse.

The GES model is key—for both men and woman—to maintaining a healthy sexuality while aging. Thus, scholarly discourses that view *mutʿa* specifically as a solution to men having high sex drives must be more nuanced and include the role forms of pleasure outside of intercourse, like touching, as key to healthy sexuality.

Scholarship on transgender sexuality further complicates discussions of sexuality. Bockting addresses this growing body of research, which is a domain where the conventional gender binary that has dominated researchers' conceptions of sexuality and sexual bodies and the physical coherence of the sexual body has been fundamentally challenged.[155] He reviews literature on identity development and the health of transgender people and demonstrates how these identities remain distinct from, albeit related to, issues of sexual orientation, attraction, and behavior. Bockting's assessment illuminates how heteronormativity and unequal gender hierarchies are forms of oppression and have shaped public policies affecting sexual rights. He demonstrates the detrimental effects such policies have had on the development of sexuality and sexual health. Interestingly, Muslim scholars have held a positive view of transgender sexuality.[156] Khomeini issued a positive fatwa on the permissibility of sex reassignment surgery for transgender people in 1964, when the struggle for transgender rights and reassignment surgery was still in its infancy in the west.[157] Not only is Iran ranked the second highest when it comes to the number of sex reassignment surgeries performed, the state also subsidizes these operations and facilitates the related bureaucracy (e.g., changing gender registration on official paperwork).[158] Given this example, Muslim scholars should also incorporate modern scientific findings on sexuality into their thinking about female sexuality and marital and sexual ethics in relation to Islamic law.

Historically, Muslims have published numerous texts on sex and sexuality. The aforementioned *Encyclopedia of Pleasure* by ʿAlī b. Nasr al-Kātib was written in Baghdad between the late tenth and early eleventh centuries. The *Encyclopedia of Pleasure* has 43 chapters and covers every conceivable sexual practice, with titles like, "On the Kinds and Techniques of Coition," "On Jealousy," "On the Advantages of Nonvirgins Over Virgins," and "On Increasing the Sexual Pleasure of Man and Woman."[159] The compendium advises its readers on female pleasure, discussing female physiology and giving detailed classifications of women's libidos and types of orgasms. It even recommends postcoital conversation and cuddling—a hallmark of civilized lovemaking and counsel present in both the Qur'an and *aḥādīth*.[160] Al-Kātib considered women's sexual desire, and it was also socially acceptable to write about it in a detailed fashion. Indeed, historically, the act of pleasing women and satisfying them belonged to the realm of refined behavior, and knowledge about female sexuality should be part of a refined man's education. Therefore, the *Encyclopedia of Pleasure* includes chapters on sexual technique, sexual health, and—remarkably—a chapter on female orgasm, with classifications of women regarding their attitudes toward sex and how they reach climax. There is no reason that this spirit should not be revived today and further informed by the science of sexuality.

Although none of the abovementioned scientific studies are conclusive, they do complicate our understanding of human sexuality. First, they point out that assumptions regarding human sexuality are based primarily on men's experiences, because most research on sexual orientation has been conducted on and by men. Therefore, these studies describe men more or less accurately, but their conclusions do not always apply to women. More specifically, such research demonstrates that female, rather than male, sexuality is fluid and plastic. These studies also show us that the nature of difference (such as women's supposedly "naturally low" sex drives and the "orgasm gap") is not necessarily biological but may have a lot to do with complex interactions between genes, hormones, maturation states, personality traits, situational factors, interpersonal influences, and cultural norms, and therefore, they are not easily designated as male or female. Juxtaposing Muslim scholars' ideas about fe/male sexuality with current scientific research exposes the gaps and contradictions present in both. Exploring the interplay between studies of the science of sexuality and Islamic law is crucial to moving Islamic law forward in a just and equitable manner. Taking the study of the science of sexuality in conjunction with Muslim feminist methodological intervention and studies of morality and ethnography allow us to examine *mutʿa* in a more holistic fashion.

CONCLUSION

The institution of *mutʿa* and its utility is complicated—different groups consider it either obsolete or cutting-edge. In this chapter, I called for a methodological reappraisal of approaches to the topic and argue that answering this query is contingent upon a deeper multidimensional study that involves: (1) intentionally utilizing Muslim feminist methodological interventions toward a new exegesis of Q 4:24; (2) conducting socio-legal ethnographic studies among Muslim men, women, and children and treating their voices as a critical source for law; (3) engaging earnestly with moral philosophy in our legal thinking; (4) taking the science of sexuality seriously in order to reevaluate gendered sexuality in Muslim scholarship; and subsequently incorporating these interventions into our thinking about sexual and marital ethics in Islamic law. These areas and approaches are not completely distinct, as each study relates to and has implications for the others. Most importantly, this calling for a reassessment of the way that the institution of *mutʿa* is understood does not go against the texts and traditions that Muslims embrace, but with them. As illustrated earlier in the chapter, historically, there has been significant room for juristic discourse to maneuver and still remain grounded in the Islamic tradition. I am hopeful that this exercise in mapping potential approaches and methodologies will not only motivate scholars and activists to heed the call but also potentially inspire us to reexamine institutions other than *mutʿa* in light of this multidimensional approach. The contemporary interpretive community can and should make choices that move us in the direction of gender justice and equitable sexual and marital ethics. This chapter presents one path that could lead us there.

NOTES

1. I also request avoiding *bidʿa*, illicit innovation, which is a paradox at the heart of *ijtihād.*
2. Sulayman b. al-Ash'at al-Sijistani Abu Dawud, *Kitab al-sunun*, trans. Ahmad Hasan (Lahore; Muhammad Ashraf, 1984), 3:1019, hadith no. 3585.
3. Kecia Ali, *Sexual Ethics and Islam: Feminist Reflections on Qur'an, Hadith, and Jurisprudence*, 1st ed. (Oxford: Oneworld Publications, 2006), 72.
4. Ali, *Sexual Ethics and Islam*, 72.
5. Hina Azam, *Sexual Violation in Islamic Law* (Cambridge: Cambridge University Press, 2015), 7.
6. Ebrahim Moosa, "Recovering the Ethical: Practice, Politics, and Tradition," in *The Shari'a: History, Ethics and Law*, ed. Amyn B. Sajoo (I. B. Tauris & Company, Limited, 2018), 47.
7. Moosa, "Recovering the Ethical," 42.
8. Ibid., 41.
9. Ibid., 47.
10. The idea that a husband could violate or commit a sexual crime against his wife simply did not arise.
11. The reader would be correct to ask if I am qualified to call myself a *mujtāhida*. As a bare minimum defense, I would respond that whether or not I am qualified, the questions I raise here, and the path to reinterpretation I present, can be considered on its own merits. Additionally, the reader might note that *fiqh* (juristic law) scholars clearly indicate that the process of *ijtihād* (the independent exercise of judgment) is human and therefore fallible and can only produce rules that are approximate articulations of *sharīʿa* (Divine Law). Thus, it follows that as long as *fiqh* is the result of sincere *ijtihād*, any conclusion qualifies as a possible and legitimate articulation of *sharīʿa*. Moreover, Muslim jurists across time have thought that to make an error in *ijtihād* is not only probable but also permissible and worthy of reward provided the

mujtahid/a is sincere and earnest in his or her attempt. This also helps me to illustrate the inherent pluralism of Islamic legal thinking.

12. For a detailed study of his *maqāṣid* work in English, see Hasan Beloushi, "The Theory of *Maqāṣid al-Sharīʿa* in Shīʿī Jurisprudence: Muḥammad Taqī al-Mudarrisī as a Model" (PhD diss., University of Exeter, 2014); and for a full intellectual biography of Mudarrasī, see chapter 2, 62–116.

13. Beloushi, "The Theory of *Maqāṣid al-Sharīʿa*," 96.

14. Ibid., 133.

15. Ibid., 191.

16. Beloushi, "The Theory of *Maqāṣid al-Sharīʿa*," 186. He writes that "the general characteristics of Mudarrisī's epistemology lie in the belief that reason is the source of truth, because reason is differentiated from desire as the source of error. He established this epistemology to be valid for all disciplines of knowledge, and therefore applied it himself in his theological as well as his jurisprudential work," Beloushi, "The Theory of *Maqāṣid al-Sharīʿa*," 131.

17. Beloushi, "The Theory of *Maqāṣid al-Sharīʿa*," 135.

18. Ibid., 144.

19. Ibid., 263.

20. Upon reading this article, Mudarrisī may or may not agree with all the paths taken, questions asked, and connections made. Maybe he will say I expand the scope of the application more than he intended, but I trust he will agree that what has taken place in this article is in the spirit of his thinking and is a good faith attempt at connecting his theory to a method. The reader might also be correct in thinking that a clear one-on-one correspondence between Mudarrisī's *maqāṣid al-sharīʿa* and the methodology I present has not been made. To this, I respond that this is a preliminary attempt. I deal with his theory in broad strokes and connect it to my methodological questions and do not dwell on the minutia.

21. Beloushi, "The Theory of *Maqāṣid al-Sharīʿa*," 322.

22. Ibid., 84–99.

23. The term "Muslim feminist" has been debated. Some Muslim feminists are reluctant to present themselves as such because of the negative connotations that the term bears since feminism is associated with colonialism. Others, however, defend their adherence to the broader category of feminism, but work within a religious framework and qualify their efforts with the descriptive adjective "Muslim." Fatima Seedat, "When Islam and Feminism Converge," *Muslim World* 103, no. 3 (2013): 406.

24. I owe this observation to conversations with Rahel Fischbach.

25. Ayesha A. Hidayatullah, *Feminist Edges of the Qur'an*, 1st ed. (Oxford: Oxford University Press, 2014). Hidayatullah writes that there are two mutually exclusive conditions for feminist approaches to the Qurʾan: we must either question the just nature of God or we must question the Qurʾan's divinity because in her final analysis, it is not possible to unread the gender inequality in the Qurʾan.

26. A summary of feminist hermeneutics of the Qurʾan developed by Riffat Hassan, Amina Wadud, Asma Barlas, and others can be found in Asma Barlas, "Women's Readings of the Qurʾān," in *The Cambridge Companion to the Qurʾān*, ed. Jane McAuliffe (Cambridge: Cambridge University Press, 2006) 255–71. The works of

Ziba Mir-Hosseni and Kecia have presented groundbreaking feminist engagements with *fiqh*. See Ziba Mir-Hosseini, "Muslim Women's Quest for Equality: Between Islamic Law and Feminism," *Critical Inquiry* 32, no. 4 (Summer 2006) 629–45; Ziba Mir-Hosseini, "The Construction of Gender in Islamic Legal Thought and Strategies for Reform," *Hawwa* 1, no. 1 (2003): 1–28; Kecia Ali, *Sexual Ethics and Islam: Feminist Reflections on Qur'an, Hadith, and Jurisprudence* (Oxford: Oneworld, 2006); and Kecia Ali, *Marriage and Slavery in Early Islam* (Cambridge, MA: Harvard University Press, 2010).

27. This method has been successfully explored by feminist scholars in connection with various issues related to women. See the work of Ziba Mir-Hosseini, Kecia Ali, Amina Wadud, Hadia Mubarak, Celene Ibrahim, Ayesha Hidayatullah, Ayesha Chaudhry, Fatima Seedat, Aisha Geissinger, Hina Azam, Zahra Ayubi, and Laury Silvers.

28. Fazlur Rahman, *Major Themes of the Qur'an* (Minneapolis: Bibliotheca, 1980), xv.

29. Hidayatullah, *Feminist Edges of the Qur'an*, 87.

30. This is not a comprehensive list of all the *āyāt* that could be brought into conversation but only a brief overview that illustrates what is meant by intratextuality; many more *āyāt* could be added to the list of those that I cover.

31. Q 2:187, "It has been made permissible for you to be intimate with your wives during the nights preceding the fast. Your spouses are a garment for you as you are for them. God knows that you were deceiving yourselves. So He has accepted your repentance and pardoned you. So now you may be intimate with them and seek what God has prescribed for you. (You may) eat and drink until you see the light of dawn breaking the darkness of night, then complete the fast until nightfall. Do not be intimate with your spouses while you are meditating in the mosques. These are the limits set by God, so do not exceed them. This is how God makes His revelations clear to people, so they may become mindful (of Him)."

32. Q 2:222, "They ask you (O Prophet) about menstruation. Say, 'Beware of its harm! So keep away, and do not have intercourse with your wives during their monthly cycles until they are purified. When they purify themselves, then you may approach them in the manner specified by God. Surely God loves those who always turn to Him in repentance and those who purify themselves.'"

33. Q 2:223,"Your wives are like farmland for you, so approach them (consensually) as you please. And send forth something good for yourselves. Be mindful of God, and know that you will meet Him. And give good news to the believers."

34. Q 4:1, "O humanity! Be mindful of your Lord Who created you from a single soul, and from it He created its mate, and through both He spread countless men and women. And be mindful of God—in Whose Name you appeal to one another—and (honour) family ties. Surely God is ever Watchful over you."

35. Q 4:3, "Of you fear you might fail to give orphan women their (due) rights (if you were to marry them), then marry other women of your choice—two, three, or four. But if you are afraid you will fail to maintain justice, then (content yourselves with) one or those (bondwomen) in your possession. This way you are less likely to commit injustice."

36. Q 4:34, "Men are the caretakers of women, as men have been provisioned by God over women and tasked with supporting them financially. And righteous women are devoutly obedient and, when alone, protective of what God has entrusted them with. And if you sense ill-conduct from your women, advise them (first), (if they persist,) do not share their beds, (but if they still persist,) then discipline them (gently). But if they change their ways, do not be unjust to them. Surely God is Most High, All-Great."

37. Q 4:128, "If a woman fears indifference or neglect from her husband, there is no blame on either of them if they seek (fair) settlement, which is best. Humans are ever inclined to selfishness. But if you are gracious and mindful (of God), surely God is All-Aware of what you do."

38. Q 4:129, "You will never be able to maintain (emotional) justice between your wives—no matter how keen you are. So do not totally incline towards one leaving the other in suspense. And if you do what is right and are mindful (of God), surely God is All-Forgiving, Most Merciful. But if they choose to separate, God will enrich both of them from His bounties. And God is Ever-Bountiful, All-Wise."

39. Q 9:71, "The believers, both men and women, are guardians of one another. They encourage good and forbid evil, establish prayer and pay alms-tax, and obey God and His Messenger. It is they who will be shown God's mercy. Surely God is Almighty, All-Wise."

40. Q 30:21, "And one of His signs is that He created for you spouses from among yourselves so that you may find comfort in them. And He has placed between you compassion and mercy. Surely in this are signs for people who reflect."

41. Q 7:189, "He is the One Who created you from a single soul, then from it made its spouse so he may find comfort in her. After he had been united with her, she carried a light burden that developed gradually. When it grew heavy, they prayed to God, their Lord, 'If you grant us good offspring, we will certainly be grateful.'"

42. Q 39:6, "He created you (all) from a single soul, then from it He made its mate. And he produced for you four pairs of cattle. He created you in the wombs of your mothers (in stages), one development after another, in three layers of darkness. That is God—you Lord! All authority belongs to Him. There is no god (worthy of worship) except Him. How can you then be turned away?"

43. Q 51:49, "And We created pairs of all things so perhaps you would be mindful."

44. Q 49:13, "O humanity! Indeed, We created you from a male and a female, and made you into peoples and tribes so that you may (get to) know one another. Surely the most noble of you in the sight of God is the most righteous among you. God is truly All-Knowing, All-Aware"

45. Q 75:39, "[P]roducing from it both sexes, male and female."

46. Amina Wadud, *Inside the Gender Jihad: Women's Reform in Islam* (Oxford: Oneworld, 2006), 192–93.

47. Asma Barlas, *Believing Women in Islam: Unreading Patriarchal Interpretations of the Qur'an* (Austin: University of Texas Press, 2002), 164–65.

48. Celene Ibrahim, *Women and Gender in the Qur'an* (Oxford: Oxford University Press, 2020).

49. Rawand Osman, *Female Personalities in the Qur'an and Sunna: Examining the Major Sources of Shi'i Islam* (New York: Routledge, 2014).

50. Asma Lamrabet, *Women in the Qur'an: An Emancipatory Reading*, trans. Myriam Francois-Cerrah (New York: Kube Publishing Ltd, 2016); and Asma Lamrabet *Women and Men in the Qur'ān*, trans. Muneera Salem-Murdock (Cham, Switzerland: Palgrave Macmillian, 2018).

51. Hadia Mubarak's forthcoming book, *Rebellious Wives, Neglectful Husbands: Controversies in Modern Qur'anic Commentaries* (Oxford: Oxford University Press, forthcoming in Jan 2022).

52. Ali, *Sexual Ethics and Islam*, 122.

53. Hidayatullah, *Feminist Edges of the Qur'an*, 85.

54. Fatema Mernissi, *Can We Women Head a Muslim State*? (Lahore, Pakistan: Simorgh, Women's Resource and Publications Centre, 1991).

55. Sa'diyya Shaikh, "Knowledge, Women, and Gender in the Hadith: A Feminist Interpretation," *Islam and Muslim-Christian Relations* 15, no. 1 (2004): 99–108.

56. N. H. Barazangi, *Woman's Identity and Rethinking the Hadith* (London: Ashgate Publishing, 2015).

57. Hidayatullah, *Feminist Edges of the Qur'an*, 86.

58. Taking the tradition seriously is not about stagnation or being against growth. It is rather embracing the intellectual heritage of Muslim scholarship while still being critical about it. I agree with the saying: tradition is not the worship of ashes but the preservation of fire. See Sherman Jackson, "Taqlīd, Legal Scaffolding and the Scope of Legal Injunctions in Post-Formative Theory," *Islamic Law and Society* 3, no. 2 (1996): 165–92, https://doi.org/10.1163/1568519962599104.

59. Ṣaḥiḥ al-Bukhārī, Kitab al-Nikah [Chapter of Marriage], volume 7 of Sahih al Bukhari, 1st ed. (Cairo: Dar al Ta'seel, 2012), 100, Hadith #522.

Sahih Muslim, Kitab Fada'il al Sahaba, volume 1 of 1st ed. (Riyadh, Saudi Arabia: Dar Tayba, 2006) 1145, hadith #2449.

60. Q 33:21, "Indeed, in the Messenger of God you have an excellent example for whoever has hope in God and the Last Day and remembers God often."

61. Kecia Ali, "'A Beautiful Example': The Prophet Muḥammad as a Model for Muslim Husbands," *Islamic Studies* 43, no. 2 (2004): 275.

62. The most famous one that causes serious concern and discomfort for Muslim feminists is the Prophet Muhammad's marriage to ʿAʾisha, who was presumably a child at the time. Legal scholars have used this example to permit child marriages between Muslim adults men and young girls. Muslim feminist have argued that "it is possible to hold that his conduct is exceptional in certain matters without thereby criticizing that conduct" (Ali, "'A Beautiful Example,'" 290). This means child marriage does not have to be considered legal in Islamic rulings because it was an exceptional case permitted only to the Prophet Muhammad.

63. Ali, "'A Beautiful Example,'" 288.

64. There are quite a few examples of *aḥādīth* that "liken them [women] to donkeys and dogs or described them as 'crooked' (from a bent rib), 'a trial' (for male Muslims), or as the majority of the inhabitants of Hell. Those that 'command' obedience of the wife to her husband and suggest that women's entry into paradise is dependent

on their husbands' pleasure are repugnant to Muslims, male and female" (Ali, "'A Beautiful Example,'" 288).

65. The Prophet is said to have had thirteen wives and concubines. All of them, except for ʿA'isha, had been previously married. All of them, except for Khadīja, were younger than him. Nine survived him. These were not marriages of lust; rather, they were marriages to cement sociopolitical ties within the Arab polity. See Barbara Freyer Stowasser, "Wives of the Prophet," *Encyclopedia of the Qur'ān*, ed. Jane Dammen McAuliffe (Brill Reference Online), 5:506–8.

66. Khaled Abou El Fadl, *Speaking in God's Name: Islamic Law, Authority, and Women* (Oxford: Oneworld Publications, 2001), 214–25.

67. Ali, "'A Beautiful Example,'" 289.

68. Shadaab Rahemtulla and Sara Ababneh, "Reclaiming Khadija's and Muhammad's Marriage as an Islamic Paradigm: Toward a New History of the Muslim Present," *Journal of Feminist Studies in Religion* 37, no. 2 (Fall 2021): 83. Masculinity, as it is used here, is not a biological fact, rather it can be understood as what it means to be a man at a certain time and place and as a product of social discourses.

69. Rahemtulla and Ababneh, "Reclaiming Khadija's and Muhammad's Marriage," 87.

70. Ibid., 89.

71. Amirah al-Azhary Sonbol, "Rethinking Women and Islam," in *Daughters of Abraham: Feminist Thought in Judaism, Christianity, and Islam*, eds. Yvonne Yazbeck Haddad and John L. Esposito (Gainesville: University Press of Florida, 2001), 138.

72. Saba Mahmood, *Politics of Piety: The Islamic Revival and the Feminist Subject* (Princeton, NJ: Princeton University Press, 2005).

73. Fazlur Rahman, *Islam and Modernity: Transformation of an Intellectual Tradition* (Chicago: University of Chicago Press, 1984), 17.

74. Hina Azam, *Sexual Violation in Islamic Law: Substance, Evidence, and Procedure* (New York: Cambridge University Press, 2015) 23–26.

75. Kecia Ali, *Marriage and Slavery in Early Islamic Law* (Cambridge, MA: Harvard University Press, 2010) 60–61.

76. Zahra Ayubi, *Gendered Morality: Classical Islamic Ethics of the Self, Family, and Society* (New York: Columbia University Press, 2019).

77. The book is based on three key Persian philosophical treatises on ethics: *Kimiya-i Saʿadat* or *The Alchemy of Happiness* by Abū Ḥāmid Muḥammad al-Ghazālī (d. 1111); *Akhlaq-i Nasiri* or *The Nasirean Ethics* by Nasīr al-Dīn Tūsī (d. 1274); and *Akhlaq-i Jalali* or *The Jalalean Ethics* by Jalāl al-Dīn Davānī (d. 1502). It not only reorients the study of Islam away from *fiqh* by focusing on philosophy but also reorients the study of Islam away from focusing on Arabic.

78. Generally speaking, women and non-elite men lack intellect and are overly emotional, a state that the authors of the texts believe is divinely ordained.

79. Sa'diyya Shaikh, *Sufi Narratives of Intimacy: Ibn 'Arabi, Gender and Sexuality* (Chapel Hill: The University of North Carolina Press 2012).

80. It must not be forgotten that feminism has political power over colonized people. See Lila Abu-Lughod, *Do Muslim Women Need Saving?* (Cambridge, MA:

Harvard University Press, 2013). For an intellectual history of Muslim feminism in North America, see Juliane Hammer, *American Muslim Women, Religious Authority, and Activism: More Than Prayers* (Austin: University of Texas Press, 2012), 57–59. See also Z. Mir-Hosseini, "Beyond 'Islam' vs. 'Feminism,'" *IDS Bulletin*, 42: 72, where she argues that Muslim feminist scholars must recognize the legacy of colonialism and western hegemony; Valentine M. Moghadam, "Islamic Feminism and Its Discontents: Toward a Resolution of the Debate," *Signs: Journal of Women in Culture and Society* 27, no. 4 (2002): 1135–71; Sa'diyya Shaikh, "Transforming Feminism: Islam, Women, and Gender Justice," in *Progressive Muslims: On Justice, Gender, and Pluralism*, ed. Omid Safi (Oxford: One World, 2003), 147–62; Omaima Abou-Bakr, "Islamic Feminism: What's in a Name? Preliminary Reflections," *AMEWS Review* 15, no. 16 (Winter/Spring 2001): 1–4.

81. The historical-critical approach arose in the west to tackle questions in the field of Biblical studies and is closely linked to secularization projects, and then it became the dominant approach in western Qur'anic studies. The aim of the historical-critical method of approaching the Qur'an and viewing it as text is to divest it of its metaphysical meaning and give power to those who believe it to have such meaning.

82. Beloushi, "The Theory of *Maqāṣid al-Sharīʿa*," 210.

83. Shahla Haeri, *Law of Desire: Temporary Marriage in Shiʿi Iran* (Syracuse, NY: Syracuse University Press, 1989.).

84. Linda S. Walbridge, *Without Forgetting the Imam: Lebanese Shi'ism in an American Community* (Detroit: Wayne State University Press, 1996).

85. This is not an exhaustive list of the types of possible relationships; it is, however, illustrative of how complicated and varied relationships can be. Monogamy (heterosexual and homosexual) is where two people are in an exclusive relationship. Throuple is a relationship where three people of any gender are in relationship with each other. There are also quads where four people of any gender are involved with one another. This is different from polygyny, where a man is married to more than one woman, which in turn is different from polyamory, where the individuals have more than one open relationship at a time. In these relationships, there can be individuals called metamours, people who an individual's partner is involved with but the individual is not. Each individual in such relationships is called a polycule. There are also open marriages, where one or both partners can seek new sexual partners outside of their marriage. These relationships work in different ways—ultimately, each one is a response to the needs of the people involved. These people claim that a traditional monogamous marriage is too restrictive.

86. Q 24:30–31, "(O Prophet!) Tell the believing men to lower their gaze and guard their chastity. That is purer for them. Surely God is All-Aware of what they do. And tell the believing women to lower their gaze and guard their chastity, and not to reveal their adornments except what normally appears. Let them draw their veils over their chests, and not reveal their (hidden) adornments except to their husbands, their fathers, their fathers-in-law, their sons, their stepsons, their brothers, their brothers' sons or sisters' sons, their fellow women, those (bondwomen) in their possession, male attendants with no desire, or children who are still unaware of women's nakedness. Let

them not stomp their feet, drawing attention to their hidden adornments. Turn to God in repentance all together, O believers, so that you may be successful."

87. Q 2:83, "And (remember) when We took a covenant from the children of Israel (stating), 'Worship none but God; be kind to parents, relatives, orphans and the needy; speak kindly to people; establish prayer; and pay alms-taxes.' But you (Israelites) turned away—except for a few of you—and were indifferent."

88. Q 2:177, "Righteousness is not in turning your faces towards the east or the west. Rather, the righteous are those who believe in God, the Last Day, the angels, the Books, and the prophets; who give charity out of their cherished wealth to relatives, orphans, the poor, (needy) travelers, beggars, and for freeing captives; who establish prayer, pay alms-tax, and keep the pledges they make; and who are patient in times of suffering, adversity, and in (the heat of) battle. It is they who are true (in faith), and it is they who are mindful (of God)."

89. Q 4:36, "Worship God (alone) and associate none with Him. And be kind to parents, relatives, orphans, the poor, near and distant neighbors, close friends, (needy) travelers, and those (bondspeople) in your possession. Surely God does not like whoever is arrogant, boastful."

90. See Anver Giladi, "Family," *Encyclopedia of the Qurʾān*, 2:173–76; "Children," *Encyclopedia of the Qurʾān*, 1:301–2; and "Parents," *Encyclopedia of the Qurʾān*, 4:20–22. See also, Talal Asad, "Kinship," *Encyclopedia of the Qurʾān*, 3:95–100.

91. Amina Wadud, *Qur'an and Woman: Rereading the Sacred Text from a Woman's Perspective*, reprint ed. (New York: Oxford University Press, 1999), 91.

92. Kecia Ali, "Destabilizing Gender, Reproducing Maternity: Mary in the Qurʾān," *Journal of the International Qur'anic Studies Association* 2 (2017): 90. In the same vein, see Aisha Geissinger, "Mary in the Qur'an: Rereading Subversive Births," in *Sacred Tropes: Tanakah, New Testament, and Qur'an as Literature and Culture*, ed. Roberta Sabbath, (Leiden: Brill, 2009), 379–92.

93. See Marcia Hermansen, "Wombs," *Encyclopedia of the Qurʾān*, 5:522–23. Examples of *āyāt* in the Qurʾan are Q 4:1, 31:34, and 47:22.

94. Not all mothers are biologically female. Although regardless of which parent is raising the child, the biologically female body has a special place and requires special consideration since it undergoes a very particular biological process of change.

95. For book length summary of some of the scholarship on this in English, see Kevin Reinharst, *Before Revelation: The Boundaries of Muslim Moral Thought* (Albany, SUNY Press, 1995); Paul Powers, *Intent in Islamic Law* (Leiden: Brill, 2006); Baber Johansen, *Contingency in a Sacred Law: Legal and Ethical Norms in the Muslim Fiqh* (Leiden: Brill, 1998). For a more recent work, which locates the textual record of the discursive mechanisms of the connection between ethics and law in *fiqh* texts, see Junaid Quadri, "Moral Habituation in the Law: Rethinking the Ethics of the Shari'a," *Islamic Law and Society* 26 (2019): 191–226.

96. Beloushi, "The Theory of *Maqāṣid al-Sharīʿa*," 225.

97. Ibid.

98. Ibid.

99. Zahra Ayubi, "De-Universalising Male Normativity: Feminist Methodologies for Studying Masculinity in Premodern Islamic Ethics Texts," *Journal of Islamic Ethics* 4 (2020): 66–97. 10.1163/24685542–12340044. Ayubi writes, "Because premodern Islamic ethics texts across multiple genres of the scriptural and intellectual tradition presume male readers and subjects, we must take male normativity, the assumption that Muslim ethics is for men, male bodies and practiced by persons marked by maleness, as our critical starting point." Ibid., 66.

100. Timo Jütten, "Sexual Objectification," *Ethics: An International Journal of Social, Political and Legal Philosophy* 27, no. 1 (2016): 27–49.

101. Alan Wertheimer, "Consent and Sexual Relations," in *The Philosophy of Sex: Contemporary Readings*, 5th ed. (Plymouth, UK: Rowan and Littlefield Publishers, Inc., 2008), 289.

102. Wertheimer, "Consent and Sexual Relations," 301–6.

103. Q 24:32, "Marry off the (free) singles among you, as well as the righteous of your bondmen and bondwomen. If they are poor, God will enrich them out of His bounty. For God is All-Bountiful, All-Knowing."

104. The *āya* also says that if the enslaved women are forced, they will not be held morally accountable for any actions performed against their will. Hina Azam, "Rape as a Variant of Fornication (Zina) in Islamic Law: An Examination of Early Legal Reports," *Journal of Law and Religion* 28, no. 2 (2012–13): 441–66. Pg 448.

105. Melanie A. Beres, "'Spontaneous' Sexual Consent: An Analysis of Sexual Consent Literature," *Feminism & Psychology* 17, no. 1 (2007): 93–108, DOI 10.1177/0959353507072914.

106. Robin West, "The Harms of Consensual Sex," in *The Philosophy of Sex: Contemporary Readings*, 5th ed. (Lanham, MD: Rowman and Littlefield Publishers, Inc., 2008), 317.

107. Anne Barnhill, "Bringing the Body Back to Sexual Ethics." *Hypatia* 28, no. 1 (2013): 1.

108. Stephanie Grant, "Why My Daughter Got (Temporarily) Married at 13," Modern Love, *New York Times*, August 27, 2021, https://www.nytimes.com/2021/08/27/style/modern-love-temporary-marriage-at-13.html.

109. "[T]he assumption [is] that all people are sexual [. . .] and [that] compel[s] people to experience themselves as desiring subjects, take up sexual identities, and engage in sexual activity." Kristina Gupta, "Compulsory Sexuality: Evaluating an Emerging Concept," *Signs: Journal of Women in Culture and Society* 41, no. 1 (2015): 131–54, pg. 132.

110. Gupta, "Compulsory Sexuality," 131.

111. Ibid., 140–45.

112. John S. Grabowski, *Sex and Virtue: An Introduction to Sexual Ethics*, vol. 2 of *Catholic Moral Thought* (Washington DC: Catholic University of America Press, 2003).

113. Grabowski, *Sex and Virtue*, 71.

114. Ibid.

115. Ibid.

116. Fredrick Elliston, "In Defense of Promiscuity," in *Philosophical Perspectives on Sex and Love*, ed. Robert M. Stewart (New York, Oxford University Press, 1995), 156.

117. This is the idea that one has to repeat choices and habituate oneself to them.

118. My thinking on this question has been shaped by a number of articles, including: Ferdinand Schoeman, "Rights of Children, Rights of Parents, and the Moral Basis of the Family," *Ethics* 91, no. 1 (1980): 6–19; James Lindemann Nelson, "Parental Obligations and the Ethics of Surrogacy: A Causal Perspective," *Public Affairs Quarterly* 5, no. 1 (1991): 49–61; Samantha Brennan and Robert Noggle, "The Moral Status of Children: Children's Rights, Parents' Rights, and Family Justice," *Social Theory and Practice* 23, no. 1 (1997): 1–26; Onora O'Neill, "Children's Rights and Children's Lives," *Ethics* 98, no. 3 (1988): 445–63.

119. I am grateful to Dr. Sherman Jackson for making me aware of this in a conversation many years ago. Currently, I regularly attend a mosque with a historically, predominantly African-American congregation—Masjid Al-Islam—and this issue comes up directly or indirectly in the Friday khutbahs.

120. Additionally, Black nationalists advocate plural marriage as a way to separate the Black community culturally and politically from mainstream American culture.

121. If anything, it has led to a rise in male violence, gang rape, and, in the case of China, abducting women and forcing them to marry—I also know of cases from Pakistan.

122. "If you fear you might fail to give orphan women their (due) rights (if you were to marry them), then marry other women of your choice—two, three, or four. But if you are afraid you will fail to maintain justice, then (content yourselves with) one or those (bondwomen) in your possession. This way you are less likely to commit injustice" (Q 4:3); "You will never be able to maintain (emotional) justice between your wives—no matter how keen you are. So do not totally incline towards one leaving the other in suspense. And if you do what is right and are mindful (of God), surely God is All-Forgiving, Most Merciful" (Q 4:129).

123. Elizabeth Brake, "Is 'Loving More' Better? The Values of Polyamory," in *The Philosophy of Sex: Contemporary Readings*, eds. Raja Halwani, Alan Soble, Sarah Hoffman, and Jacob M. Held (Lanham, MD: Rowman and Littlefield, 2017), 207.

124. Alan Soble, "Sexual Use," in *The Philosophy of Sex: Contemporary Readings*, 5th ed. (Plymouth, UK: Rowan and Littlefield Publishers, Inc., 2008), 283.

125. Beloushi, "The Theory of *Maqāṣid al-Sharīʿa*," 213.

126. Ibid.

127. Deborah L. Tolman and Lisa M. Diamond, eds., *APA Handbook of Sexuality and Psychology* (Washington DC: American Psychological Association, 2014).

128. Joseph Massad, *Desiring Arabs* (Chicago: The University of Chicago Press, 2007).

129. Ibrahim, *Women and Gender in the Qur'an*, 24.

130. Ayatollah Morteza Motahari, *Woman and Her Rights*, trans. M. A. Ansari (Islamic Seminary Publications), http://www.iranchamber.com/personalities/mmotahari/works/woman_rights_islam.pdf (accessed January 10, 2020); see also

ʿAllama Sayyid Muḥammad Muḥammad Ḥusayn Ṭabāṭabāʾī, *Shi'ite Islam*, trans. Seyyed Hossein Nasr (Albany, NY: SUNY Press, 1977).

131. Scientists have treated men's experiences as normative and have marginalized women's experiences. For example, historically, women's changing sexual patterns and discontinuities have been written off as atypical and inauthentic.

132. This is as true for sexuality as it is for any other realm of life. See Fatema Mernissi, *The Veil and the Male Elite: A Feminist Interpretation of Women's Rights in Islam* (Reading, MA: Addison-Wesley, 1991).

133. "Cliteracy," *The Huffington Post*, http://projects.huffingtonpost.com/projects/cliteracy (accessed January 14, 2020).

134. "History: The Clitoris' Vanishing Act," *The Huffington Post*, http://projects.huffingtonpost.com/projects/cliteracy/history (accessed September 26, 2020).

135. "History: The Clitoris' Vanishing Act," *The Huffington Post.*

136. Widespread misperception about orgasms leads to another perceived disparity, known appropriately as the "orgasm gap," the finding that men are more likely than women to report having orgasms as a result of heterosexual relations. The idea of an orgasm is complicated by the *definition* of orgasm; for example, if it is counted as ejaculation or if it depends on whether the individual realizes he or she has had an orgasm. This is because the definition of orgasm is an unresolved debate. Understanding the female orgasm in particular is complicated by sociocultural factors that influence women's understandings of their own bodies. The objectification of women may prevent some from understanding their sexual desires, because their sexuality develops based on how others see them, and this becomes how they evaluates themselves.

137. Ryan Anderson, "The Truth About Female Orgasms | Psychology Today," *Psychology Today*, September 17, 2015, https://www.psychologytoday.com/us/blog/the-mating-game/201509/the-truth-about-female-orgasms.

138. Navneet Magon and Sanjay Kalra, "The Orgasmic History of Oxytocin: Love, Lust, and Labor," *Indian Journal of Endocrinology and Metabolism* 15, no. 3 (September 2011): S156–61, https://doi.org/10.4103/2230-8210.84851.

139. See Inga D. Neumann, "The Advantage of Social Living: Brain Neuropeptides Mediate the Beneficial Consequences of Sex and Motherhood," *Frontiers in Neuroendocrinology* 30, no. 4 (October 2009): 483–96, https://doi.org/10.1016/j.yfrne.2009.04.012; see also, Keith M. Kendrick, "The Neurobiology of Social Bonds," *Journal of Neuroendocrinology* 16, no. 12 (December 2004): 1007–8, https://doi.org/10.1111/j.1365-2826.2004.01262.x.

140. Magon and Kalra, "Orgasmic History of Oxytocin," 483.

141. Eric Hollander et al., "Oxytocin Increases Retention of Social Cognition in Autism," *Biological Psychiatry* 61, no. 4 (February 15, 2007): 498–503, https://doi.org/10.1016/j.biopsych.2006.05.030.

142. Marla V. Broadfoot, "High on Fidelity," *American Scientist*, June 2002.

143. "Erotic plasticity" refers to the degree to which a person's sex drive can be shaped by social, cultural, and situational factors, see Roy F. Baumeister, "Erotic Plasticity," in *Encyclopaedia of Social Psychology*, eds. Roy F. Baumeister and Kathleen D. Vohs (Thousand Oaks, CA: SAGE Publications, Inc., 2007), 310–11.

144. Lisa M. Diamond, *Sexual Fluidity: Understanding Women's Love and Desire* (Cambridge, MA: Harvard University Press, 2009).

145. Diamond, *Sexual Fluidity*, 3.

146. Some works on same-sex relations in English are: Kathryn Babayan et al., *Islamicate Sexualities: Translations Across Temporal Geographies of Desire* (Cambridge, MA: Center for Middle Eastern Studies of Harvard University, 2008); Khaled El-Rouayheb, *Before Homosexuality in the Arab-Islamic World, 1500–1800* (Chicago: University of Chicago Press, 2005); Stephen O. Murray and Will Roscoe, *Islamic Homosexualities: Culture, History, and Literature* (New York: New York University Press, 1997); J. W. Wright and Everett K Rowson, *Homoeroticism in Classical Arabic Literature* (New York: Columbia University Press, 1997); Massad, *Desiring Arabs*; Scott Alan Kugle, *Homosexuality in Islam: Critical Reflection on Gay, Lesbian, and Transgender Muslims* (Oxford, UK: Oneworld, 2010). For an excellent overview of the history of same-sex relations between women in Arabic literature, see Samar Habib, *Female Homosexuality in the Middle East: Histories and Representations* (Hoboken, NJ: Taylor and Francis, 2012).

147. Fluidity is not defined as choice or the ability to shape sexuality into a pattern of one's choosing.

148. Peggy J. Kleinplatz and Lisa M. Diamond, "Sexual Diversity," in *APA Handbook of Sexuality and Psychology*, eds. Deborah L. Tolman and Lisa M. Diamond (Washington DC: American Psychological Association, 2014), 210–20.

149. Mathematicians and physicists invented dynamic system models to explain physical phenomena with states that vary over time (for example, cloud formations). This model analyzes the multiple factors that determine the state of the system in order to predict its pattern of change over time, which otherwise seems random and arbitrary. Later, this model was also used by psychologists to explain complex human phenomenon such as language acquisition and development. They were able to show that complex development happened through interactions between elements such as genes, hormones, and cognition and other elements, such as experiences, relationships, and cultural norms. The dynamic systems approach has since been applied to many fields.

150. R. F. Baumeister, K. Cantanese, and K. Vohs, "Is There a Gender Difference in Strength of Sex Drive?: Theoretical Views, Conceptual Distinctions, and a Review of Relevant Evidence," *Personality and Social Psychology Review* 5 (2001): 242–73.

151. Abdul Hassan ʿAli b. Nasr al-Kātib, *Encyclopedia of Pleasure* [*Jawamiʾ al-ladha*], ed. Salah Addin Khawwam, trans. ʾAdnan Jarkas and Salah Addin Khawwam (Toronto: Aleppo Publishing, 1977).

152. Pernilla Myrne, *Female Sexuality in the Early Medieval Islamic World: Gender and Sex in Arabic Literature* (London: I. B. Tauris, 2019).

153. Barry McCarthy and Emily J. McCarthy, *Finding Your Sexual Voice: Celebrating Female Sexuality*, 1st ed. (New York: Routledge, 2018).

154. Who defined male sex as individual performance with total control and predictability? This might work for younger men, but not for older men, married couples, or people in a monogamously partnered relationship.

155. Walter O. Bockting, "Transgender Identity Development" in *APA Handbook of Sexuality and Psychology*, eds. Deborah L. Tolman and Lisa M. Diamond (Washington DC: American Psychology Association, 2014), 739–58.

156. M. Alipour, "Islamic Shari'a Law, Neotraditionalist Muslim Scholars and Transgender Sex-Reassignment Surgery: A Case Study of Ayatollah Khomeini's and Sheikh al-Tantawi's Fatwas," *International Journal of Transgenderism* 18, no. 1 (2017): 91–103.

157. Alipour, "Islamic Shari'a Law," 96.

158. Alipour, "Islamic Shari'a Law," 101n9, 95.

159. Shereen El Feki, *Sex and the Citadel: Intimate Life in a Changing Arab World* (New York: Pantheon Books, 2013), 53.

160. El Feki, *Sex and the Citadel,* 54.

Conclusion

This book's purpose was twofold: 1) to question the veracity of Q 4:24 as a proof text for the permissibility of *mut'a* and 2) to address modern-day questions and concerns about *mut'a* and its implications for Islamic marital and sexual ethics. The first was undertaken by tracing the historical development of the exegesis of Q 4:24 in *tafsīr* literature, noting evolutions, changes, and shifts in meaning. Chapters 2, 3, and 4 were dedicated to this analysis, and each chapter highlighted important themes that are interwoven in the sources and mapped out a cultural conversation that traverses time and space. The polysemy and ambiguity traced in the exegesis of Q 4:24 opened up the path for the second purpose. I contend we must assess and rethink the conceptualization of sexual and marital ethics within interpretations of *mut'a* in particular and within Islamic law in general. An ongoing discussion of female sexuality in all its complexity is required for rethinking the role of *mut'a* in Islamic legal scholarship. Chapter 5, the final chapter, proposes one such path by advancing a four-dimensional approach: 1) taking seriously the works of Muslim feminists and the methodological approaches they have put forth to (re)think Islamic sources; 2) incorporating lived Islam though socio-legal ethnography as a testament to the significance of living Muslims; 3) considering moral questions on the issue of sexual ethics and marriage; and 4) seriously weighing the scientific findings on human sexuality.

In this conclusion, I will outline major themes covered in the book, including the role of sectarian identity in *tafsīr*, the five discursive stages of exegetical discussions on Q 4:24, and the sectarian role of hadith when claiming *mut'a* is permissible.

TAFSĪR

Examining exegetes from a variety of backgrounds and intellectual schools, as well as covering the expanse of Islamic intellectual history, allowed me to voice criticism of the interpretations of this *āya* from a hermeneutical point of view. I found that scholars consistently imposed their preconceived notions on interpretations of this *āya* and were influenced by ideologically charged interpretations and thus did not engage in impartial hermeneutical methods, with the exception pf Ibn ʿĀshūr, who was an outlier. When Shiʿi and Sunni law became institutionalized, the exegetical process was vital for creating sectarian identities. *Mutʿa* became central to communal debates. The Shiʿi attempt to use *mutʿa* to define themselves politically and religiously is clearly indicated in Shiʿi sources, and eventually also in Sunni writings. In general, it appears that a scholar's hermeneutical method has little bearing on his or her interpretation, yet an individual exegete's theological school plays a significant role. Hence, this genealogical study of the *tafāsīr* of Q 4:24 has demonstrated a powerful sectarian legacy. Amirpur explains this phenomenon in his study of Abdolkarim Soroush,[1] a contemporary author who has written on Islam and cognitive theory.[2] Cognitive theory tells us that since human cognition is changeable, individuals' understandings of their religion are also changeable because all cognition depends on the current development of collective human intellectual thought. Consequently, the interpreter plays an important role in shaping the interpretation: the interpreter's preconceived notions significantly influence the final product of interpretation (e.g., the exegetical text). Soroush argues that due to the interpreter's cognitive interests, their inner disposition is an inherent factor in the cognitive process. He calls it *savabit-i zihnī va-ittilat-i kharijī*, preconceived ideas and ideas of external origin. While Soroush considers it completely natural that exegetes have specific interests and subjugate texts to the interpretative lenses of these interests, most scholars claim to objectively follow the text to the letter and consider *tafsīr bi-l-raʾy*, exegesis according to personal opinion, an anathema. Walid A. Saleh also elaborates on this point, telling us that *tafsīr* was the first medium to provide Muslim intellectuals with a discursive space for fitting together the various parts of their worldview; *aḥādīth* were not able to do this. It is no wonder that *tafsīr* works were consistently produced, reformulated, and expanded as Islam was put in a position to (re)define itself.[3]

The reformulation and development of the genre of *tafsīr* can be observed through an analysis of exegesis on *mutʿa*. In this book, each chapter introduced exegetical formulations and discourse related to Q 4:24 that occurred over the course of 500 years. The evolution of exegesis on Q 4:24—from a contested *āya* to one used as proof text for *mutʿa*—underwent five discursive stages.

The first stage is characterized by textual openness. Classical scholars from both proto-Shiʿi and proto-Sunni schools included the variant reading of the *āya*, which included the phrase "for a predetermined time," alongside the now canonical version of it without any discussion about the need or necessity for the fixed-ness of the text. It is as if each of the two readings had equal authority. In this initial stage, exegetical texts rarely stressed the canonical reading, and the variant reading is grounded in ninth-century texts with chains of authority that date back to Ibn ʿAbbās. The fact that prominent scholars held such contradictory views proves *mutʿa*'s legitimacy was not decided at this point.[4] Eventually, however, scholars on both sides begin to minimize the variant reading. This is especially true in the modern period, where there is no mention of it—not even by Shiʿi exegetes, whose cause would be well served by the inclusion of such a discussion—most likely because the implications of having variant readings of the Qurʾan, as well as the chaos textual variants of the Qurʾan could incite, was a scholarly concern in the modern period.

The second stage is linguistic. The most important problem concerns the word *istamtaʿa*, to enjoy, in this *āya*. At the start, the normative understanding of the gramatical verb *istamtaʿa* was transformed by treating it as a noun referring to *mutʿa,* temporary marriage. The main argument for this reading is that there was a form of marriage called *mutʿa* at the advent of Islam, and it was practiced during the lifetime of the Prophet Muhammad and afterwards—it is unclear if it was prohibited by him. The rules of Qurʾanic hermeneutics require the vocabulary in the Qurʾan to adhere to meanings in use when an *āya* was revealed. Therefore, *istamtaʿa* refers to *mutʿa*, which was practiced when the Qurʾan was revealed. As time went on and the enterprise of *tafsīr* became increasingly more sophisticated, counterarguments were presented, which helped settle the case for Sunni scholars. The counterargument was that *istamtaʿa* refers to pleasure, or sexual pleasure in marriage, because the Qurʾan uses the same word to connote pleasure in other *āyāt* (Q 9:69)[5]—without any connection to *mutʿa*. The letters *sīn* and *tāʾ* are thus there for emphasis and not to create the verbal form *istafʿala*. This latter explanation removes the possibility of the word being read as connoting *mutʿa*. These counterarguments, however, were not taken seriously by Shiʿi scholars, who maintained this *āya* was a proof text for *mutʿa*. These discussions demonstrate how Q 4:24 was a focal point when the schools of Islamic jurisprudence were taking shape.

The third stage is grammatical. We see a change in these discussions as we approach the last two to three decades of the modern period—covered in chapter 4. When grammatical discussions were introduced into exegetical works, scholars commenting on the Qurʾan's grammar wrote that the second *mā*, the relative pronoun that precedes the word *istamtaʿtum* (*fa-mā istamtaʿtūm bihi minhunna*), refers to women. Sayyid Muḥammad Ḥusayn Ṭabāṭabāʾī bases his ruling for the permissibility of *mutʿa* on two arguments, one of which is that the relative pronoun *mā* refers to, and can only refer to, inanimate objects; therefore, in this case, it refers to the (inanimate) institution of *mutʿa*, not seeking pleasure from women. While it is true that Modern Standard Arabic uses the relative pronoun *mā* for inanimate objects, Classical

Arabic uses *mā* for both animate and inanimate objects, as witnessed in al-Rāzī's *tafsīr*.

The fourth discursive stage brought methodological issues to the forefront and focused on the subject of *nāsikh wa mansūkhuhu*, abrogation. In the early Islamic period, this was not understood in a linear manner. Many Companions responded to reports of Q 4:24 being used as a proof text for *mutʿa* with claims that it had been abrogated by *āyāt* on: *ṭalāq*, divorce, Q 65:1;[6] *ʿidda,* waiting period, Q 2:228;[7] *mīrāth*, inheritance, Q 4:12;[8] and how sexual intercourse can only take place with a wife or slave Q 23:5–6.[9] The *mutʿa* wife does not fit within any of these categories—some of which had been revealed before Q 4:24. Over time, Shiʿi scholars began to respond to these claims, stating abrogation could not apply to *āyāt* that precede Q 4:24; after all, how could a *āya* revealed earlier abrogate something that came later?

The fifth stage is the modernist turn and the consolidation of the rational for the permissibility of *mutʿa* in Shiʿi scholarship. Ṭabāṭabāʾī advocates a rationalistic outlook, and this plays a decisive role in his interpretation. Historically, Shiʿi exegetes have maintained that the Qurʾan does not make irrational statements. They have written page after page about the contemporary relevance of *mutʿa*, making arguments that it is permissible because it offers a realistic appraisal of human nature and sexual desire. As we saw, over time the practice went from being permissible to becoming commendable, a current interpretation that challenges previous historical understandings of the practice. A survey of modern Shiʿi literature in chapter 1 and then in the Shiʿi exegetes showed just how important this issue still is in our times and reveals recent changes and innovations in Shiʿi thought on the matter.

HADITH

In addition to grammatical, methodological, and linguistic arguments, *aḥādīth* were also used in sectarian debates about the legitimacy of *mutʿa*. The position of Shiʿi scholars on the *aḥādīth* concerning *mutʿa* is clear and unambiguous: all traditions, whether early or late, unanimously agree that this type of marriage is legal and acceptable. In fact, they insist that this practice is in line with the clear commands of the Qurʾan and the Prophet Muhammad as they understand them. As part of this effort, past and present Shiʿi scholars have collected numerous traditions that despite their great variety, all have one purpose: not just to prove the legality of *mutʿa* but also to articulate the benefits of this kind of marriage. In fact, a chronological analysis of Shiʿi hadith literature shows that with time, the quantity and quality of traditions on *mutʿa* increase dramatically.

Sunni *aḥādīth* on *mut'a* are contradictory. For example, al-Rāzī cites three that can be traced to Ibn 'Abbās. The first states that *mut'a* was allowed, the second that it was allowed under certain circumstances, and the third that it was not allowed. Al-Rāzī explains that the Shi'a base their prohibition on a hadith by 'Ali in which he claims *mut'a* was not prohibited. Al-Rāzī cites this hadith and then proceeds to cite another in which 'Ali says *mut'a* is prohibited. Thus, al-Rāzī claims that he gives contradictory statements: *mut'a* was prohibited as well as not prohibited according to 'Ali.

A key area of contestation regarding the issue of *mut'a* is the sermon of 'Umar, the second caliph, in which he outlawed *mut'a*: "Two *mut'a*s were practiced during the time of the Prophet, but I forbid both of them and will punish anyone who practices either."[10] The Sunni interpret the Companions' silence and lack of protest at this sermon to indicate their knowledge that *mut'a* had already been abrogated. The Shi'a, on the other hand, claim 'Umar's sermon demonstrates that *mut'a* was permitted during the lifetime of the Prophet Muhammad and therefore attribute the banning of *mut'a* to 'Umar and his opinion, which is not, according to them, compulsory to follow. If the Prophet Muhammad had indeed prohibited *mut'a*, then 'Umar need not have banned it. According to al-Rāzī, the claim that 'Umar falsely forbade *mut'a* is unreasonable. This would mean that not only was 'Umar an unbeliever but so were those who heard him in the sermon and failed to protest. This would have included 'Ali, since he was also present. Therefore, the logical conclusion to draw from 'Umar's prohibition is that 'Umar forbade *mut'a* because the Prophet Muhammad had done so as well.

Early Sunni texts on canonical law indicate that several of the Prophet Muhammad's Companions believed *mut'a* was not forbidden. This is a legal position that chronologically precedes the emergence of Shi'i law. In other words, the Sunni dispute concerning the legality of *mut'a* and its judicial implications predates the appearance of the Shi'i sect. Thus, one must conclude that the initial debate on this subject (during the first century AH/seventh–eighth century CE) was not connected with the Sunni-Shi'i sectarian quarrel. Nonetheless, the dispute did not remain within the confines of Sunni Islam for long and quickly spread after the appearance of the Shi'i sect. No modern Shi'i hadith collection lacks a chapter, or at least part of a chapter, containing a tradition on *mut'a*. The prominence of the subject indicates its importance in Shi'i hadith literature, which goes into extensive detail on *mut'a*, unlike Sunni hadith literature. This can perhaps be explained by the fact that *mut'a* is a defining aspect of Shi'i communal identity, and since the Qur'an is treated as a fixed text, hadith literature is the arena in which positions are more likely to be defended.

FIQH

Mutʿa is a major point of difference between Twelver *imāmī* Shiʿi *fiqh* and the legal practices of other Muslim sects. Sunni jurists do not permit *mutʿa*; and therefore, there are no legal rulings delineating a valid legal process for such a marriage. The Shafiʿi, Maliki, and Hanbali Sunni schools consider *mutʿa* completely invalid and any such contract a void contract. But the Hanafi Sunni school considers a *mutʿa*'s time limit to be invalid and converts it into a permanent marriage. The Zaydīs and Ismaʿili Shiʿi branches also do not permit *mutʿa* and subsequently do not have any legal rules or regulations regarding it. Twelver *imāmī* Shiʿa permit *mutʿa* and therefore have well-developed rules regulating *mutʿa*, which have been summarized in chapter 1, where they have also been compared with the rules for permanent marriage. Suffice it to note here that the rules for *mutʿa* in Shiʿi *fiqh* use the rules for permanent marriage as scaffolding whenever possible. The most problematic aspect of *mutʿa* rulings for gender justice is that in most places, this marriage does not need to be registered with a central authority or publicly announced, which easily leads to the abuse and abandonment of the women in these marriages. This is why Ziba Mir-Hosseini presciently labels *mutʿa* a "socially defective marriage."[11] Second, even though women are permitted to contract a *mutʿa*—that is, they can contract and be in one *mutʿa* at a time—men can contract as many simultaneous *mutʿa* marriages as they want.

CONCLUDING REMARKS

In this book, I wrestled with two main issues: 1) whether or not Q 4:24 legitimizes or legalizes the practice of *mutʿa* and 2) what the implications of such a practice are for Muslim families and marital and sexual ethics. Chapters 2, 3, and 4 undertook the enormous task of analyzing a 1,400-year history of Qurʾanic exegesis to answer the question of whether Q 4:24 can be used as a proof text for *mutʿa*. What becomes evident through the study of *tafāsīr*, related *aḥādīth*, *fiqh*, and the Qurʾan is the wide variety of interpretive possibilities that arise when trying to understand the meaning of the *āya*. This history, as well as the five stages mentioned earlier, illustrate the polysemy of Qurʾanic *āyāt*. With varying ways to interpret and examine Q 4:24, including grammatically, linguistically, and methodologically, it is impossible to arrive at one clear conclusion for how it should be understood. Exegetes existed in particular historical contexts, identified themselves with specific theological schools, and often promoted certain interpretations. This meant that the exegesis was likewise informed by an exegete's personal influences. Though the exegetes were historically, socially, and politically informed, it is important to note here that Muslim scholars hold "the possibility that an interpretation of a text such as the Qur'an could emerge that moves beyond an existing sociological reality should not be precluded a priori."[12]

Why is it important to analyze the history of exegesis about this *āya* and early opinions about a seemingly outdated practice? It is important because these discussions have actual consequences for present-day Muslim women, men, and children. First, such analyses provide the opportunity to fundamentally question the assumptions—related to marital and sexual ethics—that underlie the premises for the practice of *mut'a*. For example, men are presumed to have naturally higher libidos that may warrant several simultaneous marriages, while women are thought to be fully satisfied within one marriage and are presumed to have tamer libidos. Questioning this presumption about human sexuality allows us to question how to seriously incorporate current studies on the science of sexuality into discussions on *mut'a*. Underlying the issue of the permissibility of *mut'a* is a broader question: is sexual activity somehow tied to a Muslim's spiritual being? This moral question requires us to consider the body's impact on the soul, rather than conventional frameworks that prioritize the soul's impact on the body. Further, there has been no serious consideration of or study on how fulfilling one's sex drive through multiple temporary marriages may, for example, affect children, wives, and temporary wives, or even what it might mean for marriage as a societal concept. Therefore, it is crucial for any study conducted on *mut'a* to consider the very real implications such practices have on Muslim communities. In my book, I argued that one must not consider the Qur'an, *aḥādīth*, and *fiqh* in isolation, but indeed, we should supplement and enrich our research with additional methodologies and frameworks.

My most important intervention is a reappraisal of previous methodology regarding reinterpretations of Islamic law and posits a new four-fold, multidimensional approach—which is both interpretative and normative—that draws upon: 1) Muslim feminist methodological interventions; 2) socio-legal ethnographic study among men, women, and children; 3) the moral philosophy of sexuality; and 4) the science of sexuality. These four aspects are interlinked—how one question is answered is inextricably connected to how one answers the other and so on—and the collective answers carry considerable legal ramifications. Through this methodological intervention, I propose preliminary areas for future study and considerations that allow us as scholars to center those who are affected most deeply by this practice. I strive to consider new technologies and scientific information within the study of *mut'a* in particular and within Islamic law in general and to produce scholarship that considers the classical texts alongside contemporary research, questions, and concerns. The analysis conducted here, as well as the work that is still left to do, have serious implications for issues related to modern sexual relationships, marriage, and Islamic sexual ethics.

And God knows best.

NOTES

1. A few of Abdolkarim Sorush's writings have been translated into English by Ahmad and Mahmud Sadri, for example, see Abd-al-Karim Sorush, *Reason, Freedom and Democracy in Islam* (Oxford: Oxford University Press, 2000). Quite a number of works studying Sorush's work have been published, see Afshin Matin-Asghari, "Abdolkarim Sorush and the Secularization of Islamic Thought in Iran," *Iranian Studies* 30, (1997): 1–2, 95–115; John Cooper, "The Limits of the Sacred: The Epistemology of Abd al-Karim Soroush," in *Islam and Modernity: Muslim Intellectuals Respond*, eds. Cooper et al. (London: Tauris, 1998), 38–56; Forough Jahanbaksh, *Islam, Democracy and Religious Modernism in Iran (1953–2000): From Bazargan to Soroush* (Leiden: Brill, 2001); Ashk Dahlen, *Deciphering the Meaning of Revealed Law: The Sorushian Paradigm Shiite Epistemology* (Uppsala: University Press, 2001).

2. Katajun Amirpur, "The Changing Approach to the Text: Iranian Scholars and the Qur'an," *Middle Eastern Studies* 41, no. 3 (2005): 337–50.

3. Walid A. Saleh, *The Formation of the Classical Tafsīr Tradition: The Qurʾān Commentary of al-Thaʿlabī (d. 427/1035)* (Leiden: Brill, 2004), 191–98.

4. Arthur Gribetz provides a concise summary of the dispute concerning *mutʿa* among early legalists, see *Strange Bedfellows:* Mutʿat al-Nisāʾ *and* Mutʿat al-Ḥajj*: A Study Based on Sunnī and Shīʿī Sources of* Tafsīr, Ḥadīth, *and* Fiqh (Berlin: Klaus Schwartz, 1994), 159–60.

5. Q 9:69, "(You hypocrites are) like those (disbelievers) before you. They were far superior to you in might and more abundant in wealth and children. They enjoyed their share in this life. You have enjoyed your share, just as they did. And you have engaged in idle talk, just as they did. Their deeds have become void in this world and the Hereafter. And it is they who are the (true) losers."

6. Q 65:1, "O Prophet! (Instruct the believers:) When you (intend to) divorce women, then divorce them with concern for their waiting period, and count it accurately. And fear God, your Lord."

7. Q 2:228, "Divorced women must wait three monthly cycles (before they can re-marry). It is not lawful for them to conceal what God has created in their wombs, if they (truly) believe in God and the Last Day. And their husbands reserve the right to take them back within that period if they desire reconciliation. Women have rights similar to those of men equitably, although men have a degree (of responsibility) above them. And God is Almighty, All-Wise."

8. Q 4:12, "You will inherit half of what your wives leave if they are childless. But if they have children, then (your share is) one-fourth of the estate—after the fulfilment of bequests and debts. And your wives will inherit one-fourth of what you leave if you are childless. But if you have children, then your wives will receive one-eighth

of your estate—after the fulfilment of bequests and debts. And if a man or a woman leaves neither parents nor children but only a brother or a sister (from their mother's side), they will each inherit one-sixth, but if they are more than one, they (all) will share one-third of the estate—after the fulfilment of bequests and debts without harm (to the heirs). (This is) a commandment from God. And God is All-Knowing, Most Forbearing."

9. Q 23:5–6, "[T]hose who guard their chastity except with their wives or those (bondwomen) in their possession, for then they are free from blame."

10. Aḥmad Ibn Ḥanbal, *Musnad* (Cairo: n.p., 1971), 3:325, 356, 363.

11. Ziba Mir-Hosseini, *Marriage on Trial: A Study of Islamic Family Law*, rev. ed. (New York: I. B. Tauris, 2001), 166.

12. Mohammad Fadel, "Two Women, One Man: Knowledge, Power, and Gender in Medieval Sunni Legal Thought," *International Journal of Middle East Studies* 29 (1997): 186.

Appendix

Below is Q 4:24, first broken down so that the various parts can be parsed separtely and easily and then given in its entirety. The transliterated Arabic is followed by three translations. The first is a literal translation, the second is in clearer English—both are my translations—and the third is the translation by Mustafa Khattab.

Wa-l-muḥṣanāt min al-nisāʾ illā mā malakat imānukum

1. And [also prohibited to you are all] married women from [among] women except for what your right hand possesses [i.e., slaves].
2. Prohibited are married women except for [married] slave women.
3. Also (forbidden are) married women—except (female) captives in your possession.

kitāb Allāh alaykum

1. [This is] Allah's writ for you.
2. [This is] Allah's ordinance for you.
3. This is God's commandment to you.

wa uḥilla lakum mā wa rāʾa dhālikum

1. And lawful for you are what is besides that [i.e., all other women]
2. All other women are permitted to you
3. Lawful to you are all beyond these

an tabtaghū bi-ʾāmwālikum muḥṣinīn ghayr musāfiḥīn

1. [provided] that you seek them [women] with your wealth, with chastity, not fornication.

2. provided you seek them by means of your wealth, desiring chastity, not committing fornication.
3. as long as you seek them with your wealth in a legal marriage, not in fornication.

fa-mā istamtaʿtūm bihi minhunna

1a) So, such of them with whom you have *mutʿa* (Shiʿa);
or 1b) Those with whom you seek enjoyment (Sunni)
2) So, for the enjoyment you have enjoyed from them
3) Give those you have consummated marriage with

fa-ʾātūhunna ujūrahunna farīḍa

1. give them their wages as settled.
2. give them their dowries as settled.
3. their due dowries.

wa-lā junāḥ ʿalaykum fī-mā tarāḍaytum bihi min baʿd al-farīḍa

1. And there is no blame upon you in what you agree after the settlement.
2. There is no blame upon you for what you may mutually agree upon beyond the settlement.
3. It is permissible to be mutually gracious regarding the set dowry.

inna Allāh kāna ʿalīmman ḥakīmā

1 and 2) Indeed, Allah is All-Knowing, All-Wise.
3) Surely God is All-Knowing, All-Wise.

Wa-l-muḥṣanāt min al-nisāʾ illā mā malakat imānukum kitāb Allāh alaykum wa uḥilla lakum mā wa rāʾa dhālikum an tabtaghū bi-ʾāmwālikum muḥṣinīn ghayr musāfiḥīn fa-mā istamtaʿtūm bihi minhunna fa-ʾātūhunna ujūrahunna farīḍa wa-lā junāḥ ʿalaykum fī-mā tarāḍaytum bihi min baʿd al-farīḍa inna Allāh kāna ʿalīmman ḥakīmā

1. And [also prohibited to you are all] married women from [among] women except for what your right hand possesses [i.e., slaves]. [This is] Allah's writ for you. And lawful for you are what is besides that [i.e.,

all other women] [provided] that you seek them [women] with your wealth, with chastity, not fornication. So, such of them with whom you have *mut'a* (Shi'a). Those with whom you seek enjoyment (Sunni), give them their wages as settled, and there is no blame upon you in what you agree after the settlement. Indeed, Allah is All-Knowing, All-Wise.

2. Prohibited are married women except for [married] slave women. [This is] Allah's ordinance for you. All other women are permitted to you provided you seek them by means of your wealth, desiring chastity, not committing fornication. So, for the enjoyment you have enjoyed from them, give them their dowries as settled. There is no blame upon you for what you may mutually agree upon beyond the settlement. Indeed, Allah is All-Knowing, All-Wise.
3. Also (forbidden are) married women—except (female) captives in your possession. This is God's commandment to you. Lawful to you are all beyond these—as long as you seek them with your wealth in a legal marriage, not in fornication. Give those you have consummated marriage with their due dowries. It is permissible to be mutually gracious regarding the set dowry. Surely God is All-Knowing, All-Wise.

Bibliography

ʿAbduh, Muḥammad, and Muḥammad Rashīd Riḍā. *Tafsīr al-Qurʾān al-ḥakīm al-mashhūr bi- tafsīr al-manār*. Edited by Ibrāhīm Shams al-Dīn. 12 vols. Beirut: Dar al-Kutub al- 'Ilmiyyah, 1999. 4

Abdul, Musa O. A. "The Historical Development of Tafsir." *Islamic Culture* 50 (1976): 141–53.

Abou-Bakr, Omaima. "Islamic Feminism: What's in a Name? Preliminary Reflections." *AMEWS Review* 15, no. 16 (Winter/Spring 2001): 1–4.

Abu Khalil, As'ad. "Ideology and Practice of Hizballah in Lebanon: Islamization of Leninist Organizational Principles." *Middle Eastern Studies* 27, no. 3 (1991): 390–403.

Abū Zahra, Muḥammad. *al-Aḥwāl al-shakhṣīyya*. Cairo: n.p., 1957.

Abu-Lughod, Lila. *Do Muslim Women Need Saving?* Cambridge, MA: Harvard University Press, 2013.

Afsaruddin, Asma. "ʿĀʾisha bt. Abī Bakr." In *Encyclopaedia of Islam, THREE*, edited by Kate Fleet, Gudrun Krämer, Denis Matringe, John Nawas, and Everett Rowson. Brill Online.

Ahmad, Khurshid, and Zafar Ishaq Ansari, eds. *Islamic Perspectives: Studies in Honour of Mawlana Sayyid Abul Aʿla Mawdudi*. Leicester: Islamic Foundation, 1979.

Ahmad, Mumtaz. "Media-Based Preachers and the Creation of New Muslim Publics in Pakistan." In *Who Speaks for Islam? Muslim Grassroots Leaders and Popular Preachers in South Asia*, edited by Mumtaz Ahmad, Dietrich Reetz and Thomas Johnson, Special Report number 22. Washington, DC: The National Bureau of Asian Research, 2010.

Ahmed, Leila. "Women and the Advent of Islam." *Signs* 11, no. 4 (1986): 665–91.

Ahmed, Rashid. "Qur'anic Exegesis and Classical Tafsir." *The Islamic Quarterly* 12 (1968): 71–119.

Ahmed, Sameera. "Religiosity and Presence of Character Strengths in American Muslim Youth," *Journal of Muslim Mental Health* 4, no. 2 (2009): 104–23.

Akhondpour, Hassan, dir. *Fereshteh: Daughter of Ahmad (2016) - IMDb*, 2016. http://www.imdb.com/title/tt5643170/plotsummary.

Algar, Hamid. "Allama Sayyid Muhammad Husayn Tabatabai: Philosopher, Exegete, and Gnostic." *Journal of Islamic Studies* 17, no. 3 (March 22, 2006): 326–51. https://doi.org/10.1093/jis/etl002.

ʿAlī, Jawād. *al-Mufaṣṣal fī tārīkh al-ʿArab qabla al-Islām*. Beirut: Dār al-ʿIlm li-l-Malāyīn, 1976.

Ali, Kecia. "The Feminist Sexual Ethics Project." Brandeis University, September 26, 2003. https://www.brandeis.edu/projects/fse/muslim/articles.html.

Ali, Kecia "'A Beautiful Example': The Prophet Muḥammad as a Model for Muslim Husbands." *Islamic Studies* 43, no. 2 (2004): 273–91.

Ali, Kecia. *Sexual Ethics and Islam: Feminist Reflections on Qur'an, Hadith, and Jurisprudence*. 1st ed. Oxford: Oneworld Publications, 2006.

Ali, Kecia. *Marriage and Slavery in Early Islam*. Cambridge, MA: Harvard University Press, 2010.

Ali, Kecia. "Destabilizing Gender, Reproducing Maternity: Mary in the Qurʾān." *Journal of the International Qur'anic Studies Association* 2 (2017): 89–109.

ʿAlī, Zayd b. *Corpus Juris*. Edited by Eugenio Griffini. Milan: Ulrico Hoepli, 1919.

Ali-Faisal, Sobia. "North American Muslims & Sex Ed: Looking at Sexual Guilt with Researcher Sobia Faisal-Ali." Interview by Chelby Daigle, June 2, 2015. https://muslimlink.ca/stories/muslim-sex-ed-sexual-guilt.

Ali-Faisal, Sobia. "What's Sex Got to Do with It? The Role of Sexual Experience in the Sexual Attitudes, and Sexual Guilt and Anxiety of Young Muslim Adults in Canada and the United States." *Journal of Muslim Mental Health* 10, no. 2 (2016): 27–41. https://doi.org/10.3998/jmmh.10381607.0010.202.

Alipour, M. "Islamic Shari'a Law, Neotraditionalist Muslim Scholars and Transgender Sex-Reassignment Surgery: A Case Study of Ayatollah Khomeini's and Sheikh al-Tantawi's Fatwas." *International Journal of Transgenderism* 18, no. 1 (January 2, 2017): 91–103. https://doi.org/10.1080/15532739.2016.1250239.

Allon, J. Uhlmann. "Introduction: Reflections on the Study of Sexuality in the Middle East and North Africa," *Social Analysis: The International Journal of Social and Cultural Practice* 49, no. 2 (Summer 2005): 3–15.

Alshugairi, Noha. "Marital Trends in the American Muslim Community: A Pilot Study." *Journal of Muslim Mental Health* 5, no. 3 (2010): https://doi.org/10.1080/15564908.2010.551275.

al-ʿĀmilī, Muḥammad b. al-Ḥasan al-Ḥurr. *Wasāʾil al-Shiʿa*. Vol. 14. Edited by Ḥasan al-Amīn. Beirut: Dār al-Taʿāruf, 1986.

Anawati, G. C. "Fa k h r Al-Dīn al-Rāzī." In *Encyclopaedia of Islam, Second Edition*, edited by P. Bearman, Th. Bianquis, C.E. Bosworth, E. van Donzel, and W.P. Heinrichs. Brill Online, 2012.

Anderson, Ryan. "The Truth About Female Orgasms | Psychology Today." *Psychology Today*, September 17, 2015. https://www.psychologytoday.com/us/blog/the-mating-game/201509/the-truth-about-female-orgasms.

Asad, Talal. "Kinship." In *Encyclopedia of the Qurʾān*. Edited by Jane Dammen McAuliffe. Brill Online.

Ashraf, Ajaz. "What is Mut'a Marriage—and Why It May Be Difficult for India's Supreme Court to Invalidate It." Scroll.in, https://scroll.in/article/874702/what-is

-muta-marriage-and-why-it-may-be-difficult-for-the-supreme-court-to-invalidate-it. Last accessed September 4, 2021.

al-ʿAsqalānī, Shihāb al-Dīn Aḥmad Ibn Ḥajar. *al-Iṣāba fī tamyīz al-ṣahāba*. Edited by Khayrī Saʿīd. 8 vols. Cairo: Al Maktabah al-Tawfiqiyya, n.d.

Awde, Nicholas. *Women in Islam*. 2nd rev. ed. London: Bennett and Bloom, 2005.

al-ʿAyyāshī, Abū al-Naḍr Muḥammad b. Masʿ ūd al-Samarqandī. *al-Tafsīr li-Abī al-Naḍr Muḥammad Ibn Masʿūd al-ʿAyyāshī*. 3 vols. Qom: Maktabat al-Biʿtha, 2000.

Ayubi, Zahra. *Gendered Morality: Classical Islamic Ethics of the Self, Family, and Society*. New York: Columbia University Press, 2019.

Ayubi, Zahra. "De-Universalising Male Normativity: Feminist Methodologies for Studying Masculinity in Premodern Islamic Ethics Texts," *Journal of Islamic Ethics* 4 (2020): 66–97. https://doi.org/10.1163/24685542–12340044.

Azam, Hina. "Rape as a Variant of Fornication (Zina) in Islamic Law: An Examination of the Early Legal Reports." *Journal of Law and Religion* 28, no. 2 (2012): 441–66.

Azam, Hina. *Sexual Violation in Islamic Law: Substance, Evidence, and Procedure*. Cambridge, UK: Cambridge University Press, 2015.

al-Azami, Muhammad Mustafa. *Studies in Early Hadith Literature*. Indianapolis: American Trust Publications, 1978. Originally published in Beirut: al-Maktab al-Islāmī, 1388/1968.

Babayan, Kathryn, et al. *Islamicate Sexualities: Translations Across Temporal Geographies of Desire*. Cambridge: Center for Middle Eastern Studies of Harvard University, 2008.

Badrān, Abū al-ʿAynayn. *Aḥkam al-zawāj wa-l-ṭalāq fī al-Islām*. Cairo: Dār al-maʿārif, 1964.

al-Balkhī, Muqātil b. Sulaymān. *Tafsīr*. Edited by ʿAbd Allāh Maḥmūd Shiḥāta. 5 vols. Cairo: al- Hayʾa al-Miṣriyya al-ʿĀmma li-l-Kitāb, 1979.

Bahadur, Kalim. *The Jamaʿat-i-Islami of Pakistan: Political Thought and Political Action*. New Delhi: Chetana, 1977.

Bar-Asher, Meir M. *Scripture and Exegesis in Early Imāmī Shiism*. Leiden: Brill, 1999.

Barazangi, N. H. *Woman's Identity and Rethinking the Hadith*. London: Ashgate Publishing, 2015.

Barlas, Asma. *Believing Women in Islam: Unreading Patriarchal Interpretations of the Qur'an*. Austin: University of Texas Press, 2002.

Barlas, Asma. "Women's Readings of the Qurʾān." In *The Cambridge Companion to the Qurʾān*, edited by Jane McAuliffe, 255–71. Cambridge: Cambridge University Press, 2006.

Barnhill, Anne. "Bringing the Body Back to Sexual Ethics." *Hypatia* 28, no. 1 (2013): 1–17.

Bauer, Karen. *Gender Hierarchy in the Qur'ān: Medieval Interpretations, Modern Responses*. Cambridge Studies in Islamic Civilization. Cambridge: Cambridge University Press, 2015.

Baumeister, Roy F. "Erotic Plasticity." In *Encyclopaedia of Social Psychology*, edited by Roy F. Baumeister and Kathleen D. Vohs, 310–11. Thousand Oaks, CA: SAGE Publications, Inc., 2007.

Baumeister, R. F., K. Cantanese, and K. Vohs. "Is There a Gender Difference in Strength of Sex Drive?: Theoretical Views, Conceptual Distinctions, and a Review of Relevant Evidence." *Personality and Social Psychology Review* 5 (2001): 242–73.

Al-Bawaba. "Iran Permits Brothels Through Temporary Marriages," last modified June 7, 2010. http://www.albawaba.com/behind-news/iran-permits-brothels-through-temporary-marriages.

Ba-Yunus, Ilyas. "Divorce Among Muslims." *Islamic Horizons*, July/August 2000.

Ba-Yunus, Ilyas. "How Do Muslims in North America Divorce?" In *Muslim Family in a Dilemma: Quest for a Western Identity*, edited by M. Akhtar, 9–18. Washington, DC: University Press of America, 2007.

BBC Asian Network Reports. "Married for a Minute," May 13, 2013. https://www.bbc.co.uk/programmes/b01sdpfp.

Beres, Melanie A. "'Spontaneous' Sexual Consent: An Analysis of Sexual Consent Literature," *Feminism & Psychology* 17, no. 1 (2007): 93–108. https://doi.org/10.1177/0959353507072914.

Berg, Herbert. *The Development of Exegesis in Early Islam: The Authenticity of Muslim Literature from the Formative Period*. New York: Routledge, 2000.

Berg, Herbert. "The 'Isnād' and the Production of Cultural Memory: Ibn ʿAbbās as a Case Study." *Numen* 58, no. 2/3 (2011): 259–83.

Berger, L. "Al-Karrāmiyya." In *Encyclopaedia of Islam, THREE*, edited by Kate Fleet, Gudrun Krämer, Denis Matringe, John Nawas, and Everett Rowson. Brill Online.

Binder, Leonard. *Religion and Politics in Pakistan*. Berkeley: University of California Press, 1961.

Bockting, Walter O. "Transgender Identity Development." In *APA Handbook of Sexuality and Psychology*, edited by Deborah L. Tolman and Lisa M. Diamond, 739–58. Washington, DC: American Psychological Association, 2014.

Booth, Marilyn. "Exemplary Lives, Feminist Aspirations: Zaynab Fawwāz and the Arabic Biographical Tradition." *Journal of Arabic Literature* 26, no. 1/2 (1995): 120–46.

Bosworth, C. E. "al-Maybudī." In *Encyclopaedia of Islam, Second Edition*, edited by P. Bearman, Th. Bianquis, C. E. Bosworth, E. van Donzel, and W. P. Heinrichs. Brill Online, 2012.

Bosworth, C. E. "al-Ṭabarī." In *Encyclopaedia of Islam, Second Edition*, edited by P. Bearman, Th. Bianquis, C. E. Bosworth, E. van Donzel, and W. P. Heinrichs. Brill Online, 2012.

Bosworth, C. E. "K̲ h̲ wārazm." In *Encyclopaedia of Islam, Second Edition*, edited by P. Bearman, Th. Bianquis, C. E. Bosworth, E. van Donzel, and W. P. Heinrichs. Brill Online, 2012.

Brake, Elizabeth. "Is Loving More Better? The Values of Polyamory." In *The Philosophy of Sex: Contemporary Readings*, edited by Raja Halwani, Alan Soble, Sarah Hoffman, and Jacob M. Held, 201–20. Lanham, MD: Rowman and Littlefield, 2017.

Brennan, Samantha, and Robert Noggle. "The Moral Status of Children: Children's Rights, Parents' Rights, and Family Justice." *Social Theory and Practice* 23, no. 1 (1997): 1–26.

Broadfoot, Marla V. "High on Fidelity." *American Scientist*, June 2002.

Brockelmann, C. "Al- T h aʿlabī." In *Encyclopaedia of Islam, First Edition (1913–1936)*, edited by M. Th. Houtsma, T. W. Arnold, R. Basset, and R. Hartmann. Brill Online.

Brockelmann, C. "Al-Zamakhsharī." In *Encyclopaedia of Islam, First Edition (1913–1936)*, edited by M. Th. Houtsma, T. W. Arnold, R. Basset, and R. Hartmann. Brill Online.

al-Bukhārī, Ṣaḥiḥ. *Kitāb al-Jāmiʿ al-ṣaḥīḥ*. Leiden: n.p., 1862–1908).

al-Bukhārī, Ṣaḥiḥ. *Kitab al-Nikah* [Chapter of Marriage]. Volume 7 of *Ṣaḥiḥ al-Bukhārī*. 1st ed. Cairo: Dar al Ta'seel, 2012.

al-Burhān fī ʿulūm al-Qurʾān, n.d.

Burton, John. *An Introduction to the Hadīth*. Edinburgh: Edinburgh University Press, 1994.

al-Burūsawī, Ismāʿīl Ḥāqqī. *Tafsīr rūḥ al-bayān*. 10 vols. Beirut: Dār al-Fikr, n.d.

Calder, Norman. "Tafsīr from Ṭabarī to Ibn Kathīr: Problems in the Description of the Genre, Illustrated with Reference to the Story of Abraham." In *Approaches to the Qur'an*, edited by Gerald R. Hawting and Abdul-Kader A. Shareef, 101–40. London: Routledge, 1993.

Calmard, J. "Mardjaʿ-i Taḳlīd." In *Encyclopaedia of Islam, Second Edition*, edited by P. Bearman, Th. Bianquis, C. E. Bosworth, E. van Donzel, and W. P. Heinrichs. Brill Online, 2012.

Calmard, J. "Mudjtahid." In *Encyclopaedia of Islam, Second Edition*, edited by P. Bearman, Th. Bianquis, C. E. Bosworth, E. van Donzel, and W. P. Heinrichs. Brill Online, 2012.

Canard, M. "Daʿwa." In *Encyclopaedia of Islam, Second Edition*, edited by P. Bearman, Th. Bianquis, C. E. Bosworth, E. van Donzel, and W. P. Heinrichs. Brill Online, 2012.

Carra de Vaux, B. "Ṭafsīr." In *Encyclopaedia of Islam, First Edition (1913–1936)*, edited by M. Th. Houtsma, T. W. Arnold, R. Basset, and R. Hartmann. Brill Online.

Chapman, Aliya R., and Lauren Bennett Cattaneo. "American Muslim Marital Quality: A Preliminary Investigation." *Journal of Muslim Mental Health* 7, no. 2 (2013): http://dx.doi.org/10.3998/jmmh.10381607.0007.201.

Chatterjee, Partha. *Nationalist Thought and the Colonial World: A Derivative Discourse*. London: Zed Books, 1986.

Chaudhry, Ayesha S. *Domestic Violence and the Islamic Tradition: Ethics, Law, and the Muslim Discourse on Gender*. Oxford: Oxford University Press, 2015.

Cheraghi, Tayyebeh. "Lady Nusrat Begum Amin." Translated by Seyyeda Zahra Mirtendereski. *Message of Thaqlain* 14, no. 3 (2012): 109–29.

Clarke, Lynda. "Religious Practices: Prophecy and Women Prophets: Overview." In *Encyclopedia of Women & Islamic Cultures*, edited by Suad Joseph. Brill Online, 2014.

Clarke, Morgan. "Neo-Calligraphy: Religious Authority and Media Technology in Contemporary Shiite Islam." *Comparative Studies in Society and History* 52, no. 2 (2010): 351–83.

Cooper, John. "The Limits of the Sacred: The Epistemology of Abd al-Karim Soroush." In *Islam and Modernity: Muslim Intellectuals Respond*, edited by Cooper et al., 38–56. London: Tauris, 1998.

Cott, Nancy F. *Public Vows: A History of Marriage and the Nation*. Cambridge: Harvard University Press, 2000.

Cowan, J. Milton. *Hans Wehr: A Dictionary of Modern Written Arabic*. Librairie du Liban, 1980.

Daftary, Farhad. *The Isma'ilis: Their History and Doctrines*. Cambridge: Cambridge University Press, 1992.

Dahlen, Ashk. *Deciphering the Meaning of Revealed Law: The Sorushian Paradigm Shiite Epistemology*. Uppsala: University Press, 2001.

Daudpota, Umar b. Muhammad, and Asaf Ali Aasghar Fyzee. "Notes on *Mut'a* or Temporary Marriage in Islam." *Journal of the Bombay Branch of the Royal Asiatic Society* 8 (1932): 79–92.

Deeb, Lara. "On Representational Paralysis, Or, Why I Don't Want to Write About Temporary Marriage." *Jadaliyya*, December 1, 2010. https://www.jadaliyya.com/Details/23588.

Deeb, Lara, and Mona Harb. "Sanctioned Pleasures | MERIP." *Middle East Report* 37, no. 245 (2007): https://merip.org/2007/12/sanctioned-pleasures/. Accessed January 14, 2020.

Diamond, Lisa M. *Sexual Fluidity: Understanding Women's Love and Desire*. Cambridge, MA: Harvard University Press, 2009.

Ebied, R. Y., and M. J. L. Young. "al-Ḳurṭubī." In *Encyclopaedia of Islam, Second Edition*, edited by P. Bearman, Th. Bianquis, C. E. Bosworth, E. van Donzel, and W. P. Heinrichs. Brill Online, 2012.

Eekelaar, John M., and Mavis Maclean, eds. *A Reader on Family Law*. Oxford: Oxford University Press, 1994.

El Feki, Shereen. *Sex and the Citadel: Intimate Life in a Changing Arab World*. New York: Pantheon Books, 2013.

El-Mesawi, Muḥammad. *Treatise on Maqāsid al-Shariah*. Herndon, VA: International Institute of Islamic Thought, 2006.

El-Rouayheb, Khaled. *Before Homosexuality in the Arab-Islamic World, 1500–1800*. Chicago: University of Chicago Press, 2005.

Elliston, Fredrick. "In Defense of Promiscuity." In *Philosophical Perspectives on Sex and Love*, edited by Robert M. Stewart, 146–58. New York: Oxford University Press, 1995.

Elsadda, Hoda. "Discourses on Women's Biographies and Cultural Identity: Twentieth-Century Representation of the Life of Aisha Bint Abu Bakr." *Feminist Studies* 27, no. 1 (2001): 37–64.

Eltantawi, Sarah. *Shari'ah on Trial: Northern Nigeria's Islamic Revolution*. Oakland, CA: University of California Press, 2017.

Ende, W. "Rashīd Riḍā." In *Encyclopaedia of Islam, Second Edition*, edited by P. Bearman, Th. Bianquis, C. E. Bosworth, E. van Donzel, and W. P. Heinrichs. Brill Online, 2012.

Fadel, Mohammad. "Two Women, One Man: Knowledge, Power, and Gender in Medieval Sunni Legal Thought." *International Journal of Middle East Studies* 29, no. 2 (1997): 185–204.

Faḍl Allāh, Sayyid Muḥammad Ḥusayn. *Min waḥy al-Qur'ān*. 24 vols. Beirut: Dar al-Malak, 1998.

Fahimi, Hamid Reza, and Matthew Koushki-Melvin. "al-ʿAyyāshī." In *Encyclopaedia Islamica*, edited by Wilferd Madelung and Farhad Daftary, n.d. Accessed August 2, 2020.

Farah, Madelain. *Marriage and Sexuality in Islam: A Translation of al-Ghazali's Book on the Etiquette of Marriage from the Ihya*. Salt Lake City: University of Utah Press, 1984.

Frontline. Season 2019, episode 6. "Iraq's Secret Sex Trade," November 12, 2019, https://www.pbs.org/wgbh/frontline/film/iraqs-secret-sex-trade/.

Geissinger, Aisha. "The Exegetical Traditions of ʿĀ'isha: Notes on Their Impact and Significance." *Journal of Qur'anic Studies* 6, no. 1 (2004): 1–20.

Geissinger, Aisha. "Mary in the Qur'an: Rereading Subversive Births." In *Sacred Tropes: Tanakah, New Testament, and Qur'an as Literature and Culture*, edited by Roberta Sabbath, 379–92. Leiden: Brill, 2009.

al-Ghazālī, Abū Ḥāmid. *Iḥyā' ʿulūm al-dīn*. Beirut: Dār al-Marifat, 1981.

Giladi, Anver. "Children." In *Encyclopedia of the Qur'ān*. Edited by Jane Dammen McAuliffe. Brill Online.

Giladi, Anver. "Family." In *Encyclopedia of the Qur'ān*. Edited by Jane Dammen McAuliffe. Brill Online.

Giladi, Anver. "Parents." In *Encyclopedia of the Qur'ān*. Edited by Jane Dammen McAuliffe. Brill Online.

Gilliot, Claude. "ʿAbdallāh b. ʿAbbās." In *Encyclopaedia of Islam, THREE*, edited by Kate Fleet, Gudrun Krämer, Denis Matringe, John Nawas, and Everett Rowson. Brill Online.

Gimaret, D. "Muʿtazila." In *Encyclopaedia of Islam, Second Edition*, edited by P. Bearman, Th. Bianquis, C. E. Bosworth, E. van Donzel, and W. P. Heinrichs. Brill Online, 2012.

Godlas, Alan. "Ṣūfism." In *The Wiley Blackwell Companion to the Qur'an*, edited by Jawid Mojaddedi and Andrew Rippin, 350–61. Malden, MA: Wiley-Blackwell, 2006.

Goldfeld, Yeshayahu. "Pseudo Ibn ʿAbbās Responsa-Polemics against the Ghamiyya." *Arabica* 35, no. 3 (1988): 350–67.

Goldfield, Isaiah. *Qur'ānic Commentary in the Eastern Islamic Tradition of the First Four Centuries of the Hijra: An Annotated Preface of al-Thaʿlabī's "Kitāb al-Kashf Wa l-Bayān ʿan Tafsīr al-Qur'ān*. Acre: Scrugy Printers and Publishers, 1984.

Goldziher, Ignaz. *Introduction to Islamic Theology and Law*. Vol. 9. Princeton: Princeton University Press, 1981.

Grabowski, John S. *Sex and Virtue: An Introduction to Sexual Ethics*. Vol. 2 of *Catholic Moral Thought*. Washington DC: Catholic University of America Press, 2003.

Grant, Stephanie. "Why My Daughter Got (Temporarily) Married at 13." Modern Love, *New York Times*, August 27, 2021, https://www.nytimes.com/2021/08/27/style/modern-love-temporary-marriage-at-13.html.

Gribetz, Arthur. *Strange Bedfellows: Mutʿat al-Nisāʾ and Mutʿat al-Ḥajj: A Study Based on Sunnī and Shīʿī Sources of Tafsīr, Ḥadīth, and Fiqh*. Berlin: Klaus Schwartz, 1994.

Gupta, Kristina. "Compulsory Sexuality: Evaluating an Emerging Concept," *Signs: Journal of Women in Culture and Society* 41, no. 1 (2015): 131–54.

Habib, Samar. *Female Homosexuality in the Middle East: Histories and Representations*. Hoboken: Taylor and Francis, 2012.

Haeri, Shahla. "Temporary Marriage." In *Encyclopedia of the Qurʾān*. Edited by Jane Dammen McAuliffe. Brill Online.

Haeri, Shahla. *Law of Desire: Temporary Marriage in Shiʿi Iran*. Syracuse, NY: Syracuse University Press, 1989.

Haider, Najam I. *The Origins of the Shia: Identity, Ritual, and Sacred Space in Eighth Century Kufa*. New York: Cambridge University Press, 2011.

al-Hajjāj, Muslim b. *Tafsīr al-ṣahīh*. Cairo: n.p., 1374/1916.

Hammer, Juliane. *American Muslim Women, Religious Authority, and Activism: More Than Prayers*. Austin: University of Texas Press, 2012.

Hammer, Juliane, Dina El Omari, and Mouhanad Khorchide, eds. *Muslim Women and Gender Justice: Concepts, Sources, and Histories*. London: Routledge, 2019.

Hamza, Feras, Sajjad Rizvi, and Farhana Mayer. *On the Nature of the Divine*. Vol. 1 of *An Anthology of Qur'anic Commentaries*. Oxford: Oxford University Press, 2010.

Ḥāqqī, Ismāʿīl. *Tafsīr rūḥ al-bayān*. 10 vols. Beirut: Dār al-Fikr, n.d.

Hashmi, Farhat. "Women: خواتین." Quran for All: In Every Hand, In Every Heart. https://www.farhathashmi.com/assorted-section/women/. Accessed August 5, 2020.

Hassan, Riffat. "Islam and Human Rights in Pakistan: A Critical Analysis of the Positions of Three Contemporary Women." *Canadian Foreign Policy Journal* 10 (January 1, 2002): 131–55. https://doi.org/10.1080/11926422.2002.9673311.

Hassan, Riffat. "Islam and Human Rights." *Dawn, Review* (November 14, 2002). Available online at: http://www.columbia.edu/itc/mealac/pritchett/00islamlinks/txt_riffat_hasan/txt_riffat_hasan.htm.

al-Haythamī, Nūr al-Dīn ʿAlī b. Abī Bakr. *Majmaʿ al-zawāʾid wa-manbaʿ al-fawāʾid*. 10 vols. Cairo: Dar al-Rayyan li-l-Turath, 1987.

Heffening, W. "Mutʿa." In *Encyclopaedia of Islam, Second Edition*, edited by P. Bearman, Th. Bianquis, C. E. Bosworth, E. van Donzel, and W. P. Heinrichs. Brill Online, 2012.

Hermansen, Marcia. "Wombs." In *Encyclopedia of the Qurʾān*. Edited by Jane Dammen McAuliffe. Brill Online.

Hidayatullah, Aysha A. *Feminist Edges of the Qur'an*. 1st ed. Oxford: Oxford University Press, 2014.

Hollander, Eric, Jennifer Bartz, William Chaplin, Ann Phillips, Jennifer Sumner, Latha Soorya, Evdokia Anagnostou, and Stacey Wasserman. "Oxytocin Increases Retention of Social Cognition in Autism." *Biological Psychiatry* 61, no. 4 (February 15, 2007): 498–503. https://doi.org/10.1016/j.biopsych.2006.05.030.

Howard, I. K. A. "*Mut'a* Marriage Reconsidered in the Context of the Formal Procedures for Islamic Marriage." *Journal of Semitic Studies* 2, no. 1 (1975): 82–92. https://doi.org/10.1093/jss/XX.1.82.

Ibn Abī Shayba, ʿAbd Allāh b. Muḥammad. *al-Musannaf*. Beirut: n.p., 2004.

Ibn ʿAshūr, Muḥammad al-Ṭāhir. *al-Taḥrīr wal-tanwīr*. Vol. 5. Tunis: al-Dār al-Tūnisiyya lil-Nashr, 1984.

Ibn al-Humām, Kamāl al-Dīn. *Fatḥ al-qadīr*. Vol. 3. Cairo: al-Maktaba al-Tijāriyya al-Kubrā, 1974.

Ibn Dāwud. *Arkān al-nikāḥ wa-shurūṭuhu*. Cairo: Maktabat al-tarbiya al-islamiya, 1963.

"Ibn Ḥaiyān." In *Encyclopaedia of Islam, First Edition (1913–1936)*, edited by Houtsma, M. Th., T. W. Arnold, R. Basset, and R. Hartmann. Brill Online.

Ibn Ḥanbal, Aḥmad. *Musnad*. Vol. 3. Cairo: n.p., 1971.

Ibn Hishām, ʿAbd al-Malik. *The Life of Muhammad: A Translation of Isḥāq's* Sīrat Rasūl Allāh. Translated by Alfred Guillaume. Karachi: Oxford University Press, 1978.

Ibn Manzūr, Muḥammad b. Mukarram b. *Lisān al-ʿArab*. Beirut: Dār al-Sadir, 1990.

Ibn Saʿd, Abū ʿAbd Allāh Muhammad. *Kitāb al-Ṭabaqāt al-kabīr*. Edited by Eduard Sachau. 9 vols. Leiden: E. J. Brill, 1904.

Ibn ʿAbbās, ʿAbd Allāh. *Tanwīr al-miqbās min tafsīr Ibn ʿAbbās*. Beirut: Dār al-Kutub al- ʿIlmiyya, 2000.

Ibn ʿAbd al-Barr, Yusūf b. ʿAbd Allāh. *Jām bayān al-ʿilm*. Cairo: n.p., 1346.

Ibrahim, Celene. *Women and Gender in the Qur'an*. Oxford: Oxford University Press, 2020.

Iran Rooyan. "Trafficking Fact Sheet," n.d. http://iranrooyan.org/wp-content/uploads/2011/12/TRAFFICKING-FACT-SHEET-final.pdf.

"Iran Unveils State-Approved Dating App to Promote Marriage." BBC News, July 13, 2021, https://www.bbc.com/news/world-middle-east-57818758.

Jackson, Sherman. "Taqlīd, Legal Scaffolding and the Scope of Legal Injunctions in Post-Formative Theory." *Islamic Law and Society* 3, no. 2 (1996): 165–92. https://doi.org/10.1163/1568519962599104.

Jahanbaksh, Forough. *Islam, Democracy and Religious Modernism in Iran (1953–2000): From Bazargan to Soroush*. Leiden: Brill, 2001.

Jameelah, Maryam. *Who Is Maudoodi?* Lahore: Mohammad Yusuf Khan, 1973.

al-Jazīrī, ʿAbd al-Rahmān. *al-Fiqh ʿalā al-madhāhib al-arbaʿa*. Vol. 4. Cairo: n.p., 1969.

Jeffery, Arthur. *Materials for the History of the Text of the Qur'an: The Old Codices*. Leiden: E. J. Brill, 1937.

Johansen, Baber. *Contingency in a Sacred Law: Legal and Ethical Norms in the Muslim Fiqh*. Leiden: Brill, 1998.

Jütten, Timo. "Sexual Objectification." *Ethics: An International Journal of Social, Political and Legal Philosophy* 27, no. 1 (2016): 27–49.

Juynboll, G. H. A. "Khabar al-Wāḥid." In *Encyclopaedia of Islam, Second Edition*, edited by P. Bearman, Th. Bianquis, C. E. Bosworth, E. van Donzel, and W. P. Heinrichs. Brill Online, 2012.

Juynboll, G. H. A. *Muslim Tradition: Studies on Chronology, Provenance and Authorship of Early Ḥadīth*. Cambridge: Cambridge University Press, 1983.

Kalmbach, Hilary. "Social and Religious Change in Damascus: One Case of Female Islamic Religious Authority." *British Journal of Middle Eastern Studies* 35, no. 1 (2008): 37–57.

Kāshānī, ʿAbd al-Razzāq. *Tafsīr al-Qurʾān al-karīm*. 2 vols. Beirut: Dār al-Yaqẓa al-ʿArabiyya, 1968.

Kassamali, Sumayya. "A Politics of Submission: Conditional Agents and Canadian Threats at the Al-Huda Institute of Islamic Education for Women." Master's thesis, University of Toronto, 2009.

al-Kātib, Abdul Hassan ʿAli b. Nasr. *Encyclopedia of Pleasure [Jawamiʾ al-ladha]*. Edited by Salah Addin Khawwam. Translated by ʾAdnan Jarkas and Salah Addin Khawwam. Toronto: Aleppo Publishing, 1977.

Katz-Wise, Sabra L., and Janet S. Hyde. "Sexuality and Gender: The Interplay." In *APA Handbook of Sexuality and Psychology*, edited by Deborah L. Tolman and Lisa M. Diamond. Washington, DC: American Psychological Association, 2014.

Keeler, Annabel. "Exegesis iii, In Persian." In *Encyclopedia Iranica*, December 15, 1999. https://www.iranicaonline.org/articles/exegesis-iii.

Keeler, Annabel. "Ẓāhir and Bāṭin in Maybudī's Kashf al-Asrār." In *Proceedings of the Third European Conference of Iranian Studies, Part 2: Medieval and Modern Persian Studies*, edited by Charles Melville, 167–78. Wiesbaden: Otto Harrassowitz, 1999.

Keeler, Annabel. *Sufi Hermeneutics: The Qurʾan Commentary of Rashīd al-Dīn Maybudī*. Oxford: Oxford University Press, 2006.

Kendrick, Keith M. "The Neurobiology of Social Bonds." *Journal of Neuroendocrinology* 16, no. 12 (December 2004): 1007–8. https://doi.org/10.1111/j.1365–2826.2004.01262.x.

Kern, Soeren. "Britain: Islamic Temporary Marriages on the Rise." Gatestone Institute, http://www.gatestoneinstitute.org/3748/uk-islamic-temporary-marriages, last modified June 4, 2013.

Khaleeli, Homa. "I Was a Temporary Bride." *The Guardian*, July 11, 2015. https://www.theguardian.com/lifeandstyle/2015/jul/11/i-was-a-temporary-bride-in-iran.

Khānum, Nuṣrat. *Makhzan al-ʿirfān dar tafsīr-i Qurʾān*. Vol. 4. Iṣfahān: Anjuman-i Ḥimāyat az Khānavādah'hā-yi Bī'sarparast-i Īrānī, 1990.

Khattab, Mustafa, trans. *The Clear Quran: A Thematic English Translation of the Message of the Final Revelation*. Lombard, IL: Book of Signs Foundation, 2016.

Khikmatiar, M. Azkiya. "Muqatil Bin Sulaiman, Pengarang Kitab Tafsir Al-Kabir." Islami[dot]co, September 24, 2018. https://islami.co/muqatil-bin-sulaiman-pengarang-kitab-tafsir-al-kabir/.

Khomeini, Ruhollah. *A Clarification of Questions: An Unabridged Translation of Resaleh Towzih al-Masael*. Translated by J. Borujerdi. 1st ed. Boulder: Westview Press, 1984.

Kleinplatz, Peggy J., and Lisa M. Diamond. "Sexual Diversity." In *APA Handbook of Sexuality and Psychology*, edited by Deborah L. Tolman and Lisa M. Diamond, 210–20. Washington, DC: American Psychological Association, 2014.

Kohlberg, E. "Al-Ṭabrisī." In *Encyclopaedia of Islam, Second Edition*, edited by P. Bearman, Th. Bianquis, C. E. Bosworth, E. van Donzel, and W. P. Heinrichs. Brill Online, 2012.

Kohlberg, Etan. "Imam and Community in the Pre-Ghayba Period." In *Authority and Political Culture in Shi'ism*, edited by Arjomand Said Ami. Albany: State University of New York Press, 1988.

Kramers, J. H., C. E. Bosworth, O. Schumann, and Ousmane Kane. "Sulṭān." In *Encyclopaedia of Islam, Second Edition*, edited by P. Bearman, Th. Bianquis, C. E. Bosworth, E. van Donzel, and W. P. Heinrichs. Brill Online, 2012.

Kugle, Scott Alan. *Homosexuality in Islam: Critical Reflection on Gay, Lesbian, and Transgender Muslims*. Oxford: Oneworld, 2010.

al-Kulaynī, Muḥammad b. Yaʿqūb. *al-Furūʿ min al-kāfī*. Vol. 5 of 8. Tehran: Dār al-Kutub al-Islāmiyya, 1968.

Künkler, Mirjam, and Roja Fazaeli. "The Life of Two *Mujtahidah*s: Female Religious Authority in Twentieth-Century Iran." In *Women, Leadership and Mosques: Changes in Contemporary Islamic Authority*, edited by Masooda Bano and Hilary Kalmbach, 127–60. Leiden: Brill, 2016.

Kut, Günay Alpay. "Ismāʿīl Ḥaḳḳī." In *Encyclopaedia of Islam, Second Edition*, edited by P. Bearman, Th. Bianquis, C. E. Bosworth, E. van Donzel, and W. P. Heinrichs. Brill Online, 2012.

Kynsilehto, Anitta. *Islamic Feminism: Current Perspectives*. Tampere: Tampere Peace Research Institute, 2008.

Labi, Nadya. "Married for a Minute." *Mother Jones*, March/April 2010. https://www.motherjones.com/politics/2010/03/temporary-marriage-iran-islam/.

Lamrabet, Asma. *Women in the Qur'an: An Emancipatory Reading*. Translated by Myriam Francois-Cerrah. New York: Kube Publishing Ltd, 2016.

Lamrabet, Asma. *Women and Men in the Qur'ān*. Translated by Muneera Salem-Murdock. Cham, Switzerland: Palgrave Macmillian, 2018.

Lane, Andrew J. *A Traditional Muʿtazilite Qurʾān Commentary: The Kashshāf of Jār Allāh al-Zamakhsharī (d. 538–1144)*. Leiden: E. J. Brill, 2006.

Leehmuis, Frederik. "Codices of the Qur'an." In *Encyclopedia of the Qurʾān*. Edited by Jane Dammen McAuliffe. Brill Online.

Levit, Nancy, and Robert M. Verchick, eds. *Feminist Legal Theory: A Primer*. New York: New York University Press, 2006.

Lewis, B. "al-ʿAyyāshī." In *Encyclopaedia of Islam, Second Edition*, ed. P. Bearman, Th. Bianquis, C. E. Bosworth, E. van Donzel, and W. P. Heinrichs. Brill Online, 2012.

Lings, Martin. *Muhammad: His Life Based on the Earliest Sources*. New York: Inner Traditions, 2006.

Macdonald. "ʿAbd Al-Razzāḳ." In *Encyclopaedia of Islam, First Edition (1913–1936)*, edited by T. W. Arnold, R. Basset, and R. Hartmann. Brill Online.

Madelung, Wilferd. "al-Mahdī." In *Encyclopaedia of Islam, Second Edition*, edited by P. Bearman, Th. Bianquis, C. E. Bosworth, E. van Donzel, and W. P. Heinrichs. Brill Online, 2012.

Madelung, Wilferd. "al-Zamakhsharī." In *Encyclopaedia of Islam, Second Edition*, edited by P. Bearman, Th. Bianquis, C. E. Bosworth, E. van Donzel, and W. P. Heinrichs. Brill Online, 2012.

Madelung, Wilferd. "Imāma." In *Encyclopaedia of Islam, Second Edition*, edited by P. Bearman, Th. Bianquis, C. E. Bosworth, E. van Donzel, and W. P. Heinrichs. Brill Online, 2012.

Madelung, Wilferd. "Ismāʿīliyya," in *Encyclopaedia of Islam, Second Edition*, edited by P. Bearman, Th. Bianquis, C. E. Bosworth, E. van Donzel, and W. P. Heinrichs. Brill Online, 2012.

Madelung, Wilferd. "Ḳarmaṭī." In *Encyclopaedia of Islam, Second Edition*, edited by P. Bearman, Th. Bianquis, C. E. Bosworth, E. van Donzel, and W. P. Heinrichs. Brill Online, 2012.

Madelung, Wilferd. "Shīʿa." In *Encyclopaedia of Islam, Second Edition*, edited by P. Bearman, Th. Bianquis, C. E. Bosworth, E. van Donzel, and W. P. Heinrichs. Brill Online, 2012.

Madelung, Wilferd. "Zaydiyya." In *Encyclopaedia of Islam, Second Edition*, edited by P. Bearman, Th. Bianquis, C. E. Bosworth, E. van Donzel, and W. P. Heinrichs. Brill Online, 2012.

Madelung, Wilferd. "Shi'a Attitudes Towards Women as Reflected in Fiqh." In *Society and the Sexes in Medieval Islam*, edited by A. L. S. Marsot, 69–79, n.d.

Madelung, Wilferd. *Der Imam al-Qasim Ibn Ibrahim Und Die Glaubenslehre Der Zaiditen*. Berlin: Walter de Gruyter, 1965.

Magon, Navneet, and Sanjay Kalra. "The Orgasmic History of Oxytocin: Love, Lust, and Labor." *Indian Journal of Endocrinology and Metabolism* 15, no. 3 (September 2011): S156–61. https://doi.org/10.4103/2230–8210.84851.

Mahmood, Saba. *Politics of Piety: The Islamic Revival and the Feminist Subject*. Princeton, NJ: Princeton University Press, 2005.

Mahmood, Shabnam, and Catrin Nye. "I Do, for Now Anyway." *BBC News*, May 13, 2013, sec. UK. https://www.bbc.com/news/uk-22354201.

al-Majlisī, Muḥammad Bāqir b. Muḥammad Taqī. *Biḥār al-anwār*. 104 vols. Beirut: Mu'assasat al-Wafa, 1983.

"Marriages Down, Divorces Increase in Turkey." *Daily Sabah*, February 26, 2020. https://www.dailysabah.com/turkey/marriages-down-divorces-increase-in-turkey/news.

Massad, Joseph. *Desiring Arabs*. Chicago: The University of Chicago Press, 2007.

Matin-Asghari, Afshin. "Abdolkarim Sorush and the Secularization of Islamic Thought in Iran." *Iranian Studies* 30 (1997): 1–2, 95–115.

Mawdūdī, Sayyid Abū al-Aʿlā. *Towards Understanding the Qurʾān: Abridged Version of Tafhīm al-Qurʾān*. Translated and edited by Zafar Ishaq Ansari. Leicester, UK: The Islamic Foundation, 1988.

Mawdūdī, Sayyid Abū al-Aʿlā. *Tafhīm al-Qurʾān*. 6 vols. Lahore: Idāra-i Tarjumān al-Qurʾān, 2000.

Maybudī, Abū al-Faḍl Rashīd al-Dīn. *Kashf al-asrār wa-ʿuddat al-abrār*. Edited by ʿAlī Aṣghar Hikmat. 10 vols. Tehran: Tehran University Press, 1952.

McCarthy, Barry, and Emily J. McCarthy. *Finding Your Sexual Voice: Celebrating Female Sexuality*. 1st ed. New York: Routledge, 2018.

McEvers, Kelly. "Abuse Of Temporary Marriages Flourishes In Iraq." NPR, October 19, 2010. https://www.npr.org/templates/story/story.php?storyId=130350678.

Mernissi, Fatema. *Can We Women Head a Muslim State*? Lahore, Pakistan: Simorgh, Women's Resource and Publications Centre, 1991.

Mernissi, Fatema. *The Veil and the Male Elite: A Feminist Interpretation of Women's Rights in Islam*. Reading, MA: Addison-Wesley, 1991.

Mir-Hosseini, Ziba. *Marriage on Trial: A Study of Islamic Family Law*. Rev. ed. New York: I. B. Tauris, 2001.

Mir-Hosseini, Ziba. "The Construction of Gender in Islamic Legal Thought and Strategies for Reform." *Hawwa* 1, no. 1 (2003): 1–28.

Mir-Hosseini, Ziba. "Muslim Women's Quest for Equality: Between Islamic Law and Feminism." *Critical Inquiry* 32, no. 4 (Summer 2006) 629–45.

Mir-Hosseini, Ziba. "Beyond 'Islam' vs 'Feminism.'" *IDS Bulletin* 42 (2011): 67–77. https://doi.org/10.1111/j.1759–5436.2011.00202.x.

Mir-Hosseini, Ziba, et al., eds. *Men in Charge?: Rethinking Authority in Muslim Legal Tradition*. London: Oneworld, 2015.

Mir-Hosseini, Ziba, et al., eds. *Gender and Equality in Muslim Family Law: Justice and Ethics in the Islamic Legal Tradition*. New York: I. B. Tauris, 2017.

Modahl, C., L. Green, D. Fein, M. Morris, L. Waterhouse, C. Feinstein, and H. Levin. "Plasma Oxytocin Levels in Autistic Children." *Biological Psychiatry* 43, no. 4 (February 15, 1998): 270–77. https://doi.org/10.1016/s0006-3223(97)00439–3.

Modarressi, Hossein. *Crisis and Consolidation in the Formative Period of Shiʿite Islam: Abū Jaʿfar Ibn Qiba al-Razi and His Contribution to Imamite Shiʿite Thought*. Princeton, NJ: Darwin Press, 1993.

Moghadam, Valentine M. "Islamic Feminism and Its Discontents: Toward a Resolution of the Debate." *Signs: Journal of Women in Culture and Society* 27, no. 4 (2002): 1135–71.

Moosa, Ebrahim. "Recovering the Ethical: Practice, Politics, and Tradition." In *The Shari'a: History, Ethics and Law*, edited by Amyn B. Sajoo, 40–57. London: I. B. Tauris and Company, Ltd., 2018.

Mortezai, Sudabeh. dir., *In The Bazaar of Sexes*, FreibeuterFilm, 2019. Trailer available at: https://www.filmplatform.net/product/in-the-bazaar-of-sexes/.

Motahari, Ayatollah Morteza. *Woman and Her Rights*. Translated by M. A. Ansari. Islamic Seminary Publications. Available online at: http://www.iranchamber.com/personalities/mmotahari/works/woman_rights_islam.pdf. Accessed January 10, 2020.

Moṭahharī, Murtaẓa. *The Rights of Women in Islam*. Tehran: World Organization for Islamic Services, 1981.

Motzki, Harald. "Marriage and Divorce." In *Encyclopedia of the Qurʾān*, edited by Jane Dammen McAuliffe. Brill Online.

Mubarak, Hadia. "Intersections: Modernity, Gender, and Qur'anic Exegesis." Phd diss., Georgetown University, 2014.

Mubarak, Hadia. "Change through Continuity: A Case Study of Q. 4:34 in Ibn ʿĀshūr's *al-Taḥrīr wa'l-tanwīr*." *Journal of Qur'anic Studies* 20, no. 1 (2018): 1–27.

Mubarak, Hadia. *Rebellious Wives, Neglectful Husbands: Controversies in Modern Qur'anic Commentaries*. Oxford: Oxford University Press, forthcoming January 2022.

Muhammad, al-Qadi Numan b. *Ikhtilāf uṣūl al-madhāhib*. 2 vols. Edited by Sham'un T. Lokhandwalla. Shimla: Indian Institute for Advanced Studies, 1972.

Murata, Sachiko. *Mutʿa: Temporary Marriage in Islamic Law*. Qum: Ansariyan Publishers, 1986.

Murray, Stephen O., and Will Roscoe. *Islamic Homosexualities: Culture, History, and Literature*. New York: New York University Press, 1997.

al-Murtaḍā, al-Sharīf. *al-Intiṣār*. Najaf: Manshūrat al-Matbaʿa al-Ḥaḍāriyya, 1971.

Mushtaq, Faiza. "A Day with Al-Huda." *Contexts* 6, no. 2 (2007): 60–61.

Muslehuddin, Mohammad. *Mutʿa: Temporary Marriage*. Lahore: n.p., 1974.

Muslim, Ṣaḥiḥ. *Kitab Fadaʾil al-Sahaba*. Vol. 1. 1st ed. Riyadh, Saudi Arabia: Dar Tayba, 2006.

Muslim Ibn al-Ḥajjāj, *al-Ṣaḥīḥ*. Cairo: n.p., 1374–75/1955–56.

Myrne, Pernilla. *Female Sexuality in the Early Medieval Islamic World: Gender and Sex in Arabic Literature*. London: I. B. Tauris, 2019.

Nafi, Basheer. "The Rise of Islamic Reformist Thought and Its Challenge to Traditional Islam." In *Islamic Thought in the Twentieth Century*, edited by. Suha Taji-Farouki and Basheer Nafi, 28–60. London, New York: I. B. Tauris, 2004.

Nafi, Basheer. "Ṭāhir Ibn ʿĀshūr: The Career and Thought of a Modern Reformist *ʿālim*, with Special Reference to His Work of *Tafsīr*." *Journal of Qurʾanic Studies* 7, no. 1 (2005): 1–32.

Najibullah, Farangis, and Kayumars Ato. "Tajik Mullahs Warn of New Threat in Temporary Marriages." RadioFreeEurope/RadioLiberty, last modified June 17, 2012, https://www.rferl.org/a/tajik-mullahs-warn-against-temporary-marriages/24616875.html.

Nasr, Seyyed Hossein. "Ṭabāṭabā'ī, Muḥammad Ḥusayn." In *The Oxford Encyclopaedia of the Modern Islamic World*, edited by John L. Esposito. Oxford Islamic Studies Online, http://www.oxfordislamicstudies.com/article/opr/t236MIW/e077 (accessed November 22, 2021).

Nawa, Fariba. "Divorce Turkish Style." *The New York Review of Books*, February 20, 2019. https://www.nybooks.com/daily/2019/02/20/divorce-turkish-style/.

Nelson, James Lindemann. "Parental Obligations and the Ethics of Surrogacy: A Causal Perspective." *Public Affairs Quarterly* 5, no. 1 (1991): 49–61.

Neumann, Inga D. "The Advantage of Social Living: Brain Neuropeptides Mediate the Beneficial Consequences of Sex and Motherhood." *Frontiers in Neuroendocrinology* 30, no. 4 (October 2009): 483–96. https://doi.org/10.1016/j.yfrne.2009.04.012.

Newitz, Annalee. "How Iran Became One of the World's Most Futuristic Countries." Gizmodo, May 2, 2014. https://io9.gizmodo.com/how-iran-became-one-of-the-worlds-most-futuristic-count-1570438769.

Newman, Andrew J. *The Formative Period of Twelver Shi'ism: Ḥadīth as Discourse Between Qum and Baghdad*. Richmond, Surrey: Curzon Press, 2000.

Niemeijer, A.C. "Khilāfa." In *Encyclopaedia of Islam, Second Edition*, edited by P. Bearman, Th. Bianquis, C. E. Bosworth, E. van Donzel, and W .P. Heinrichs. Brill Online, 2012.

O'Neill, Onora. "Children's Rights and Children's Lives." *Ethics* 98, no. 3 (1988): 445–63.

Osman, Rawand. *Female Personalities in the Qur'an and Sunna: Examining the Major Sources of Shi'i Islam*. New York: Routledge, 2014.

Paret, R. "al-Ṭabarī." In *Encyclopaedia of Islam, First Edition (1913–1936)*, edited by M. Th. Houtsma, T. W. Arnold, R. Basset, and R. Hartmann. Brill Online.

Patai, Raphael. *Golden River to Golden Road: Society, Culture, and Change in the Middle East*. Philadelphia: University of Pennsylvania Press, 1967.

Peters, R. "Zinā or Zināʾ." In *Encyclopaedia of Islam, Second Edition*, edited by P. Bearman, Th. Bianquis, C. E. Bosworth, E. van Donzel, and W. P. Heinrichs. Brill Online, 2012.

Pink, Johanna. "Tradition, Authority and Innovation in Contemporary Sunnī Tafsīr: Towards a Typology of Qur'an Commentaries from the Arab World, Indonesia and Turkey." *Journal of Qur'anic Studies* 12, no. 1–2 (2010): 56–82.

Planet Iran. "Temporary Marriage Has Turned into a Career and Source of Income in Iran." *Iran Press News*, August 9, 2010. http://planet-iran.com/index.php/news/21112.

Plessner, M., and A. Rippin. "Muḳātil b. Sulaymān." In *Encyclopaedia of Islam, Second Edition*, edited by P. Bearman, Th. Bianquis, C. E. Bosworth, E. van Donzel, and W. P. Heinrichs. Brill Online, 2012.

Poonawala, I. "Taʾwīl." In *Encyclopaedia of Islam, Second Edition*, edited by P. Bearman, Th. Bianquis, C. E. Bosworth, E. van Donzel, and W. P. Heinrichs. Brill Online, 2012.

Powers, Paul. *Intent in Islamic Law*. Leiden: Brill, 2006.

al-Qaraḍāwī, Yūsuf. *Zawāj al-misyār*. Cairo: Maktabat wahba, 1999.

Quadri, Junaid. "Moral Habituation in the Law: Rethinking the Ethics of the Shari'a." *Islamic Law and Society* 26 (2019): 191–226.

Quale, G. Robina. *A History of Marriage Systems*. Westport: Greenwood, 1988.

Qureshi, Sameera. "I'm a Muslim Sexual Health Educator. 'Ramy' Shouldn't Surprise You." *Medium*, July 10, 2020. https://medium.com/@sameeraq/im-a-muslim-sexual-health-educator-ramy-shouldn-t-surprise-you-a144de565863.

al-Qurṭubī, Abū ʿAbd Allāh. *al-Jāmiʿ li-aḥkām al-Qurʾān wa-l-mubayyin li-mā taḍammana min al-sunna wa-āyāt al-furqān*. Beirut: al-Risāla Publishers, 2006.

Rahemtulla, Shadaab, and Sara Ababneh. "Reclaiming Khadija's and Muhammad's Marriage as an Islamic Paradigm: Toward a New History of the Muslim Present." *Journal of Feminist Studies in Religion* 37, no. 2 (Fall 2021): 83–102.

Rahman, Fazlur. *Major Themes of the Qur'an*. Minneapolis: Bibliotheca, 1980.

Rahman, Fazlur. *Islam and Modernity: Transformation of an Intellectual Tradition.* Chicago: University of Chicago Press, 1984.

al-Rāzī, Abū Ḥātim. *Kitāb Al-Zīna Fī al-Kalimāt al-ʿArabiyya al-Islamiyya*. Edited by Ḥusayn b. Fayḍ Allāh al-Ḥamdānī. 2 vols. Cairo: Dār al-Kitāb al-ʿArabī, 1957–58.

al-Rāzī, Abū Ḥātim. *Aʿlam Al-Nubuwwa*. Edited by Salah al-Sawi and Ghulam Rida Awani. Tehran: Imperial Academy of Philosophy, 1977.

al-Rāzī, Abū Ḥātim. *Kitāb Al-Iṣlāḥ*. Edited by Hasan Minuchihr and Mahdi Muhaqqiq. Montreal: McGill Institute of Islamic Studies, 1998.

al-Rāzī, Fakhr al-Dīn Muḥammad b. ʿUmar. *Mafātīḥ al-ghayb aw al-tafsīr al-kabīr*. 32 vols. Tehran: Dār al-Kutub al-ʿIlmiyya, n.d.

Reda, Lolwa. "On Marriage and Divorce in Egypt." *Egypt Today*, February 28, 2019. http://www.egypttoday.com/Article/6/66379/On-Marriage-and-Divorce-in-Egypt.

Rehman, Sofia Abdur. "ʿĀ'isha's Corrective of the Companions: A Translation and Critical Ḥadīth Study of al- Zarkashī's *al-Ijāba li-Īrādi mā Istadrakathu ʿĀ'isha ʿala al Ṣahāba*." PhD diss., University of Leeds, 2019.

Reinharst, Kevin. *Before Revelation: The Boundaries of Muslim Moral Thought.* Albany: SUNY Press, 1995.

Rios, Lorena. "'Biased' Changes To Egypt's Divorce Laws Over Custody Prompt Outcry." *Huffington Post*, January 26, 2017. https://www.huffpost.com/entry/egypt-divorce-laws-custody_n_588a0396e4b0737fd5cbaf46.

Rippin, Andrew. "Ṭafsīr." In *Encyclopaedia of Islam, Second Edition*, edited by P. Bearman, Th. Bianquis, C.E. Bosworth, E. van Donzel, and W.P. Heinrichs. Brill Online, 2012.

Rippin, Andrew. "al- T̲ h̲ aʿlabī." In *Encyclopaedia of Islam, Second Edition*, edited by P. Bearman, Th. Bianquis, C. E. Bosworth, E. van Donzel, and W. P. Heinrichs. Brill Online, 2012.

Rippin, Andrew. "Ibn ʿAbbās's *al-Lughāt fī al-Qurʾān*." *Bulletin of the School of Oriental and African Studies* 44, no. 1 (1981): 15–25.

Rippin, Andrew. "Al-Zukhrī, *Naskh al-Qurʾān* and the Problem of Early *Tafsīr* Texts." *Bulletin of the School of Oriental and African Studies* 47 (1984): 22–43.

Rippin, Andrew. "*Tafsīr Ibn ʿAbbās* and Criteria for Dating Early *Tafsīr* Texts." *Jerusalem Studies in Arabic and Islam* 18 (1994): 38–83.

Robinson, F. C. R. "Mawdūdī." In *Encyclopaedia of Islam, Second Edition*, edited by P. Bearman, Th. Bianquis, C. E. Bosworth, E. van Donzel, and W. P. Heinrichs. Brill Online, 2012.

Robson, J. "Ḥadīth." In *Encyclopaedia of Islam, Second Edition*, edited by P. Bearman, Th. Bianquis, C. E. Bosworth, E. van Donzel, and W. P. Heinrichs. Brill Online, 2012.

Rutner, Maryam. "Religious Authority, Gendered Recognition, and Instrumentalization of Nusrat Amin in Life and after Death." *Journal of Middle East Women's Studies* 11, no. 1 (2015): 24–41.

Sachedina, Abdulaziz. *Islamic Messianism: The Idea of Mahdī in Twelver Shīʿism*. Albany: State University of New York Press, 1981.

Saleh, Walid A. *The Formation of the Classical Tafsīr Tradition: The Qurʾān Commentary of al-Thaʿlabī (d. 427/1035)*. Leiden: Brill, 2004.

Saleh, Walid A. "The Last of the Nishapuri School of Tafsīr: Al-Wāḥidī (d. 468/1076) and His Significance in the History of Qur'anic Exegesis." *Journal of the American Oriental Society* 126 (2006): 223–43.

Saleh, Walid A. "Preliminary Remarks on the Historiography of Tafsir in Arabic: A History of the Book." *Journal of Qur'anic Studies* 12 (2010): 6–40.

Saleh, Walid A. "Marginalia and Peripheries: A Tunisian Historian and the History of Qurʾanic Exegesis." *Numen* 58, no. 2/3 (2011): 284–313.

Saleh, Walid A. "Exegesis viii. Nishapuri School Quranic Exegesis." In *Encyclopedia Iranica*, January 1, 2020, http://www.iranicaonline.org/articles/exegesis-viii-nishapuri-school-quranic-exegesis.

Samimi, Mehrnaz. "Online 'Sigheh' in Iran: Revolutionary or Restricting?" *HuffPost*, November 18, 2014. https://m.huffpost.com/us/entry/6182110/amp.

al-Sarṭāwī, Maḥmūd ʿAlī. *Sharḥ qānūn al-aḥwāl al-ahakhṣiyya*. Amman: Dār al-Fikr, 1997.

Sayeed, Asma. "Women and Ḥadīth Transmission: Two Case Studies from Mamluk Damascus." *Studia Islamica* 95 (2002): 71–94.

Sayeed, Khalid bin. "The Jamaat-i-Islami Movement in Pakistan." *Pacific Affairs* 30, no. 1 (1957): 59–68.

Schacht, Joseph. "Abū Ḥanīfa al-Nuʿmān." In *Encyclopaedia of Islam, Second Edition*, edited by P. Bearman, Th. Bianquis, C. E. Bosworth, E. van Donzel, and W. P. Heinrichs. Brill Online, 2012.

Schacht, Joseph. *Origins of Muhammadan Jurisprudence*. Oxford: Clarendon Press, 1950.

Schacht, Joseph. *An Introduction to Islamic Law*. Oxford: Oxford University Press, 1982.

Schacht, J., A. Layish, R. Shaham, Ghaus Ansari, J. M. Otto, S. Pompe, J. Knappert, and Jean Boyd. "Nikāḥ." In *Encyclopaedia of Islam, Second Edition*, edited by P. Bearman, Th. Bianquis, C. E. Bosworth, E. van Donzel, W. P. Heinrichs. Brill Online, 2012.

Schoeman, Ferdinand. "Rights of Children, Rights of Parents, and the Moral Basis of the Family." *Ethics* 91, no. 1 (1980): 6–19.

Sciolino, Elaine. "Love Finds a Way in Iran: 'Temporary Marriage.'" *New York Times*, October 4, 2000, sec. World. https://www.nytimes.com/2000/10/04/world/love-finds-a-way-in-iran-temporary-marriage.html.

Seedat, Fatima. "When Islam and Feminism Converge." *Muslim World* 103, no. 3 (2013): 404–20.

Sells, Michael. *Approaching the Qur'án: The Early Revelations*. Ashland, OR: White Cloud Press, 2007.

Shaikh, Khanum. "Gender, Religious Agency, and the Subject of Al-Huda International." *Meridians* 11, no. 2 (2011): 62–90.

Shaikh, Sa'diyya. "Transforming Feminism: Islam, Women, and Gender Justice." In *Progressive Muslims: On Justice, Gender, and Pluralism*, edited by Omid Safi, 147–62. Oxford: One World 2003.

Shaikh, Sa'diyya. "Knowledge, Women, and Gender in the Hadith: A Feminist Interpretation." *Islam and Muslim-Christian Relations* 15, no. 1 (2004): 99–108.

Shaikh, Sa'diyya. *Sufi Narratives of Intimacy: Ibn 'Arabī, Gender, and Sexuality*. Chapel Hill: University of North Carolina Press, 2012.

Sharma, Betwa. "Islam's Sex Licenses." *Daily Beast*, last modified April 29, 2009. https://www.thedailybeast.com/islams-sex-licenses.

al-Shīrāzī, Muḥammad al-Ḥusaynī. *al-Fiqh: Mawdū'a istidlāliyya fī al-fiqh al-Islāmī*. Beirut: Dār al-'Ulūm, 1988.

Shmuluvitz, Shoshana. "Temporary Marriage in Islam: Exploitative or Liberating?" *Tel Aviv Notes* 6, no. 5 (March 11, 2012). http://dayan.org/content/tel-aviv-notes-temporary-marriage-islam-exploitative-or-liberating.

"Sībawayh." In *Encyclopedia Britannica*, January 8, 2015, https://www.britannica.com/biography/Sibawayh.

Siddiqui, Samana. "Divorce Among American Muslims: Statistics, Challenges & Solutions." Sound Vision. https://www.soundvision.com/article/divorce-among-american-muslims-statistics-challenges-solutions. Accessed August 9, 2020.

al-Sijistani, Abu Dawud Sulayman b. al-Ash'at. *Kitab al-sunun*. Translated by Ahmad Hasan. Vol. 3. Lahore: Muhammad Ashraf, 1984.

Sindawi, Khalid. *Temporary Marriage in Sunni and Shi'ite Islam: A Comparative Study*. Wiesbaden: Harrassowitz Verlag, 2013.

Smith, Martyn. "Review of The First Muslims: History and Memory by Asma Afsaruddin." *International Journal of Middle East Studies* 41, no. 3 (2009): 524–26.

Smith, William Robertson. *Kinship and Marriage in Early Arabia*. Boston: Beacon Press, 1903.

Soble, Alan. "Sexual Use." In *The Philosophy of Sex: Contemporary Readings*, 259–88. 5th ed. Plymouth, UK: Rowan and Littlefield, 2008.

Sonbol, Amira A. *Women, the Family, and Divorce Laws in Islamic History*. 1st ed. Syracuse: Syracuse University Press, 2007.

Sonbol, Amirah al-Azhary. "Rethinking Women and Islam." In *Daughters of Abraham: Feminist Thought in Judaism, Christianity, and Islam*, edited by Yvonne Yazbeck Haddad and John L. Esposito. Gainesville: University Press of Florida, 2001.

Sorush, Abd-al-Karim. *Reason, Freedom and Democracy in Islam*. Oxford: Oxford University Press, 2000.

Spellberg, D. A. *Politics, Gender, and the Islamic Past: The Legacy of A'isha Bint Abi Bakr*. New York: Columbia University Press, 1994.

Srivastava, Rol. "Indian Child Brides Sold in 'Package Deals' to Men from Gulf States." *Thomson Reuters Foundation*, October 10, 2017. https://www.reuters.com/article/us-india-trafficking-marriage/indian-child-brides-sold-in-package-deals-to-men-from-gulf-states-idUSKBN1CF1F7.

Stern, Gertrude H. *Marriage in Early Islam*. London: The Royal Asiatic Society, 1939.

Stern, S. M. "Abū Ḥātim Al-Rāzī." In *Encyclopaedia of Islam, Second Edition*, edited by P. Bearman, Th. Bianquis, C. E. Bosworth, E. van Donzel, and W. P. Heinrichs. Brill Online, 2012.

Stowasser, Barbara Freyer. "Wives of the Prophet." In *Encyclopedia of the Qur'ān*, edited by Jane Dammen McAuliffe. Brill Online.

al-Suyūṭī, Jalāl al-Dīn. *al-Itqan fī 'ulūm al-Qur'ān*. 2 vols. Beirut: Dār al-Kutub al-'Ilmiyya, 1987.

al-Suyūṭī, Jalāl al-Dīn. *al-Taḥbīr fī 'ilm al-tafsīr*. Beirut: Dār al-Fikr, 1983.

al-Ṭabarī, Abū Ja'far Muḥammad b. Jarīr. *Jāmi' Al-Bayān Fī Ta'wīl al-Qur'ān*. Volume 8. Edited by Muhammad Shākir and Ahmad Shākir. Cairo: al-Hay'a al-Miṣriyya al-'Āmma li-l-Kitāb, 1954.

Ṭabāṭabā'ī, Allāma Ḥusayn Mudarrissī. *al-Mizān fī tafsīr al-Qur'ān*, 20 vols. Beirut: Mu'assasat al-A'lamī li-l-Maṭbū'āt, 1973–1974. Translated by Sayyid Sa'īd Akhtar Rizwī as *Al-Mizān: An Exegesis of the Qur'ān*. 8 vols. Tehran: World Organization for Islamic Services, 1983–92.

Ṭabāṭabā'ī, 'Allama Sayyid Muḥammad Muḥammad Ḥusayn. *Shi'ite Islam*. Translated by Seyyed Hossein Nasr. Albany: State University of New York, 1977.

al-Tabātabā'ī, Muhammad Alī. *Riyād al-masā'il*. 2 vols. Tabriz: n.p., 1990–91.

Ṭabāṭabā'ī, Muhammad Husayn. *The Quran in Islam: Its Impact and Influence in the Life of Muslims*. Translated by A. Yates. London: Zahra, 1987.

al-Ṭabrisī (Ṭabarsī), Al-Faḍl b. al-Ḥasan. *Majma' al-bayān fī tafsīr al-Qur'ān*. Vol. 3. Beirut: Dār al-Murtada, 2006.

al-Ṭabrisī, al-Faḍl b. al-Ḥasan. *Majma' al-bayān fī tafsīr al-Qur'ān*. Edited by Hāshim al-Rasūlī and Faḍl Allāh al-Ṭabāṭabā'ī al-Yazdī. 10 vols. Mashhad: al-Ma'ārif al-Islāmiyya, 1976.

Tait, Robert. "Iranian Minister Backs Temporary Marriage to Relieve Lust of Youth." *The Guardian*, June 4, 2007. https://www.theguardian.com/world/2007/jun/04/iran.roberttait. Accessed August 9, 2020.

Talbi, M. "Ibn 'Āshūr." In *Encyclopaedia of Islam, Second Edition*, eds. P. Bearman, Th. Bianquis, C. E. Bosworth, E. van Donzel, and W. P. Heinrichs. Brill Online, 2012.

Tandon, Surabhi. "'Temporary' Marriages Still Going on in Kerala State." Television newscast, FRANCE 24 English, November, 18, 2013, https://www.youtube.com/watch?v=lyLvD2Hneco.

Tappan, Robert. "Beyond Clerics and Clinics: Bioethics and Assisted Reproductive Technology in Iran." Phd diss., University of Virginia, 2011.

al-Tha'labī, Aḥmad b. Muḥammad. *al-Kashf wa-l-bayān 'an tafsīr al-Qur'ān*. Edited by 'Alī 'Āshūr. Beirut: Dār Iḥyā' al-Turāth al-'Arabī, 2002.

al-Tirmidhī, Abū 'Īsā Muḥammad. *Ṣaḥīḥ*. Cairo: n.p., 1350–53/1931–34.

al-Tirmidhī, Abū 'Īsā Muḥammad. *Sunan* [*al-Jami al-Ṣaḥīḥ*]. Edited by Aḥmad Muḥammad Shākir. Cairo: Muṣṭafā Bābī al-Ḥalabī, 1978.

The Huffington Post. "History: The Clitoris' Vanishing Act," accessed September 26, 2020, http://projects.huffingtonpost.com/projects/cliteracy/history.

The Huffington Post. "You Don't Know What You Don't Know About the Clitoris," accessed January 14, 2020, http://projects.huffingtonpost.com/projects/cliteracy.

Tolman, Deborah L., and Lisa M. Diamond, eds. *APA Handbook of Sexuality and Psychology*. 2 vols. APA Handbooks in Psychology. Washington DC: American Psychological Association, 2014.

al-Ṭūsī, Abū Ja'far Muḥammad b. al-Ḥasan. *al-Tibyān fī tafsīr al-Qur'ān*. Edited by Āghā Buzurg al-Ṭihrānī. 10 vols. Najaf: al-Maṭba'a al-'Ilmiyya, 1957–63.

al-Ṭūsī, Abū Jaʿfar Muḥammad b. al-Ḥasan. *Taḥdhīb al-aḥkām*. Vol. 7. Najaf: n.p., 1380/1960–61.

al-Ṭūsī, Abū Jaʿfar Muḥammad b. al-Ḥasan. *al-Mabsūt fi fiqh al-imāmiyya*. Tehran: n.p., 1967.

Vajda, G. "Isrāʾīliyyāt." In *Encyclopaedia of Islam, Second Edition*, edited by P. Bearman, Th. Bianquis, C. E. Bosworth, E. van Donzel, and W. P. Heinrichs. Brill Online, 2012.

Versteegh, C. H. M. "al-Zamakhsharī." In *Encyclopaedia of Islam, Second Edition*, edited by P. Bearman, Th. Bianquis, C. E. Bosworth, E. van Donzel, and W. P. Heinrichs. Brill Online, 2012.

von Kügelgen, Anke. "ʿAbduh, Muḥammad." In *Encyclopaedia of Islam, THREE*, edited by Kate Fleet, Gudrun Krämer, Denis Matringe, John Nawas, and Everett Rowson. Brill Online.

Wadud, Amina. *Qur'an and Woman: Rereading the Sacred Text from a Woman's Perspective*. Reprint ed. New York: Oxford University Press, 1999.

Wadud, Amina. *Inside the Gender Jihad: Women's Reform in Islam*. Oxford: Oneworld, 2006.

Walbridge, Linda S. *Without Forgetting the Imam: Lebanese Shi'ism in an American Community*. Detroit: Wayne State University Press, 1996.

Walker, Ashley Manjarrez, and Michael A. Sells. "The Wiles of Women and Performative Intertextuality: 'A'isha, the Hadith of the Slander, and the Sura of Yusuf." *Journal of Arabic Literature* 30, no. 1 (1999): 55–77.

Walker, Paul E. "Dāʿī (in Ismāʿīlī Islam)." In *Encyclopaedia of Islam, THREE*, edited by Kate Fleet, Gudrun Krämer, Denis Matringe, John Nawas, and Everett Rowson. Brill Online.

Wansbrough, John. *Quranic Studies*. London: Oxford University Press, 1977.

al-Wāqidī, Muḥammad b. ʿUmar. *Kitāb al-Maghāzī*. 2 vols. London: Oxford University Press, 1966.

Watt, W. Montgomery. "ʿĀʾisha Bint Abī Bakr." In *Encyclopaedia of Islam, Second Edition*, edited by P. Bearman, Th. Bianquis, C. E. Bosworth, E. van Donzel, and W. P. Heinrichs. Brill Online, 2012.

Watt, W. Montgomery. *Muhammad at Medina*. Oxford: Oxford University Press, 1962.

Wertheimer, Alan. "Consent and Sexual Relations." In *The Philosophy of Sex: Contemporary Readings*, 289–316. 5th ed. Plymouth, UK: Rowan and Littlefield Publishers, Inc., 2008.Robin West, Robin. "The Harms of Consensual Sex." In *The Philosophy of Sex: Contemporary Readings*, 317–24. 5th ed. Plymouth, UK: Rowan and Littlefield Publishers, Inc., 2008.

Westermarck, Edward. *The History of Human Marriage*. New York: The Allerton Book Company, 1922.

Westermarck, Edward. *A Short History of Marriage*. New York: Macmillan, 1926.

Wheeler, Brannon. "Representations: Qurʾān: Overview." In *Encyclopedia of Women & Islamic Cultures*, edited by Suad Joseph. Brill Online, 2014.

Wright, J. W., and Everett K. Rowson. *Homoeroticism in Classical Arabic Literature*. New York: Columbia University Press, 1997.

Yazigi, Maya. “Defense and Validation in Shiʿi and Sunni Tradition: The Case of Muḥammad b. Abī Bakr.” *Studia Islamica* 98/99 (2004): 49–70.

Zalat, Maḥmūd al-Qasabī. *Fiqh al-usra*. Beirut: Dar al-Qalam, 1999.

al-Zamakhsharī, Jār Allāh Maḥmūd b. ʿUmar. *al-Kashshāf ʿan ḥaqāʾiq al-tanzīl wa-ʿuyūn al-aqāwīl fī wujūh al-taʾwīl*. 4 vols. Beirut: Dār al-Maʿrifa, 2009.

al-Zarkashī, Badr al-Dīn Abū ʿAbdullah Muḥammad b. ʿAbdullah b. Bahādur. *Zahr al-ʿArīsh fī Tahrīm al-Hashīsh,* study and verification by A. Faraj. Dār al-Wafā’ wa al-Nashr wa al-Tawzī. 1970.

al-Zarkashī, Badr al-Dīn Abū ʿAbdullah Muḥammad b. ʿAbdullah b. Bahādur. *al-Ijāba li-Īrādi mā Istadrakathu ʿĀʾisha ʿala al Ṣahāba*. Edited by Saʿīd al-Afghānī. 2nd ed. Beirut: Al-Kutub al-Islāmī, n.d..

al-Zarkashī, Muhammad b. ʾAbdullāh. *al-Burhān fī ʿulūm al-Qurʾān*. Beirut: Dār al-fikr, 1988.

Zia, Afiya Shehrbano. “The Reinvention of Feminism in Pakistan.” *Feminist Review* 91 (2009): 29–46.

Index

Ababneh, Sara, 125
ʿAbbās, 13
ʿAbd Allāh b. Muḥammad b. Khālid al-Ṭayālisī al-Tamīmī, 58
ʿAbdallāh b. ʿUmar, 44
ʿAbd al-Razzāq al-Kāshānī, 81–82
Abduh, Muḥammad, 91–95
abortion, 100
Abū Bakr, 17, 20, 33n61, 44–45, 56; ʿAʾisha and, 44; al-Ṭabarī and, 55
Abū Basīr, 21
Abū Dāwud, 18
Abū Ḥanīfa, 18
Abū Ḥātim al-Rāzī, 60, 68n88
Abū Jaʿfar, 59
Abū Qays b. al-Aslat, 42
Abū Yaʿqūb al- Sijistānī, 68n88
Abū ʿAbdallāh Muḥammad b. Karrām, 85n6
Abū ʿAmr al-Kishshī, 58
adab (literature), 81
al-ʿadam al-haraj (protection against distress and constriction), 24
ʿadm al-mirāth (absence of inheritance), 13
al-Afghānī, Sayyid Jamāl al-Dīn, 92
aḥādīth (variant readings), 4, 164–65; Companions on, 44; Faḍl Allāh on, 101; feminism and, 122–24, 127, 151n64; Hāshmī on, 102–3; Ibn ʿAbbās on, 49–50; on marriage, 11, 46–47; al-Māwardī on, 118; Maybudī on, 79–80; *mutʿa* and, 19–20, 32n49, 47–48; Nuṣrat Amīn on, 108; Q 4:24 and, 7; al- Rāzī on, 76; of Successors, 18; Sunni Islam and, 165; on *tafsīr,* 40; al-Zamakhsharī on, 73
ahl al-bayt (people of the house), 95
Aḥmad b. Ḥanbal, 18
Aḥmad b. ʿAlī, 56
ajal (fixed duration), 13
ajar (recompense), 13
ajr (compensation or wages), 43, 75; ʿAbduh and, 94
akhbār, 18
akhlāq, 126
al-ʿAlawī, Aṣīl al-Dīn ʿAbd Allāh, 81
alfaja (to become bankrupt), 93
Ali, Kecia, 7, 117, 119, 120–21, 123, 125, 126, 131
ʿAlī al-Riḍā, 58
ʿAlī b. Abī Ṭālib, 33n68, 44–45, 124
Ali-Faisal, Sobia, 10
Alshugairi, Noha, 9
APA Handbook of Sexuality and Psychology, 140
ʿaqd (contract), 11, 13

About the Author

Dr. Roshan Iqbal hails from a small hamlet of 20 million–Karachi, Pakistan. She received her PhD in Islamic Studies from Georgetown University. Prior to this she read for her MPhil at the University of Cambridge. She has studied in Pakistan, the US, Morocco, Egypt, Jordon, the UK, and Iran. Her research interests include gender and sexuality in the Qur'an, Islamic Law, Film and Media Studies, and modern Muslim intellectuals. As an associate professor at Agnes Scott College, she teaches classes in the Religious Studies department and also classes that are cross-listed with Women, Gender, and Sexuality Studies and Film Studies. When she is not working, she loves talking to her family and friends on the phone (thank you, unlimited plans), tracking fashion (sartorial flourishes are such fun), watching films (love! love! love!), reading novels (never enough), painting watercolors (less and less poorly), and cooking new dishes (sometimes successfully).